"Robert Jolles has written an interesting an___ ily ____ book on corporate training and trainers. It contains much valuable information about how to become an effective trainer based on his experience at Xerox and with many other companies. He writes clearly and offers helpful guidance to all those responsible for running seminars and workshops."

> *Edward I. Colodny*
> Former Chairman and CEO
> U.S. Air

"I am not a professional speaker, but when I walk on stage—it matters! Watching and then reading Rob Jolles has taught me that powerful presentations are no accident. In his book, he lays down the principles and techniques that can make great presentations second nature. If you want to maximize your effectiveness when you take to the lectern, read this book."

> *R. Scott West*
> Senior Vice President
> Van Kampen Merritt

"After witnessing the extraordinary effect Rob Jolles had on the Xerox Train-The-Trainer program I wondered if he could transform that energy and talent into text. I wonder no more. He has truly captured the skills conveyed to our Xerox trainers, managers and key personnel and brought them to life in this book. If you can't see him work a room live, this truly is the next best thing!"

> *Gary Aslin*
> Director of Training
> Xerox Corporation

"In this book, Rob has successfully assembled a very thought-provoking and practical list of knowledge, skills and behaviors that contribute to the continuous improvement process in the corporate training profession and offers it in a very readable and entertaining way!"

"This is must reading for anyone earning their living in 'the pit'—the corporate classroom."

> *Theodore J. Zemper*
> President
> SDA Corporation

HOW TO RUN
SEMINARS

AND
WORKSHOPS

PRESENTATION SKILLS FOR CONSULTANTS, TRAINERS, AND TEACHERS

Robert L. Jolles

John Wiley & Sons, Inc.
New York • Chichester • Brisbane • Toronto • Singapore

Copyright © 1993 by John Wiley & Sons, Inc.

All rights reserved. Published simultaneously in Canada.

This publication is designed to provide accurate and authoritative information in regard to the subject matter covered. It is sold with the understanding that the publisher is not engaged in rendering legal, accounting, or other professional services. If legal advice or other expert assistance is required, the services of a competent professional person should be sought. *From a Declaration of Principles jointly adopted by a Committee of the American Bar Association and a Committee of Publishers.*

Library of Congress Cataloging in Publication Data:

Jolles, Robert L., 1957–
    How to run seminars and workshops : presentation skills for consultants, trainers, and teachers / Robert L. Jolles.
        p.   cm.
    Includes index.
    ISBN 0-471-59478-4 (cloth). — ISBN 0-471-59477-6 (pbk.)
    1. Seminars—Handbooks, manuals, etc.   2. Workshops (Seminars)—Handbooks, manuals, etc.   3. Meetings—Handbooks, manuals, etc.
    I. Title.
    AS6.J65   1994
    658.4'56—dc20   93-5051

Printed in the United States of America

10 9 8 7 6 5 4 3 2 1

This book is dedicated to my wife Ronni
who supported, assisted, and endured the
trials of this project; to the thousands of
trainees who allowed a struggling trainer
to learn his trade and ultimately learn his
lessons in humility and compassion; and to the
memory of my dear friend Tony Fox.

PREFACE

Welcome to the world of stand-up delivery. Whether you are a trainer, seminar leader, guest speaker, or just someone who occasionally must deliver an idea by addressing a group of people, this book was created to show you not only the importance of presentation skills but many of the nuances that will allow you to direct a group of strangers so that they come together as a team and can accomplish a common goal.

There are many misunderstandings surrounding the training profession. I hope to answer many of those questions. There are many opinions regarding right and wrong. As a trainer, I hope to give you definitive answers based on my experiences. As with any class I teach, I hope you find the book both informative and fun. I hope also that you will find support and motivation within these pages. That is one of the true values of a good Train-The-Trainer and that is what this book is about.

After I had finished school at the University of Maryland, my first job was for the New York Life Insurance Company. In four days, I was taught how to be an insurance salesman. I was taught the difference between term and whole life insurance. I was taught about preexisting conditions and other key areas of health insurance. I was even taught about disability insurance and the "curse of the living death." Very scary! Four days later, when they were all through teaching me about insurance, I was shown the door and told, "two apps a week, ten apps a month. Go get 'em, tiger!" I was trained. My training failed me. I was taught about my product, but no one ever told me how to sell it.

Most people who become trainers or presenters, fall into the same trap. *They are taught what to teach, but rarely how to teach it.* They appear in front of their trainees as ill prepared as I was initially selling insurance. Customers want more than product knowledge, and so do trainees. There lies the importance of having information on not just what to teach, but how to teach it.

It has been 13 years now of teaching Train-The-Trainer courses. Thirteen years of active stand-up delivery training is kind of like dog years; that is, about 91 years of Train-The-Trainer to you and me! I have delivered these courses while employed by three major corporations as well as for myself as an entrepreneur. In those years, I have developed a love–hate relationship with a topic that I find fascinating. The love portion of Train-The-Trainer is connected to seeing thousands of presenters just like me—groping for new methods, validating and replacing old ideas, and sometimes just hanging around to get their batteries recharged. The hate portion of Train-The-Trainer centers around its unforgiving nature. In just about any seminar taught, it is more than acceptable to misplace an overhead, forget a trainee's name, or even lose your train of thought. When teaching someone "How it is done," there is very little forgiveness for errors. It is a challenge. It will also age you a bit.

I view this book, as I do a good Train-The-Trainer, as a kind of vitamin. When you take a vitamin, your body uses what it needs and only absorbs what it can use. In this book, my intention is to give you too many ideas. Each may be appropriate depending on your topic, seminar size, personality, style, and any number of other factors. Take what you need and disregard what you do not find acceptable to your situation.

You will be reading and relating to "real world" situations and solutions. Let me give you a quick taste of "real world" in the life of a presenter. Recently I was asked to speak in front of about 100 managers for one of the largest insurance companies in the country. This presentation was set to last for six hours. The individual who coordinated the presentation on behalf of the insurance company had come to me only weeks before the presentation date telling me the presentation was "no big deal," and to just "walk the group through some simple sales skills." Well, as a professional trainer, I have learned that *all* presentations are a "big deal," and I've spent 13 years guarding against the temptation to not take presentations as seriously as they need to be taken. My preparation was thorough and disciplined following the techniques taught in this book. Minutes before the presentation was set to begin, my contact person informed me that there would be a couple of visitors in the room. These visitors happened to have the title "Senior Vice President." At that time, I was also informed that instead of six hours, they would like to stretch the presentation to eight hours. "No problem" was my response. The reserve material that *always* accompanies my presentations took care of the time, and my mental preparation took care of the Senior Vice Presidents. By the way, Senior Vice Presidents rarely sit for seminars without a motive. As I suspected, that presentation acted as an audition for Xerox and its training capabilities. The results? As of this writing, the potential for somewhere in the neighborhood of a half million dollars in training revenue for Xerox.

That story is a microcosm of what it is to be a trainer and why throughout this book you will see references to the word "underfire." Whether you are speaking in front of Senior Vice Presidents or senior citizens, 150 customers or 15 customers, the pressure is always there. The potential for triumph or trouble is always there. The opportunity for success or failure is always there. Each room is a puzzle that you need to figure out. As a professional trainer, you can die from the pressure or thrive under it. One other reference you will also see from time to time is a reference to the "pit." This is the area in front of the lectern that separates the presenter from the trainees. Depending on the size of the audience, this is where presenters (with the help of a wireless microphone or a booming voice), need to live to stay connected with their audience. This book is dedicated to teaching you how to understand the pressure of going "underfire" and thrive in the "pit"!

One last point before you read what awaits you. Please remember that in no way do I wish you to walk away from what you are about to read with a desire to change your style. The greatest lesson I ever learned about style came mercifully early in my career. There are many who claim to be the greatest salespeople who ever lived. You can pick from any number who have written books, put out tapes, or deliver seminars. Each is good in his own way, and far be it from me to knock what they do.

For example, when it comes to my view of the greatest salesperson who ever lived, I select a man named Ben Feldman. In 1979, while I was with New York Life, Ben led the industry in sales. That is all the insurance companies, not just mine. Actually, it is unfair to say he led the industry, he dominated it. The top nine agents were all fairly close to each other. Ben Feldman tripled the next closest competitor. What a legend! From the big metropolis of Youngstown, Ohio, this man was rewriting the record books in sales. I had never seen a picture of Ben, but I imagined what he looked like. Tall, aggressive, good looking. I sensed he looked a lot like me (OK, minus some of those attributes). One day we received a tape of Ben Feldman in the office. I got dressed up the day I was scheduled to watch the tape, and my life changed. The

Ben Feldman on the tape was about 5'4", somewhat overweight, balding, and spoke with a lisp. Not quite what I had expected; however, something made me watch on. Within seconds, I was drawn to the techniques that Ben Feldman was using. It was then and there I learned the most valuable lesson I would ever receive in my life regarding style: I could not be Ben Feldman; I could, however, focus on his *techniques* and continue to ask myself, "How can I do that so it sounds like Rob Jolles?" Rob Jolles cannot do Ben Feldman, and Ben Feldman cannot do Rob Jolles.

As you read this book, continue to ask yourself, "How do I implement these ideas so they sound like me?" If you commit to your own style and implement some of the ideas and techniques recommended in the following pages, I believe you will do just fine. The makeup of your audience will determine the nature of your participants, so in an attempt to speak to as many of you as possible, I will refer to your participants as trainees. With that in mind, sit back, and remember that what is presented in the pages to follow is real world. Let's get ready to rumble!

ROBERT L. JOLLES

ACKNOWLEDGMENTS

I would like to acknowledge the following people:

Bill "Scooter" Leathwood who introduced me to the training profession and whose actions inspired me to become a trainer.

Robert C. Camp, author of *Benchmarking,* for showing me that a project of this nature can be done.

Mary Ellen Silk for her careful maneuvering around my "fragile writer's ego" and providing the editing assistance I so badly needed.

Emmett Reagan and Larry Domonkos for graciously filling the roles of mentor and role model, showing me what it is to be a Xerox trainer.

Xerox Corporation for putting their faith and trust in me as a trainer, allowing me to touch so many wonderful trainees inside and outside the company. For this opportunity I am eternally grateful.

CONTENTS

■ Contents ■

1

GETTING STARTED

Chapter 1

Working with Adult Audiences

When I was about six years old, I wanted very badly to grow up and be a basketball player. I was totally hooked on the sport and longed to be tall and famous. As I grew, so did my aspirations of adulthood. I passed through various stages of wanting to be a football player, an astronaut, a doctor, a lawyer, even the President of the United States. In fourth grade, however, these dreams took on a more serious focus.

I wanted to be a teacher. I had a fourth-grade teacher named Ms. Tuttweiler. She was everything a teacher should be. She was compassionate, she was kind, and she was sensitive to the needs of your typical 10-year-old. She had a spunky side, too! If you were caught chewing gum, Ms. Tuttweiler made you wear it on your nose. If you talked too much, she made you talk to yourself for a few minutes back in the coat closet. She even discouraged note passing by reading that private little message in front of the class. The funny thing is, even with all those "punishments," everybody loved good old Ms. Tuttweiler. I liked her so much that I actually felt an inspiration to teach. Unfortunately, for most of us who are drawn to corporate training, this harmless role model can often expose us to some potentially dangerous situations.

The first, and most important point that you have to understand, is that what worked with a child will not work with mature audiences. When asked to conduct training, the first instinct new presenters have is to draw on their previous experiences in the classroom. It is not that most of us do not have corporate training experiences to utilize. It is just that for every hour of adult training, there have been about 500 hours of other schooling. Assuming a schedule that allows for five to seven hours of schooling in a day, an approximate number of hours of schooling from kindergarten through four years of college would be about 21,420. In a corporate environment, to have structured training for 40 hours in a year can be viewed as excessive. Not only do those early schooling years represent numerous hours, but as a child you are more vulnerable to change.

With this in mind, try asking an adult to put a piece of gum on his nose if you do not allow gum chewing. Read aloud a message that an adult is passing to another adult in the seminar. Needless to say, these ideas would backfire horribly in a training environment. For most presenters though, what other experiences do they have to draw on?

Adults must be dealt with in a mature manner, and with that in mind, I would like to show you some basic needs that adults have that are different from those of a child. It should be noted, however, that these are ideas that I would like to see implemented with the way my children are presently being taught. Unfortunately, as you will read, there are certain things we can get away with when teaching children that we cannot get away with when training adults.

This chapter illustrates the differences in working with adults as opposed to children. I will point out these differences, and why they are important. I will not go over the solutions to some of these problems. Later on, when the creation of effective training is covered, we will also cover a process that will speak to these differences with concrete solutions in mind.

CREATE AN ATMOSPHERE CONDUCIVE TO TRAINING

One of the first major differences between teaching a child and training an adult is the necessity of attention to surroundings. Children are really exceptional when it comes to the atmosphere in which they learn. If you drive past most schools, you will notice a rather peculiar sight. It looks as if the larger buildings have actually spawned some children of their own. Those odd structures are referred to as "temporary classrooms." Speak to children about the difficulties of learning in a small, cramped environment, typically too warm in the summer and too cold in the winter, and they will politely respond by telling you, "It's neat."

Not so for an adult. For whatever reason you choose, adults come to training with a different attitude. Anything less than first class becomes an immediate knock of the training itself. You can have the best curriculum, the best presenter, and the best combination of students. Often, if the surroundings are not appropriate, your message will fall on deaf (or distracted) ears.

A classic example of inappropriate atmosphere is the case of on-site training conducted in a field office. Thousands of dollars are being spent for participant guides, trainees' time out of the field, a presenter's time and travel expense, but to save those last few pennies, the training is conducted on-site. Typically, you can count on physically losing every student in your training session at least once for an extended period of time. Training is constantly interrupted for "emergency phone calls," and with students coming back from breaks and lunch late because of "important problems." The distractions are endless. For a few more dollars, the training could be moved across the street (although I would suggest across town), eliminating this problem.

Try to establish an atmosphere that is relaxed yet businesslike. If this sounds like walking a rather precarious tightrope, you are right! For an inexperienced presenter, the desire is often to create that relaxed atmosphere at all costs. What can start off being an attempt for a relaxed atmosphere can often wind up turning into a total lack of discipline. I can remember early in my career a time when I was asked to step out in the hallway by an observer who had just watched my seminar. I had worked extremely hard to create an atmosphere that was relaxed. I had done such a good job, that as the observer was going over his evaluation, the students could be heard in the other room tossing things about, ringing bells, buzzers, and any other objects I had left behind. I sheepishly looked at the observer and muttered, "Perhaps I did too good a job creating a relaxed atmosphere."

I have also observed instructors who lean too heavily to the opposite extreme. In an attempt to create a businesslike atmosphere, the seminar room takes on the look of a prison. The presenter creates a threatening environment. Students do not speak unless spoken to; the presenter's word is all that matters, and little interaction occurs. Not only does the seminar not benefit from other experiences and points of view from the participants, there is an air of resentment among the students.

The presenter's role is to walk the tightrope between relaxed and businesslike. This can often mean crossing back and forth depending on the situation. I often refer to the role of a presenter as more of a "teflon" position. For example, sometimes the joke that is told by a student can and should be laughed at by the presenter. Other times, depending on its appropriateness, despite the punch line, it cannot be laughed at.

I am not suggesting that presenters should not be human, merely that they constantly must exercise careful judgment.

You are the role model: You are the one who must keep the seminar on an even keel. As the presenter, it is your responsibility to use your best judgment to create the kind of atmosphere most conducive to good learning. When in doubt, leave it out!

BUILD AND MAINTAIN INTEREST

When a child is not kept interested in school, the mischief that child can get into is generally containable. Sometimes it may mean a trip to the principal's office or some other threat. The mischief an adult can get into can be a lot more damaging to the training that is being conducted.

As mentioned earlier, threats are not an effective way to maintain an adult's interest. As a matter of fact, the only effectiveness threats may have within your training is to initiate contact between student and presenter. Additionally, adults can be more openly hostile about their lack of interest within the training. With the potential for a full range of audience emotions playing a part within your training, it is important to try and keep the trainees' interest any way you can. Unfortunately, this can sometimes result in an unfair level of stress on the presenter.

One rule of thumb I usually follow, when working with a new group of trainees, is not to worry about being instantly interesting. It is unrealistic and can contribute to the type of stress that burns out so many presenters so quickly. I have often fantasized about walking into a room of trainees I have never met before, approaching the lectern, slowly opening the curriculum, and being met with a crescendo of applause. Good fantasy. The only thing lacking is reality. In fact, when a presenter walks into the room, the tension and anxiety of the trainees goes up a notch. There are a number of unknowns and other factors that will soon be touched upon contributing to this anxiety, but it is certainly not the stuff that fantasies are made of.

The goal I establish for myself, and suggest for others, is a little more modest. I assume that when a group of trainees first meet me, there will not be much interest. I will give them time to worry about what they are wearing, where they are sitting, what I look like and so forth. By the first break, I would like to think that I have created a spark of interest. By lunchtime, maybe a couple of head nods of approval. By the end of the day, we have interest. By the end of the second day, we have a lot of interest. By the end of the third day, they cannot wait to start the next day. By the end of the program, it is my hope, they have just completed the best training they have ever attended.

A number of techniques can be used to get and maintain interest, which I will systematically outline in Chapter 9. The key point is simply this. If you are going to establish a goal regarding the interest you intend to generate within your training, let it be this: From the first minute to the last, at no time will you allow the interest you are working for to take a step backward. Forward, ho!

CAPITALIZE ON THE EXPERIENCE OF ADULT TRAINEES

One of the greatest aspects of working with adults is the abundance of experiences they bring to the training room. I am not, however, necessarily referring to their experience within your given subject matter. Subject matter experience is definitely a positive in most situations, but it is the trainees' *other* experiences that can often be the diamond in the rough a lot of presenters miss out on. These experiences can be just the link that is needed to teach a difficult concept.

Let me provide you with an example. When I came out of college, the first job I ever had was as an insurance salesman for the New York Life Insurance Company. I had certain strengths and weaknesses as a salesman, but my ability to, as I used to call it, "teach the sale," served me well. An example of this was my ability to explain the difference between whole life insurance and term insurance. As an Apprentice Field Underwriter, I watched intently as certain agents would spend literally hours trying to explain the difference to customers who made the unfortunate mistake of asking. Like any good trainee, when the explanation became endless, customers would fake their best "Oh, now I get it," and the salesman would move on, mercifully putting that topic out of its misery. The reality is, these salesmen rarely made the sale. If a presenter does this, the presenter will rarely get his point across.

An experienced salesman then told me to draw on the customer's experience to get the point across. He suggested using an example of purchasing a house. Many adults have either purchased or considered purchasing a home. Using that experience is what made the point easier to understand. My explanation sounded something like this:

The differences between *whole life insurance* and *term insurance* are similar to the differences between owning a home and renting a home. When you own a home, you pay more up front and your monthly payments are higher. As a trade-off, your payments remain consistent and although no one can guarantee exactly how much money you will make, chances are if you stay in the home for three to five years, you should make a significant profit. *Whole life insurance* is very similar in concept. Your monthly payments will be higher but never increase. No one can guarantee exactly how much cash value your policy will earn, but after three years it should be significant.

When you rent a home, the initial rent is usually considerably less than what a mortgage would be on a similar structure. However, rents are raised at various times, and when you leave, other than perhaps the repayment of a security deposit, you receive nothing. *Term insurance* is similar. Premiums are lower, but they can be raised through the years, and when you leave or quit the policy, you receive nothing.

Now I am not claiming to have made anyone an insurance expert, but in the 30 seconds or so that it took you to read the example, you gained a basic understanding of the concept. When was the last time your insurance agent tried to explain the difference, how long did it take, and how well did you understand it?

Another example that I use a lot in the more technical training assignments that I have worked on involves the computer. Many trainees who are forced to incorporate the computer into their training suffer from the dreaded illness referred to as "computerphobia." To soften this fearful device, my approach was to break it down into understandable experiences and terms they can all relate to.

See this computer keyboard? It is a lot like a typewriter keyboard that all of you have probably used at one time or another. The monitor is a lot like the television set you curl up with at night, and the central processing unit acts like the brain.

Once, while conducting a Train-The-Trainer in Eqypt, I was having a great deal of trouble communicating a difficult concept. Most Egyptians are clueless to many of our customs and sports, as I was to theirs. Finally, we found soccer (referred to as football by the Egyptians), and I found myself happily clinging to soccer examples to illustrate key points for the remainder of the course.

Some trainees will exhibit mental blocks relating to certain information. It is the presenter's job not only to become aware of this but to find a way to communicate the information to the trainee. It may be your analogy of a golf swing, a reference to a book that you read, or maybe even a movie that both of you have seen. Unlike a child, an adult has a wealth of experience you can relate your information to. It is that common ground of experiences that you must find to facilitate effective learning.

STRUCTURE YOUR PRESENTATION LOGICALLY

To list logic as one of the key components to working with adult audiences may seem a bit obvious, but it is critical just the same. Curriculum developers often have limited experience in the subject they are writing about because they are sought after for their writing ability.

When curriculum is developed, subject matter experts are called on to help with the creation of a course. Their involvement is usually to get the writers up to speed as quickly as possible and then step aside. Even when the development is carefully monitored, reading curriculum is one thing, teaching it is a whole different story. This is why pilots exist. One of the intents of a pilot is to take what is technically correct and determine if it is being presented in a logical manner.

One of the first points I look for when handed a new course to study is whether I need more information than what is available to understand it. I have often said that the first emotions experienced by a presenter sitting through a seminar he is to teach can be the most valuable. Whatever emotions you perceive, the students most likely will feel, too, at the exact same spot. What's more, if while teaching the material, you find yourself wishing you could refer to material that has yet to be taught, you probably are experiencing a clue that there may be a logic problem.

When trying to figure out curriculum logic, often a presenter can walk away unsure which came first, the chicken or the egg. Sometimes, despite consistent confusion among trainees, a presenter will become so out of touch with the fact that there has been constant trouble in one area (dating back to when he first taught the material), he will mistakenly begin to believe his own excuses as to why certain messages are not working. Trust your initial instinct, and do not be afraid to try to reshuffle your curriculum to deliver a more logical message.

USE ACTIVITY TO PROMOTE INVOLVEMENT

Not everyone in this world has a Type A (or slightly hyper) personality, but when it comes to training, one thing is certain among all personality types: Adults cringe at the thought of sitting for extended periods of time. Unfortunately, due to less-than-creative previous teachers or presenters, most of us assume that attendance at a training session will mean nonstop sitting. The truth is, successful training can be so much more.

There are three basic reasons to get adults involved in activities when conducting training. The first is *morale*. Let's face it; hearing from a presenter that the course you are attending will be a 16-hour lecture is enough to make the strongest stomach weak. Remember, in the business of training, the presenter is guilty until proven innocent. In other words, if students previously had a bad experience with a similar course, they will assume they are in for the same treatment again. If the training previously dragged, had no interaction, or was boring, the students naturally assume it will probably happen again. Morale is damaged before the presenter even opens his mouth.

The second reason for wanting to involve adults in activities is *to stimulate interest*. What are some of the most memorable and interesting courses you ever attended? What made them that way? I am willing to bet the success of this course centered around some kind of activity.

An example of a successful activity-centered session involved a course that I started teaching for Xerox. I was reluctant to teach it because I had taken it as a student years before and disliked it. My memories of the class were that it was dull and that it was filled with hours of useless theory. What's more, everyone I knew who had taken this course shared my opinion. While being coaxed to teach the class, I was promised that some changes had been made. I was still skeptical, however, because I knew the curriculum content could not be drastically altered. Despite the course's poor reputation, when I finally taught it, it was a tremendous success due to a small, but significant *delivery* change. Although the *curriculum* did not change, a simulation had been added to the course, tying together the previous three days' material. The students loved the activity and loved the course. Even though the simulation did not begin until the third day of the program, the anticipation of the coming activity made the course exciting.

The third benefit of involving adults in activities is *to increase retention*. Again, think back on some of the lessons you learned and still remember from the classroom; I have a sneaking suspicion there was an activity run around that lesson. There is an old saying that goes something like this:

What people hear, they forget.
What people see, they remember.
What people do, they learn.

Activity to promote involvement within the curriculum is a technique used by many top curriculum writers and presenters. *Performing* a task, rather than being told about the task, benefits the trainee's morale, interest, and ability to retain the information taught.

SET DEFINITE GOALS

In any type of training, there is an overall goal involving what is being taught. This is sometimes referred to as "the big picture." What is it that you want the students to get out of the seminar? Adults demand to know this.

The issue really can be traced back to a simple fact about working with adults. For many, it has been a long time since they have attended a training seminar, and frankly, many have forgotten how to learn. We are often not dealing with a college student who has been conditioned to follow and absorb a professor's lecture. We are dealing with possible confusion and anxiety relating to what is, and is not, important. The signs are often obvious early in a presentation. All the trainer needs to do is watch the trainees' note taking for the first clue. Often I will start a seminar by passing out a participant package. Some trainees immediately uncap the highlighter like a drawn weapon. As I welcome the students to the course, I can spot trouble from trainees who have already highlighted the participant package cover to capture the course name and other housekeeping information.

"Glad to have us here, hope our trip was a good one, gotcha!"

Boy, I would hate to miss that critical information in my notes! Given a little time, the trainees' materials begin to turn the color of that poor, overworked highlighter. Even when I make eye contact with these individuals, there is a sense of note-taking pride. This look is not much different than that of a young child's proud gaze, as he brought home that first clay pot made in school. Could there be a finer pot anywhere? The only difference is the trainee's eyes are saying, Is there a finer note taker anywhere?

I would like to think that in every seminar I teach, everything is critical information. In fact, that is unrealistic. In a well-written movie, some parts are filled with action and other parts are designed to let the audience collectively catch its breath. This also allows the audience to better focus on the key portions of the story. Curriculum is written in much the same way. There are what is referred to as "nice to knows" and "need to knows" within the material. This assists trainees in focusing in on critical information. By giving trainees "the big picture," and informing trainees of the goals of your training, you are in a better position to influence their perception of what is and is not as important.

Without a sense of the goal of your training, your trainees may experience problems focusing on the really important portions of the curriculum. Many of us just cannot maintain that level of concentration for long lengths of time, especially if it has been a long time since we attended school where these skills were necessary. Clear the air and let students know you will be sure to emphasize the "need to knows" and share with them the overall goals of your training. While you are at it, give those boxes of highlighters to another seminar.

USE REPETITION TO INCREASE RETENTION OF CRITICAL INFORMATION

One of the most basic techniques used when working with adults, as well as children, is to incorporate a steady diet of repetition. It probably is no mystery to you that the chances of increasing retention go up substantially the more you repeat a message. What a lot of presenters do not know, however, is there is an art to using repetition effectively within a seminar room. The mistake many presenters make is never reconnecting their curriculum with the experience. Eventually the trainee has to start using the presenter's terms and not his own.

To help clear this up, let's use an example I mentioned earlier relating to learning the names of certain pieces of computer hardware. After detecting some "computerphobia" among our students, we decided to simplify these terms a bit and reference their experiences with a typewriter. One of the goals for this module may well have been for the trainees to be able to comfortably use the terms associated with computer hardware. Let's face it, although the trainees might now understand the various pieces of hardware, I would not be real keen for them to leave my seminar calling the central processing unit a "brain." Here is an area where you can rely on repetition to help you. Each time you have the trainees repeat these terms tighten up their explanations. What follows is a possible dialogue:

PRESENTER: OK, now what is this called?

TRAINEE: The brain.

PRESENTER: Right, also referred to as the central processing unit.

Later

PRESENTER: Now what is this called again?

TRAINEE: The brain.

PRESENTER: Also referred to as?

TRAINEE: The central processing unit.

PRESENTER: Excellent.

Repetition allows the presenter to "clean up" the responses being provided by the trainees. The intent is to provide a bridge using the trainee's experiences. You can begin to remove that bridge using repetition and have the trainees using the terms and concepts that they need to keep the new material clear in their minds when they leave the seminar.

The advantages of repetition also relate to another concept previously covered. Repetition helps the adult learner focus on particular goals of the training. Repetition provides tremendous, yet subtle assistance in guiding student thinking. When you keep repeating a message, it begins to unconsciously look like a "need to know" item. Make sure you carefully choose which pieces of curriculum you want to repeat so that the trainees better grasp the importance of the information.

Repetition is a powerful tool to assist in adult learning. It not only increases retention but, selectively used, it allows you to "fix" areas of curriculum that need tightening and guide the trainees in learning critical information.

TELL TRAINEES WHAT YOU REQUIRE OF THEM

If you listen carefully when working with adults, sometimes you might actually hear a faint ticking sound. That noise is a time bomb that could have been set as recently as the last training session the trainee attended or as long ago as a bad experience from this trainee's schooldays. It involves the element of surprise. A successful tactic in war. A misery with the adult learner.

Remember how you felt being informed of a "pop quiz"? I can still hear the groans from my schoolmates and feel the knot in the pit of my stomach. After announcing a pop quiz to an adult learner, you may find that knot on the top of your head! Adults hate surprises. Frankly, if I felt surprises would assist your training in the least bit, I would not be so hard on this tactic. They do not.

Adults have much larger egos than children. Without carefully going over what trainees can anticipate within your training, you run the risk of badly embarrassing them. Embarrass a child, and that child may just tell his parents. Embarrass an adult, and you are looking at possible aggressive behavior either immediately or down the road within your training.

Although it may appear obvious that a presenter should avoid tests or quizzes without first telling trainees of his intentions, other requirements are less apparent and are just as upsetting to adults:

■ Will there be any form of involvement during the seminar itself?
■ If so, will your feedback be based on the trainees' level of participation?
■ Do you want the trainees to take notes throughout?
■ Will the seminar cover the same old stuff as last year's session?

Then there is the question of feedback:

■ Will any formal or informal feedback be provided to the trainee's mentor or manager?
■ What affects that level of feedback, either positively or negatively?

This factor has the potential to be a highly emotional issue.

The frustrating element to the issue of establishing requirements with adults is that most adults will not request this information.

Therefore, it is easy for the presenter to skip over telling the trainees what is anticipated of them. In a perfect world, regardless of the last time the trainee attended a seminar, this information would be provided up front and fairly. The problem is, this is not a perfect world: This information is rarely provided up front, and trainees become scarred from these "surprises." That is why I mentioned the ticking of a time bomb. It is hard to predict, but an adult is going to accept the unfair practices of attending courses without a clear set of requirements for only so long. Then he is going to blow! The real kicker is that this explosion may come before the presenter barely opens his mouth. Bad luck? Bad trainee? Once again, the presenter simply becomes guilty until proven innocent.

Allowing the trainees to know, up front, the requirements of the course and what they can anticipate is an intelligent way to start a seminar. Not only does it give the trainees a road map of what to expect, it reduces the chances of aggressive behavior toward the presenter. Establishing requirements also allows you to guide the trainees' thinking from the "nice to know" to the "need to know." If I know up front that I am going to be tested on certain pieces of information, it will be no coincidence that I focus a little harder when that information is discussed.

MOTIVATE ADULT TRAINEES TO LEARN

In my mind, perhaps one of the biggest differences between working with children and working with adults is the motivation to learn. With children, the motivation is rather typical. Do well, get good grades. Do poorly, get bad grades. All of us can remember the sickening depression of taking that long walk home with an occasional bad grade. I would like to believe that my children's teachers motivate them, but the fact of the matter is, they do not have to because the motivation is automatically built in. As the child grows, the motivation shifts from having your parents see your report card to having college admission offices see your report card.

With adults, there is rarely anything that even resembles a report card. Oh, yes, sometimes when written feedback is recorded, a copy is sent on to the trainee's mentor, but more often it is not. In the instances where the feedback is sent on to the mentor, I would still not recommend using it as the primary motivator. When working with adults, it usually boils down to one point. What type of motivation does the presenter bring into the training room with him? Techniques for establishing motivation in the beginning as well as throughout your presentation will be addressed later in this book when we look at a process to assist your training. For right now, let's agree that if you, the presenter, are upbeat and positive about the material you are asked to deliver, this has a strong effect on the motivation the trainees will feel.

The question of providing motivation to trainees becomes a question of technique and attitude. Both of these skills are controlled by the presenter. The most basic point is that it is a mistake to think the trainees will automatically be motivated by the value of the curriculum. It is not the responsibility of the trainee to attend the training motivated. It is the responsibility of the presenter to find a way to provide that motivation. The reward for you is a highly interactive, participative group of trainees who are eager to face the next challenge.

MAKE THE PRESENTATION VISUAL

When writing about adult learning, another critical factor to consider is how your message is designed to appeal to the senses of the trainees in the room. One- or two-hour lectures may be fine in a university setting, but they do not work well in the corporate training world.

How much do you still remember from those large lecture classes? What you do remember is often a result of the teacher's ability to affect more than one of your senses during the presentation. When examining how your senses affect what you learn, we must consider not only which senses are most critical, but strategies for using these senses as well.

Let me pose a question to you. Which senses do you think are most critical in our learning process? A great deal of research has been done in this area, with some pretty interesting results. If you were able to ask an infant, he would tell you the sense of touch is critical. It does not take too many lessons in touching the stovetop for this infant to realize it is hot. As the child grows, everything begins to go into the mouth. The sense of taste becomes a critical factor. Finally, reaching adulthood, we become bombarded with different educators lecturing to us, appealing to the sense of sound. That would be all well and good, if our sense of sound were not such a poor sense to rely on.

Numerous studies have been conducted to try and pinpoint just what percentage of learning comes through which sense. Most break the numbers down approximately this way:

Taste	3%
Smell	3%
Touch	6%
Sound	13%
Sight	75%

The numbers are rather staggering when you consider how much time is often expended trying to get "the words" of a presentation together. I am not saying that the words we use will not influence what is going to be learned; I am merely interpreting these numbers to say that if you want people to remember your message, you had better be visual. Certainly, using the two senses of sight and sound together make for a very effective combination.

I also want to warn against overreacting to the sense of sight. One of the biggest mistakes made by inexperienced presenters is to attempt to be too visual. There is an old saying that pertains to the use of visuals:

If you emphasize everything, you emphasize nothing!

Hopefully, now I have begun to make you a believer in visual presentations. Let me now suggest that you choose wisely not only the frequency of how many visuals you use, but the variety as well. Later in this book, we will look at the positives and negatives of various presentation aids. For now, simply understand that varying the presentation aids you choose will certainly enhance their effectiveness.

Appealing to the various senses to better communicate your message is a time-tested success story. At times, when teaching students this point in a seminar, I will purposely not be visual in certain areas and visual in others. When we review in the morning, guess which group has the most trouble remembering the information taught? You got it;

the group that was not exposed to any visual aids. Although in reading this book you are actually flooding only one sense, close the book and see if you can remember which percentage of learning comes through which sense. I am willing to bet you will be closer than you think. You would not do nearly as well if those numbers were recited to you in a lecture.

SATISFY THE INFORMATION NEEDS
OF THE TRAINEES

When I was growing up, I was one of those kids who saved the best part of his dinner for the end (truth be known, I still do). When it comes to working with an adult learner, I have also saved the most important part for last. How often have you as a trainee, heard someone groaning about why he really should not be in the seminar? Perhaps he feels he already knows the material, or feels it will be a waste of his time. He may not want to be there for any number of reasons. Maybe, that someone has been you. One thing is for certain. If someone feels he will not benefit in any way by attending your training, nothing else really matters. You can put together that best curriculum, recruit the best presenter, provide the best visuals, and attempt to satisfy all the other adult learning principles. The bottom line is there will not be anyone there who is listening. This also means a much higher chance of aggressive behavior from the trainee toward the presenter.

What needs to be accomplished is to answer one question that may or may not be asked out loud. You need to provide the trainees with a "W.I.F.M.". No, that is not a radio station's call letters, nor did I sneeze. The acronym "W.I.F.M." stands for a question the majority of trainees ask themselves before attending any type of training: "What's In it For Me?"

Does this point sound a little selfish to you? Ask yourself, why would you want to attend training if you felt there was absolutely nothing in it for you? This sense of greed actually becomes a basic human need. This issue was brought out in a rather famous speech in one of my all-time favorite movies, *Wallstreet*. In this movie, Michael Douglas delivers a presentation to a couple hundred people at a shareholders' meeting. Douglas's character, Gordon Gecco, redefines being underfire in an apparently hopeless attempt to convince his audience that a buyout of their company is beneficial. As he starts his presentation, he is jeered and booed. The title of his presentation is, appropriately enough, "Greed Is Good." If you ever want to watch a master speaker give an effective "W.I.F.M." watch this movie. By reminding his audience that most of them are attempting to be as successful as possible, and connecting his message to their success, he convinces the audience that in fact, greed is good! The audience ends up convinced, cheering his efforts and supporting his plan.

The question then becomes; is this form of selfishness or greed a bad characteristic? I say no! I want trainees who are greedy and selfish. I want trainees who want to get the most possible out of training. Who would you rather do business with, someone who is greedy, or someone who is not? I choose the greedy individual. I make that choice because as long as this individual is ethical, he is certainly easier to understand and satisfy. Most people who are successful in business have found a way to channel their greed professionally. If I can appeal to that sense of greed and show how my product can make them more successful, I too will be successful. It is a basic message that is accepted in the training field as well.

I believe that the people in my audience are in fact greedy. They want as much as they can get out of what I have to say. I do not believe they would be as successful if they did not have this goal. We are all greedy to a point. I would much rather have students attending my classes who are greedy and want to know "what's in it for me?" If I am able to answer that question, I will be in a better position to achieve my goals of providing the best training this individual has ever received.

With that said, and the point made that you must convince your trainees there is a need to learn, the question now becomes, how. Before entering the body of the curriculum, how do you "hook" trainees into your curriculum and give them a need to learn? Ah . . . pardon my own rather obvious "hook," but the formula for that will be carefully outlined in Chapter 6, "The Secret of Success: Selling Your Presentation." I will give you a hint though; remember the word, "utility."

I hope this talk of selfishness and greed did not offend anyone. I assure you, I am both ethical and honest as a businessman. My intent was to point out a very basic need that most of us have regarding training or any other service. You must be able to answer the question, "What's in it for me?" Hopefully, I have been able to provide a little bit of insight as to where that need comes from.

SUMMARY

Working with adults can be a challenging and rewarding experience. The most basic point presenters must know is that their early school experiences are not as big a help as they may first appear. Studying some of the differences between children and adults will make your approach to working with adults more successful and satisfying. It will also provide a rationale for a structured process in the training of adults.

Chapter 2

Recognizing Trainees' Levels of Behavior

$\mathbb{P}$robably the best place to begin would be to look at your trainees' current level of behavior. In everything we do, including training, everyone's behavior falls within one of the four levels outlined in this chapter. Have you ever been taught a particular skill or idea and thought to yourself, "I have been doing that correctly all along"? One somewhat confusing aspect to training is that trainees come to seminars and workshops performing at various levels of behavior as well. What makes this issue potentially confusing is that these levels can literally change like the wind. It is therefore important to understand four basic levels of performance.

LEVEL ONE—THE UNCONSCIOUS INCOMPETENT

At this first level, the trainee is ineffective and unaware. I also refer to this level as the "blissfully ignorant stage." Often on the first day of training, a lot of trainees actually start at this level. The good news is that if you are at this stage right now, you would not even know about it! For example, all of us have known someone who got on everyone's nerves in the office, and had absolutely no idea those around them felt this way.

One of the problems with individuals at this first level is that these people generally do not seek training as a solution. Why would you want to learn to do something you feel you already know how to do well? Presenters who see individuals at this stage have to be careful that they begin to move these individuals slowly to the next stage. It is difficult to accept suggestions about something you currently feel good about.

Some jobs have built-in safeguards that keep people from staying in this stage too long. In selling, you can convince yourself how well you are doing for only so long. When the commission checks are cut, reality often sets in. Presenters can operate at the unconscious incompetent stage also. A presenter at this first stage is usually difficult to work with. One reason I say this is the nature of a presenter's work. It is not a position where individuals who are unsure of themselves survive long. Also at this level, the presenter has absolutely no idea there is even the hint of a problem. All I can say is thank goodness for evaluation forms!

LEVEL TWO—THE CONSCIOUS INCOMPETENT

At this level, things begin to get a little more interesting. The trainee is still ineffective, however, he is now aware of these deficiencies. If you have ever attended a training course, listened to the presenter, and thought to yourself, "Hey, I do that! I didn't know that was wrong," you were passing from the Unconscious Incompetent level to the Conscious Incompetent level.

If there is a problem with individuals at this level, it might be that sometimes there is resistance to moving on. Some people even revel in being consciously incompetent. Have you ever known individuals who seem to take pride in informing you that they do not do a particular task very well? There is no mention of wanting to improve, just the fact that they do not do this task particularly well. Many times, these individuals have preached about their ineffectiveness for so long and the impossibility of ever fixing it, their myth becomes a reality. They proudly remain Consciously Incompetent forever.

Fortunately, that problem is much more the exception to the rule than the norm. Training is typically created with the Conscious Incompetent in mind. Once an individual comes in touch with his own deficiencies, he is much more receptive to the idea of training.

Many presenters that I work with when I teach a Train-The-Trainer course start out with me at this stage. This is because we do not live in a perfect world, and the majority of new presenters are forced to conduct seminars before they have ever been taught anything about how to teach. It is often a case of product or curriculum knowledge without any training skills. This is another one of many reasons why I refer to the realities of training as being an "Underfire" position. After a presenter takes his lumps a few times in front of an audience, he is usually very much in touch with some of his incompetent areas. Practice, preparation, and confidence instilled by the presenter who is working with these individuals usually helps a great deal to move these new presenters to the next level. If a trainee is open to change, this level should not be visited for long.

LEVEL THREE—THE CONSCIOUS COMPETENT

Level Three indicates that an individual is both effective and aware of exactly what it is that is making him effective. There are a couple of different schools of thought as to whether this is the optimum level of performance. Remember, not only are you effective, you are keenly aware of everything you are doing to make you effective. Sounds about perfect . . . almost.

There is one issue that must be discussed when dealing with the Conscious Competent. Just how conscious do you really want to be when you are performing a given task? Think back on the last time you attended training and learned a new skill. When you left that training you were the picture of conscious competency. You did not make a move without checking that manual, or going through that given checklist. You were probably able to methodically produce what you were taught, step by step. No steps missed by you, no sir. You were a machine! That, unfortunately, is where the weakness is on this level. One of the frustrations often experienced by new trainees is that while they feel good about the process they have just learned, they want to know when they will be able to implement it without using their notes or sounding like an encyclopedia. I have often felt that this level should be renamed the "Mechanical Competent."

There is certainly nothing wrong with attempting to be effective and aware of what makes you that way. This is the Conscious Competent. When just starting out, or learning new curriculum, most presenters prefer to teach a couple of seminars before being observed. The reason for this is that by practicing and rehearsing, they are often attempting to push through Level Three and move to the next level.

LEVEL FOUR—THE UNCONSCIOUS COMPETENT

At this fourth and final level, people are effective but no longer aware of certain things they are doing right. They are quite simply producing the expected results without having to think about what they are doing to achieve these results. The mechanical part of what they have learned to do has given way to a more natural, relaxed ability.

The Unconscious Competent level does not necessarily mean we have achieved utopia. Some trainees actually arrive at training with many Unconscious Competent abilities. Have you ever attended a seminar and thought to yourself as the presenter was going over a new concept, "Hey, I do that. I didn't know you were supposed to. I must be pretty good!" This happens to be another basic reason for training, particularly in areas that involve subjective training.

Many trainees will show up ready to learn how to learn a new trade because they showed certain abilities as they were growing up. Someone probably patted them on the back and said, "You ought to be a _____ [fill in the blank], you are so good at _____ [fill in the blank]." When you hear this enough times, it does a couple of things. First, it instills a confidence that assists you in doing whatever the task is, and second, these comments are probably a tipoff that you are showing some instinctive abilities in that area. Sometimes, these trainees are referred to as "naturals." In sports, they are the natural athletes.

Natural Unconscious Competents would seem to have it made if it were not for one problem. Without ever being consciously aware of what it is they are doing correctly, they fall prey to second-guessing themselves when things do not go well. It is rare to find anyone whose position does not leave them susceptible to a slump of some kind. In selling, sales may drop off from time to time. In training, maybe a few extra-negative evaluations are received. We are all subject to ups and downs within our given occupations. A Natural Unconscious Competent who has no idea what is causing the slump he is experiencing, is often left second-guessing everything he is doing and ends up attempting to fix the wrong problems. It is certainly understandable to witness a panic when faced with poor performance he cannot explain. This is one of the reasons that even trainees who are performing at an optimum level should receive training up through Conscious Competency to teach them what it is they are doing right. Perhaps now, not only will they be better prepared in the event of a downturn in performance, they will be better in touch with what it is they are doing right and maximize this strength. This may also be why historically in the world of sports, "natural athletes" make poor coaches. To me, it is not much of a mystery at all.

Take the career of a natural baseball player as an example. Since he was a boy, he had a natural ability to play baseball. Some say that hitting a major league baseball is one of the most difficult tasks to master, but to him, it was a piece of cake. The sport came easily to him from Little League on up. Ask him about the science of hitting a baseball, and he will tell you, "Swing and it will go." That is an Unconscious Competent. Years later, this baseball player retires and decides to take a crack at coaching.

A slumping hitter looks through the batting cage out at the new coach and asks, "Any tips, Coach?"

"Ya," the coach replies, "Swing and it will go!"

Not much of a lesson. It is not surprising who typically make the finest coaches. It is usually the player who had a mediocre career at best. Oh, this player quite often played in the big leagues . . . for a week or two. Usually, most of his career was spent struggling to make it. They were not blessed with natural ability. Any success they experienced was due to literally kicking, biting, clawing, and bleeding to bring out every ounce of talent they possessed. They trained themselves to be Conscious Competents.

Ask this second new coach how to hit a baseball and he will tell you, "Get your bat back, keep your eye on the ball and shift your weight," among other things. He has made a science out of hitting a baseball from struggling with his own limitations. Typically, being more in touch with his own abilities allows him to be better able to communicate these ideas to others. While there are exceptions to this rule, one point is clear: Learning what it is you do well and do not do well can only improve the natural abilities you possess.

THE FOUR LEVELS OF BEHAVIOR IN ACTION

Now, let's look at another example that will illustrate all four levels in action. The game of golf immediately comes to mind. After breaking my hand in two places a couple of years ago playing basketball, I decided to take up a safer, less physical sport, the game of golf. I chose golf for one other reason. After watching various golf tournaments on television, I was convinced that the game would be easy and fun. Now that is what I call an Unconscious Incompetent. I had absolutely no idea how misguided I was. A friend of mine suggested I might want to take a few lessons, or at least hit a bucket of balls on a driving range, but I would have none of it. Until I stepped out on the golf course, I was totally unaware just how ineffective I was going to be.

I approached the first tee calmly and ready for action. There was a crowd of golfers building behind us as we waited our turn. Little did I know, this would be the last time I approached the first tee without butterflies in my stomach. I believe it was the third time that I swung and missed the teed-up ball that I began to move to Level Two, the Conscious Incompetent. It began to appear quite clear to me that I was not the natural I had thought I was going to be. All of a sudden, lessons did not sound like such a bad idea.

After what seemed like the three days it took me to finish that first humiliating round of golf, I signed up for a series of lessons. I was given the 500 or so necessary tips required to play the game at a beginner's level, and began to practice. As with most people who are moving toward Conscious Competency, I began to experience the excitement of some improvement. I was ready to take my show on the road, and try my golf game out on a real course again. This time, I would show the waiting gallery! When it became my turn, I began to methodically go through the lessons I had learned. I fell into my hypnotic golf trance and began to mumble my instructions.

Left arm straight.
Eyes on the ball.
Keep your head still.
Let the club do the work.
Slow back swing.
Turn your hands over.
Point your left shoulder toward the target.
Turn like you're turning in a barrel.

It was right about here that I heard someone in the gallery shout, "Oh my God, he just took lessons!" A groan escaped from many of those around this golfer. It sounded as if a few of the groans came from my own foursome as I continued on. I am not sure if this second round actually moved any faster than my first, but I did show improvement.

Unfortunately, because I was so mechanical and slow, it was not the most enjoyable experience I ever had. I, like most new golfers, had settled into Level Three, the Conscious Competent. It was nice becoming a student of the game and learning what I was doing right and wrong. The only problem was that I was driving all those around me crazy. I was determined to stick with it, however, so I kept playing.

Gradually, the more I played, the smoother my swing became and my game began to speed up. I remembered my golf pro telling me that if I kept at it, I would achieve what he called "muscle memory." I call it Level Four, Unconscious Competency. At this level, I finally could swing a club fairly effectively, and not have to repeat my massive collection of directions. Achieving Unconscious Competency is a goal most trainees have when they are learning a new skill or process. To achieve this level requires patience by the trainee and encouragement by the presenter.

THE NEXT LEVEL

Much has been written about the four levels of behavior, and all the discussions lead us to believe that the process stops at Level Four, Unconscious Competency. No argument from me that Level Four is our ultimate goal, however, I do disagree that the process stops here. It is unrealistic to assume we simply stop at Level Four and remain there. I would instead refer to these levels of behaviors as more of a cycle. What would you guess the next level would be for most of us after Level Four, Unconscious Competency? You are right if you said Level One, Unconscious Incompetency.

If there is a problem with Unconscious Competency, it is that you are susceptible to complacency. Remember, you are now performing effectively, and you do not even have to think about what you are doing to achieve these results. Think back and recall the first customer you ever worked with. You were probably the model of Conscious Competency. As a matter of fact, after you recovered from the shock of actually making a sale, you most likely brushed back a tear and in a choked up voice assured the customer you would be there to make sure all that you promised would happen. Make no mistake about it either, you were there! After a few more of these experiences, you settled nicely into your Unconscious Competency role of providing good, solid service. Now, let's move forward about 50 customers. Did you give them the same level of service you gave the first person? I doubt it. You actually slipped into Level One, Unconscious Incompetency. After a couple of signals (or complaints), you became Consciously Incompetent, took steps to fix this problem, brushing through Conscious Competency, and resumed your role as an Unconscious Competent. These behaviors are in no way stagnant as the cycle repeats itself over and over again in everything you do.

Chapter 3

The Personality Parade: Training All Different Types of People

Some people say that training must be a rather boring career. From the looks of it, without ever having been involved in a long-term training project, they appear to be right. Often, presenters find themselves teaching the same curriculum, running the same role play, monitoring the same labs over and over again. How can anyone teach the same materials week after week, in what is often an environment that does not change, without getting bored? It is an interesting question, and one I would probably have trouble answering if it were not for one obvious variable. Although the courses seldom change, *the trainees do*. With those changing groups of trainees comes an assortment of personalities, making the job of a presenter anything but boring!

So much can be learned from working with various personality types that it is not unusual for companies actually to use training positions as stepping-stones to management. The reasoning is quite simple. Anyone who spends a year or two in the classroom, juggling a different assortment of personalities every week or two, and finding ways to keep all those in attendance from killing each other, knows a few things about management. As a matter of fact, I would rate the people skills of most tenured presenters to be extremely acute. As with any team that may be inherited to manage, there is generally a hodgepodge of personalities to try and take care of. A presenter's ultimate dream is to repair whatever personality flaw exists within the trainee, and literally heal that trainee. Reality says that a reasonable goal is to minimize any potential distractions due to personality conflicts and allow both the trainees and the presenter to survive!

■ 29 ■

There are a couple of flaws to the theory that presenters are ready to step in as managers after a stint in the classroom. If I were to rate a typical presenter on management skills, there is no doubt that when it came to working with personality types, he would get an "A+". The problem is that although having the skills to get the most out of any type of individual is critical, so are other generic management skills such as giving recognition and delegation. Without a management training program intact for other basic management skills, they would get a "C−". Combining a management program *with* training works wonderfully in preparing a presenter to be a manager.

Trainees come in different shapes and different sizes with an entire array of personalities. Certain personalities are attracted to various types of training. All presenters will experience a full assortment of personalities. There are two ways to approach this phenomenon. The first is to react to whatever presents itself to you and take your best instinctive shot at dealing with it. The second, and more preferred, is to arm yourself now in a more proactive stance to the realities of training. With a proactive strategy in mind, I would now like to present to you eight basic personality types, the potential problems that might arise, and solutions. I would also hope that you will feel a little less apprehensive about working with these personalities to keep potential difficulties from ever surfacing within your training.

THE LONER TRAINEE

The first type of trainee that may appear in your seminar is a student that I call the *loner*. As the name indicates, this is a trainee that prefers to be pretty much left alone and considers himself self-reliant. While in class, the trainee typically is attentive and participative, often showing what may appear to be the perfect trainee personality. The only catch is that these trainees often prefer to have as little involvement as possible with the other trainees, can tend to isolate themselves, and may appear somewhat aloof. These trainees are often quite capable as students, which may account for some of their resistance in working with others. My guess would be that if you were able to check back to a report card written as this individual was growing up, you would probably see good grades with a comment that says, "Joey is a fine student; however, he doesn't play well with others."

This type of trainee is not as easy to spot as a lot of the other personality types. A loner is usually very good at coming up with excuses as to why they will be unable to work with other students. They will try and wriggle their way out of any type of group work by saying things like, "if it isn't too much trouble, I would like to work on this exercise alone. I find I am able to concentrate better." Many presenters will not even notice this type of trainee in their seminar because of his participation. As presenters, our primary focus is on seminar activities and the involvement of the trainees. Within the seminar, and in front of the presenter, these trainees appear to be model students. This makes it difficult to look at these trainees with a watchful eye. It is my recommendation that you do! An experienced presenter will tell you that part of his job is to manage the material taught, and another major part is to manage the personalities receiving this information. What possible harm can come from a near model student who does not necessarily interact with the other trainees? Plenty.

One of the biggest problems that can occur within your seminars as a result of a loner is what I refer to as distancing. Trainees will only go so far out of their way to accept another trainee. After the initial gestures of friendship are rebuffed, the other trainees will back away and distance themselves. Then, a strange phenomenon occurs. The class can actually turn against the loner and become hostile. One reason for this is that trainees often are attending a seminar that others in their firm have attended as well. All of us want to enjoy our training experiences, and a part of that joy involves the closeness that is shared among classes. Many trainees expect that "family" type feeling. A complicating factor is that other classes in town at the same time may be experiencing that desired feeling. "Our seminar? We're like brothers and sisters!" Now, here is your seminar, that with the exception of one trainee, gets together at night for drinks, lab work, or practice of some sort. A strange type of resentment occurs. It almost seems as if the trainees become jealous that their experience is not measuring up to that of other classes, and it is the loner's fault. Classmembers stop trying to include the loner and deliberately distance themselves from this trainee. What's more, slowly, little side comments start being made by the other trainees in the seminar like, "All of us got together last night, well *almost* all of us got together, to work on this piece." Once these types of comments start, they usually only get worse. Be on the lookout for such behavior and take action.

When dealing with a loner trainee, you can try a couple of tricks. To begin with, make it a basic rule not to go into too much detail when overviewing a course and going over a course calendar. In other words, until you have a handle on the personality types within your training, be intentionally vague regarding the methods you intend to use within your training. This allows you some freedom in coping with a loner. The solution I recommend to deal with such trainees does not interfere with what you will be teaching, only how you intend to teach it. Any curriculum has some poetic license to it. To work with a loner, it will be necessary to exercise some of that license. In other words, lying! Create activities where there are none to force loners into the mainstream of the class.

For example, let's look at an evening activity. In my curriculum it might say for the trainees to look over a reading for tomorrow. Lo and behold, it tends to come out of my mouth as a group project requiring two assigned groups to get together in the evening and come up with a couple of questions to ask the other group based on what they have read. I will even go so far as to suggest they take this project to the bar or a suitable relaxing environment. Depending on the setup of your training, you may want these activities to occur in the seminar. Create small group activities or teams to accomplish tasks that may be written to be done individually. In no way is this solution intended to represent a punishment for the rest of the class. Your job is to make sure that all students get the most they can possibly get out of the seminar you are conducting. As long as you do not tell the trainees all the evening or seminar activities you have planned, the assignments will not be perceived as anything out of the ordinary.

When working with a loner, you do not want to react too slowly to the situation. Some of the off-the-cuff comments that are often made in the seminar can have a terrible effect on the morale of the loner and the rest of the class. Sadly, by the time a presenter actually hears these comments, it may be too late. Most curriculum developers will state exactly what material should be covered. How to accomplish this task is often the presenter's business. Hold back on any early commitments as to activities and evening work until you have had some time to carefully analyze your participants.

THE QUIET TRAINEE

There are a few constants in this world that we all know and probably feel comfortable with. What goes up, must come down. When considering real estate, the three most important factors are location, location, and location. When conducting a training seminar, you are going to have *quiet* trainees. The fact of the matter is that some people in this world are simply quieter than others. Is that a problem in training? Usually not. As a matter of fact, most of the time if these trainees actually do become a problem, it is a result of presenter's inappropriate handling.

The mistake so many presenters make is demanding equal participation from the quiet trainees. Where is it written that all trainees must answer the same number of questions in class? In a few outdated books, that's where! Try to understand that some people are quiet people. They are not slow. They are not troubled. They are certainly not trying to undermine the presenter in any way. They are just quiet people. For some reason, these trainees can unnerve a presenter. Quiet trainees should pose no real threat; however, a few potential problems should be considered.

To begin with, let's look at how the rest of the class may feel about a quiet trainee. Usually, the other trainees feel a sense of empathy for this trainee. Students will often band together to help the quiet trainee. When a presenter begins to work the quiet trainee hard with questions, there can be animosity toward the presenter from the entire class. At no time do you want to appear to be picking on the quiet trainee.

Another side to the argument regarding the frequency of questions to a quiet trainee is this. If you do not ask questions of the quiet trainee, it becomes awkward for the rest of the class. Some trainees begin to feel as if one student is receiving preferential treatment. "How come he doesn't have to answer questions?" the other trainees begin to think. What's worse, the longer the presenter goes without asking a question of a quiet trainee, the more difficult it actually becomes for this student to participate at all. His shyness becomes compounded the longer the trainee goes without talking.

I have a couple of recommendations for working with quiet trainees. The first involves looking at the size of your seminar. Some trainees are quiet when there are 10 or 15 students in the seminar. Their confidence is not very high, and they may feel vulnerable. Try introducing a few small group exercises to the seminar. You would be shocked and amazed at how many quiet trainees come alive when the size of their group shrinks to four or five. It may be a ratio quiet trainees will be more comfortable with. One last point about small groups. Ask that the trainees in the groups take turns with different roles such as the leader and presenter. This will also force your quiet trainee to assume a leadership role within his small group and begin to interact with the rest of the class as well. Make sure you have enough small projects so that your quiet trainee gets a turn at the key roles.

My second recommendation, when working with quiet trainees, involves the kinds of questions you ask. Especially early on in your training, stay away from questions that can put the quiet trainee on the spot. Questions involving remembering particular facts could wind up being disastrous. Try some easier questions involving his opinion. Be extremely supportive (without being artificial) of responses. Even saying things like, "Good answer!" or "Now that's what we are looking for!" can do wonders. The basic point I want to make here is to start slowly and gradually work to build confidence in the quiet trainee.

Instilling confidence within a quiet trainee can be one of the more rewarding aspects of training. Seeing a trainee literally blossom and come out of his shell often becomes one of the many success stories a presenter clings to. "Real world" says this is not the norm, however. What you should look for is creating an environment that allows quiet trainees to break out if they so desire, and if not, to at least actively participate at a percentage slightly below the rest of the class.

THE AMIABLE TRAINEE

Next up in your personality parade of trainees comes the *amiable* trainee. Typically found as new hires, these trainees are about as close to model trainees as you will find. Obedient and ready to carry out the wishes of the presenter, they sit and await your next command. You say jump, and they really will say how high. Whatever you say or do as a presenter must be right. Pinch me, these students sound too good to be true! OK, here is the pinch.

If I have a concern with the "amiable trainee," it involves their blind trust. If the presenter were to say "The sky is green," this trainee would shoot back with "You bet!" I realize this may sound like a dream come true to some of you, but if you take your role as a presenter seriously, this has to disturb you.

The reality of training is that the presenter plays an important role in the professional survival of many trainees. Mastering the skills provided by the presenter may be their lifeline to individual success. Yes, I want the training to be a tremendous experience for my trainees, and I want to be loved by all. I also want these trainees to have long and prosperous careers with the company. It is therefore my responsibility to do all within my power to make sure that the skills I teach can be reproduced by the trainee in the field . . . when I am not there. The fear I have when working with amiable trainees is that I am not always sure they will be able to think on their own. It would be impossible, in most forms of training, to present every possible scenario to the trainees. Hopefully, teaching some type of process should help. Nonetheless, a skilled presenter must also teach the trainees to think out of the box. I do not think a student's agreeing with my every statement accomplishes that goal.

The solution is rather simple; it is not, however, an intuitive one. Most presenters will question amiable trainees to make sure they can think on their own. The problem is, they ask the wrong kinds of questions. If you ask an amiable trainee a question that requires a factually based response, you will most likely get the answer you are looking for. At no time did I say amiable trainees are slow. As a matter of fact, because they are typically new hires, there is a good chance they will be among your quickest trainees. This can be attributed to either just finishing school and being adapted to a classroom environment, or simply working harder to impress, because they are new. Many presenters think this is a way to get an amiable trainee thinking on his own. I do not.

A second type of question often asked of amiable trainees is opinion based. The idea here is to solicit the trainee's opinion to a question that has no right or wrong answer. On paper, this appears to be a pretty good solution to getting amiable trainees to think on their own. Unfortunately, the reality is that most amiable trainees will attempt to anticipate the opinion of the presenter and provide that response as their answer. Once again, you are left with trainees who still are not fully prepared to think on their own feet.

The correct type of question for an amiable trainee is a case history question. Remember, the concept of a case history question is to present a scenario using information you have just taught. What the case history question does, however, is ask questions that have not been addressed but can be solved using the information taught. It is not unusual to hear an amiable trainee respond by saying, "You haven't taught us that yet." If an amiable trainee says that to you, congratulations. You are doing beautifully. Your job as a presenter is to teach the information necessary to allow the trainee to attempt a logical response. Be supportive of the amiable's answer to encourage future thinking out of the box by your trainee.

The good news about amiable trainees is that of all the personality types identified in this chapter, I would probably most prefer to be "stuck" with these trainees. Other than the potential for the difficulties discussed previously and perhaps a little bit of boredom because they are so obedient, there really is not much to complain about. Keep a watchful eye that they are not too obedient, mix in a couple of case history questions to test the waters and count your lucky stars. You are going to have an enjoyable couple of days!

THE SNIPPETY SNIT

Let's now turn from the excitement and enthusiasm of an amiable trainee to the negative gloominess of the *snippety snit*. You are dealing with a personality type that is often depressed and discouraged and brings these feelings to your seminar. The causes of this behavior can be numerous, but one thing is definitely clear. The snippety snit trainee will waste little time making you and the rest of the class aware of his feelings.

The causes for this behavior are endless. It could be that the trainee was forced to attend a training seminar he did not want to attend. Some managers who still live in the dark ages use basic training as a punishment. It could be a fear of failure. Some trainees will mask this fear with a rude, insensitive attitude. He could be a trainee who is on the way out of the company due to any number of reasons, and for some reason has ended up in your room. Fact number one is this: it is not unusual to have a snippety snit trainee in your training room. Fact number two: you had better do something about fact number one in a hurry.

The reason I recommend that you act in a hurry is to combat the basic nature of the snippety snit. These trainees love company. Think back to when you started a new job. You were eager and willing to tackle any challenge that lay ahead of you. You were excited about the new challenges and fearful of the change that you had initiated within your life. For you, and for the rest of us, it can probably be traced as one of the most emotional times in your life. Then *they* approached you. *They* are the representatives of the "I hate it here and so should you" club. The membership drive started the moment you started your first day. In the blink of an eye, you were informed how miserable it was to work with whoever, for whoever, and the fragile emotional calm you were experiencing was shattered. Perhaps you fought back, but many do not.

Now let's take this experience and relate it to the seminar or work-shop you are conducting. Here is a room full of various personalities. Certainly the most vulnerable are your amiable trainees. They want to fit in so badly. Before you know it, what was once an ideal personality is now racked with cynicism and doubt. This gloom can spread across your training room like a cancer.

Fortunately, spotting snippety snits is usually easy. No matter what question you ask them, their responses always seem to have a depressed sound to them. This is no accident. What this trainee is really asking, or should I say pleading, is for someone to listen to him. The mistake so many presenters make is not the failure to recognize this personality type, or even to deal with it immediately. The mistake made is in how they deal with it.

The first error involves listening to the snippety snit. The good news is that most presenters will, in fact, hear out this trainee early in their training. The bad news is they have this conversation in front of the en-tire class. The snippety snit would like nothing better than to air his dirty laundry in front of the class at the urgings of a presenter. What a perfect scenario . . . for him. This is where I would like to introduce you to a technique that will be used for a couple of the more aggressive personality types; it is called the "Let's have coffee" technique. Nothing deep, mind you, but you would be surprised at what the conversation will sound like when the snippety snit has no audience to perform in front of. A simple "How's it going?" will usually do the trick. What I particularly like about working with this personality type is that if you ask "How's it going?" the snippety snit will tell you!

Be prepared to defuse some anger, so a couple of points need to be made here. First, do not apologize, or say you are sorry. The reality is, no one is really satisfied with an apology. It does not usually change the situation anyway. The snippety snit has probably heard apologies along the way. In addition to that, the words, "I'm sorry," usually cause people to affix blame. The majority of the difficulties that the snippety snit tells you about have absolutely nothing to do with anything you have done. Studies have shown that when customer service representatives say "I'm sorry" over the phone, they usually get it from the customer with both barrels. What people really want to hear is an acknowledg-ment of their problem. A simple "I can understand your frustration," and a restatement of the snippety snit's concern is typically more than enough to satisfy this individual. Being a good listener helps, and a nonthreatening reminder of your role as an instructor will more often than not defuse this trainee's anger.

The second common error when working with a snippety snit trainee involves the presenter's attempt to make it to the break without calling attention to the problem at hand. One of two things can happen. The presenter can stay away from questioning the snippety snit. In that event, the presenter may be sending some unwanted signals to the class that there is a problem they want no part of. Staying away from the snippety snit, in a sense, can alleviate his plight and give him a sort of martyr status. The other possibility is that the presenter can try to soften his questions too much by feeding the snippety snit opinion-based questions. By asking a snippety snit trainee his opinion, you run the risk of allowing him to literally climb up on a soapbox and vent his frustrations in front of the class. Sorry, not for me. I want the best of both worlds. Involvement within the seminar, but no venting. The solution involves a more careful use of the questions you choose. Make it a rule to stick solely to fact-based questions. Right or wrong, black or white. Frankly, I am not interested in opinions at this time. We will save that for our coffee break.

Snippety snit trainees appear to present a major obstacle toward successful training. Handled carefully, this simply is not true. Averting any displays in front of the class and taking a genuine interest in their difficulties goes a long way to achieving a workable solution. Be careful of the questions you use, do not delay in the tactics you choose, and the snippety snit trainee will not pose any real threat to your training.

THE ENLIGHTENER TRAINEE

Most training sessions are not complete without someone in the seminar who seems to "know it all." We will call this person the *enlightener*. How many times have you sat through a seminar and watched someone continue to enlighten the class with his enormous experience in whatever topic is being discussed. They can relate to what you are explaining to the class. They have a story that needs to be told. They have an experience that may help you get your point across better. The enlightener brings to the seminar a whole array of potential problems for the presenter.

To begin with, the enlightener poses a major threat to your *timing* of the curriculum. Timing is an issue that will be gone over in more detail later in this book; however, it is critical to a presenter's success. Enlighteners can throw a wrench into the careful timing of a presentation. This, in turn, can cause seminars to run long and force presenters to sacrifice critical material to make up for the lost time. The seminar can take on the appearance of being rushed and hurried.

A second problem that can occur from the well-informed enlightener, is damage to your *control* of the seminar and your *credibility* as a presenter. What often happens when the enlightener gets on a roll is the trainees' attention begins shifting from you to the enlightener. They begin to ask questions of the enlightener and not of you. What's even more frustrating is when questions are answered by you and the class looks to the enlightener for *his* approval.

The final distraction that enlighteners can cause is their uncanny ability to throw off your rhythm. A presenter who is working effectively begins to establish a sort of rhythm. The enlightener's interjections seem to appear in a Murphy's Law manner. Count on the distraction to occur as you are trying to make your most critical point.

Not only can the enlightener's action create difficulties for the presenter, they can irritate the other class members as well. It does not take very long to notice other trainees eyes beginning to roll as the enlightener brings forth another all-important point. The other trainees can get so frustrated by the enlightener their participation and morale begins to drop along with their interest in your presentation. Something needs to be done about this right now!

Fortunately, working with enlighteners is fairly easy. To make sense of the solution, first let's look at the typical cause for their behavior. It can be summed up in one, three-letter word: ego. Enlightener's consciously or unconsciously want all those in the room to be aware of how bright they are regarding whatever topic you are discussing. Their behavior is not malicious, nor is it generally intended to create any problems. They often just want to be acknowledged. No harm; that is exactly what you should do with the enlightener. In your acknowledging, you had better choose your words carefully.

For example, you would not want to silence your enlightener by saying, "OK, Frankie, you know a lot about skydiving. I want to hear from someone else now. Do you mind?" As ridiculous as that may sound, it is easy to get to a frustrated point and have your words come out a little hostile. Try it this way, instead. "Well, it looks like Frankie has a lot of experience in this area. I am going to be looking forward to having you share that with us, but I want to hear from the rest of you as well. Come on, don't make Frankie do all your work for you." This type of statement accomplishes two things. It provides your enlightener with an ego stroke, and it brings the rest of your class back into the conversation.

One of the more traditional approaches to working with enlighteners is to simply move up and slightly into their personal space while they are talking. I am not suggesting you pick a fight or anything, just appear very interested, and move in. This approach is especially useful for enlighteners who do not necessarily speak often, but rather just have a tendency to ramble. Your movements forward will send an unconscious signal for them to net out whatever they are talking about. If that does not work, be prepared to jump right into their monologue with a statement of your own relating to their point. Then, tie it back to your topic and hang on for dear life.

An example of such an exchange would sound like this:

ENLIGHTENER: . . . which can make a difference in how you want to handle this situation. Now, when I was a child . . . .

PRESENTER: So, in handling this situation, you would first work with the administrator. You know, you make a good point when you relate how you would want to handle this. In fact, that is what we want to accomplish in this module. People who need people . . .

If I appear to be a little harsh with the enlightener trainee, it is because I have seen them innocently drive many a presenter up a wall. I would be terribly remiss if I did not mention that a great deal of the time enlightener trainees are fantastic to have in a seminar. They certainly can assist in helping you break down the Monday morning barriers that you so desperately need to remove. It is amazing how one trainee who is participating in and enjoying your seminar can make others jump in as well. When the class begins to drift away late in the day, it is the enlightener who is ready to speak at any time. Managed properly, the enlightener can be a presenter's best friend!

THE JOKER TRAINEE

Similar to the enlightener is a trainee whose personality is rarely kept a secret for long. I am referring to the old class clown who grew up into a corporate environment and who we will now refer to as the *joker*. Quick-witted and potentially aggressive, it pays to spend a moment or two getting to know this character.

There are many reasons why an individual behaves as a joker trainee. The first, and most basic reason might be that something struck him as funny. Just because a trainee makes a couple of humorous remarks does not necessarily mean there is a personality problem within your seminar. It might be just the comic relief your seminar has been looking for.

When the joker trainee's behavior becomes more constant, the reasons may be a little more complicated. Perhaps it is an ego problem or the way this individual deals with stress. Let's again look at possible problems and then at some solutions that will allow us to work with the joker trainee in a peaceful manner.

The first problem that you should beware of is the joker's effect on the timing of your seminar. As with the enlightener trainee, the joker is not shy about chiming in on a discussion. Murphy's Law of training would say that these comical additions can come at the most inopportune times. It seems that every time there is a serious point to be made or an emotional statement to be addressed, here comes the joker. Sometimes a presenter builds a presentation to a powerful climax only to see it shattered by an assault from the joker. Potential powerful magical moments are ruined by an ill-timed joke.

Another concern with the joker involves feelings. Feelings of the trainees or the presenters are often on the line every time a joker opens his mouth. When you actually stop and consider the odds of having just one trainee who may be offended by a joke you begin to understand the danger of a joker. It could be a harmless joke about New Yorkers, Californians, or any other topic of your choice. You never know who may have a connection to the topic. Especially early on, there is no way to tell the sensitivity levels of your trainees. The joker has a dangerous approach to assisting you in finding out in a hurry. What makes matters worse, many curriculum writers actually still write into the curriculum suggestions to have a different student start the seminar each day with a joke. These suggestions do not typically stay in the curriculum too long once they have been used underfire!

Understanding how to work with a joker requires just a little basic psychology. Why is it that some people require and almost thrive on attention? The answer often found here is simply to make up for some feelings of uncertainty. Therefore, as with the enlightener trainee, the best approach to working with a joker trainee is to do a little boosting of his ego, actually give him an opportunity to perform, but only on your terms. This may come by way of selecting a volunteer or strategically using the joker in a case study. There are only so many of those situations around so I would recommend that you let your joker know that he is going to be involved well before the actual event. This helps to placate the joker's need to be noticed.

Another approach to working with joker trainees again involves movement from the presenter. As with the enlightener, some movement toward the individual can often help to send out the unconscious signals for the trainee to net out his story and finish up.

If that does not work, there is still always the coffee break method of asking politely for the individual to hold back their humorous comments. Be warned. Jokers do not respond well to being singled out and attacked in class. It is not recommended to try and publicly outwit a trainee whose strengths lie in these types of clashes.

Finally, screening a joker's jokes before allowing them to be aired in front of the room may help to avoid any other serious problems. Remember, these trainees are usually high spirited, emotional people who have a lot to offer a seminar. Working to channel that enthusiasm in constructive ways can help to harness that energy and put it to work for you. No student personality has a greater potential to warm up a seminar faster and more effectively than the joker.

THE RELIANT TRAINEE

One of my favorite, and most challenging personality types is the *reliant* trainee. I say this because watching a genuine reliant trainee work his magic is like appreciating a unique art form. This trainee is so good at what he does, most presenters do not realize they have been had until it is far too late.

When was the last time you felt confident doing a certain task, and the procedures changed? How did you handle not knowing all there was to know about your topic any more? Many people will find creative approaches to keep from looking foolish and learning new procedures. Reliant trainees are masters of this form of manipulation. Their appearance is one of confidence and coolness regarding everything except what you are teaching. That is where reliants begin to work their real magic. They are usually outwardly confident in many areas but when it comes to other tasks, they will have not participated and will rely heavily on others. Thus the name. Often there is almost a sense of pride from reliant trainees regarding their resistance to learn certain information. They sneak their way out of learning with well-polished phrases such as, "If you could just do this for me one time, I know I will be able to do it on my own in the future." The only procedures reliant trainees every really learn are the steps it takes to find someone else to do their work.

You have probably unwittingly assisted many reliant trainees in your time. Maybe it is the friend who "just doesn't do well with that type of customer," or someone who "just wanted you to type that memo this one time." The problem is, there is an office full of people who will offer certain types of assistance on an occasional basis. Take my father for instance. He could probably build a house from scratch. From top to bottom, there is almost nothing he could not do . . . except work with electricity. For some strange reason, he not only refused to work with electricity, he took a strange sense of pride in telling you he neither understood nor wanted to learn about electricity. This, of course, then became my speciality out of necessity. After a number of shocks through my lifetime, I later wondered how convenient this stubbornness really was.

A common problem that creeps up with many of the personalities discussed, including the reliant trainee, involves time. Unlike many of the other personalities that cause a seminar to slow down, reliant trainees usually have little to say during a seminar. The time problem they cause involves the presenter's time when the seminar is not in session. Before the seminar, during breaks, at lunchtime, and after the seminar, the reliant trainee attacks. It starts with "Could you just take a second to read over this?" and soon becomes "I still can't get it. Could you do one for me?" Before you know it, all your free time is being spent with one trainee. I want to emphasize here that I am in no way opposed to working out of class with a student. I maintain it is a luxury and not a right to have uninterrupted time without students while at your training facility. My argument is that it just is not fair to have one trainee monopolize all your individual time.

This brings me to the second, and most important problem a reliant trainee can cause a training department. Falling for a reliant trainees' manipulation fails to correct his behavior and can impact on the credibility of your training. Remember, often reliant trainees can get away with their behavior for only so long before those around them begin to catch on to their tricks. Training is then suggested to try and correct this deficiency. Unfortunately, it is rare to receive any type of biographical information regarding the shortcomings of your trainees. I have never had a reliant trainee come to town telling me they have had a history of manipulation and are ready to mend their evil ways! If the trainee comes back without the skills to correct his performance, it is *your* training that is considered a failure.

Working successfully with a reliant trainee requires the use of a couple of training skills. Start by taking a hard look at your curriculum and see if you can get a sense for certain areas that attract reliant trainees. Perhaps it is an area that you have noticed gives trainees trouble or even a more technical process that you sense may cause anxiety. After teaching a curriculum a couple of times, these pieces become fairly obvious. Once you get a sense for where these areas are located, lay out a process for how you will work with people regarding these areas. You may start that particular module with something like this:

Today we are going to learn a new skill that will be used in introducing yourself to your customer. I will want you to write out your introductions on your own and use them in the role plays that will be conducted tomorrow. I will not look at them until after you have used what you have once in the role play. After I hear what you have worked on, I will make written comments and ask that you continue to work on them alone. After three of these role plays, if you still do not feel comfortable with the process, I will be more than happy to sit down and work with you until you do.

Making a statement like this accomplishes a couple of things. First, it lays down the ground rules establishing how and when help will be given. This allows you to back off and encourage the reliant trainee to work on his own. Second, it reassures the reliant trainee that he will not be abandoned and in fact will receive help after he has made some attempts on his own. Be prepared to be positive and encouraging to whatever attempts are made by reliant trainees. The better job you can do convincing trainees they are improving, the better the chances are that they will develop the confidence to use these skills on their own.

Laying out the ground rules in advance is a successful proactive approach. There are also some effective reactive approaches that can be implemented while underfire. A favorite trick used by reliant trainees in front of the other trainees is to ask the presenter how he would do a certain task. That certain task is of course the task they themselves need to do. Using the Reverse technique by bouncing the question back to such trainees and stroking whatever answer you receive will assist you in getting them to do their own work. The conversation may sound something like this:

TRAINEE: How would your introduction sound to a typical customer?

PRESENTER: That's a good question. What approach do you think I should take?

TRAINEE: Uh . . . well . . . maybe just a simple third-party reference and a well thought out initial benefit statement.

PRESENTER: There you go! Now that would certainly get the customer's attention and allow us to proceed. Good job.

When working with reliant trainees, it is critical that the presenter first and most importantly identify what is going on. Teaching trainees by allowing them to "crawl before they walk" and "walk before they run," builds confidence along the way. Perhaps the ultimate irony is that it is not unusual for an enlightener trainee to become a reliant trainee once he leaves his area of expertise. Call it a bonus if you want to, but you will have to probably work to turn off this trainee initially and then work to turn him back on again later. Whenever you get frustrated, however, remember back when you tried to get someone to do your work for you that "one time." This may help with the empathy that is ultimately required when working with the reliant trainee.

THE SNIPER

Perhaps the most dangerous trainee of all is the *sniper*. The sniper got this name because many of the comments made from this trainee are not blatantly aggressive. Often the intent is clear, but the sniper trainee can put on an innocent front if challenged. Like a real sniper, this trainee fires shots, his cover being the rest of the students in the seminar.

I have many concerns about snipers. The first deals with the effect this trainee can have on the morale of a seminar. It can be disturbing, to say the least, when a trainee comes to a seminar and begins picking a fight with the presenter. For many trainees, this unsettling experience can ruin their training experience. Amiable trainees are particularly susceptible to the negativity a sniper can spread.

Timing is another concern when faced with a sniper. By dragging presenters into petty and trivial conversations, snipers can throw a carefully timed curriculum into a tailspin. By the time the presenter has attempted to settle such discussions, he may have to sacrifice other more important pieces of material.

Another concern I have about snipers has to do with the presenter working too hard to placate this trainee. You can literally spend an entire week attempting to win over a sniper and lose the rest of the trainees in the process.

My final concern with a sniper, as you might have guessed, deals with the presenter's well-being. Whether presenters want to admit it or not, the situation they generally fear the most is dealing with a sniper while in front of a class. Without the proper preparation, the fight certainly appears to be an unfair one. The sniper, while using the cover of the rest of the class, gets to take shots at the presenter. Maintaining his professionalism, the presenter gets to fight back with only one disadvantage. It often appears the presenter is fighting back with his professional hands tied behind his back. It is the presenter's responsibility to maintain control of the seminar and display professional behavior. A confrontation in front of the class exhibits neither of these responsibilities. That does not sound like a very fair fight to me. As a result, I have seen presenters retreat from the pit and never return. I have seen still other presenters witness a sniper attack in cross-training situations and quit their jobs to avoid the possibility of facing this potentially humiliating situation. I will leave to your imagination the ramifications of bottom line loss of revenue when a corporation loses a trainer for this reason.

In working out solutions, let's first take a closer look at what makes a sniper tick. To begin with, most snipers, ironically, are created by presenters. No, you did not misread that last statement. It is my strong belief that roughly 80 percent of the contact a presenter receives from a sniper is initiated by the presenter. In truth, because so many presenters want to discuss the more aggressive personalities of trainees, I discuss the sniper as a personality trait. The problem is, I have almost never met a trainee who actually woke up in the morning with the intent to maliciously harm a seminar and its presenter. I have, however, seen many of the other personality traits that have been previously discussed handled poorly creating a catalyst effect on the trainee. Embarrass an enlightener or a joker or just about any trainee in front of the class, even inadvertently, and you may create a sniper. Ask the wrong type of question to the wrong trainee, and you may create a sniper. Simply not addressing certain issues up front in your training can create a sniper. How do you know what critical issues you may need to discuss up front? That question will be addressed when we look at how to structure a presentation. Suffice it to say, there are a number of reasons why a trainee can assume the role of a sniper. The real question becomes, how are you going to deal with this trainee under fire?

I would like to examine two basic scenarios to prepare you in handling a sniper. The first scenario involves contact with a sniper who you already know will be in your room. This is not an uncommon situation. Snipers usually establish reputations for their actions. The second, and more difficult scenario, will look at the same case study, but without the luxury of advanced knowledge of a sniper's presence.

How to Handle Snipers Whose Reputation Precedes Them

Let me start by presenting you with what I consider to be a classic case study.

_____ **The Tale of Rotten Rob Rolles** _____

Rob Rolles is one tough individual. Just ask him. He is intelligent and capable of doing outstanding work. He has been with Widgets 'R Wonderful for over 20 years and unfortunately usually conveys an attitude of boredom. He is generally thought of, by those who work with him, as a fearless employee who tells it like it is. He is also regarded by his supervisor as an employee with an abundance of natural skills. Rob would have been promoted long ago if it wasn't for his tendency to be negative and critical. In his mind, there always seems to be a better way to do things and Rob enjoys laying it on. His approach often takes the form of needling questions that tend to disrupt the flow of discussions. He does this interrupting with an air of innocence with comments such as, "It won't work!" and "Not this old tired idea again!"

Well, how do you like my sniper? Most trainees who look at this case study just sigh and say they know this worker all too well. In examining the first scenario, the question becomes, what are you going to do about this situation since you know this individual is going to be in your seminar?

When you carefully examine the case study, you find in the second sentence a valuable clue. Usually snipers are not unintelligent people who have nothing to offer. Actually, this intelligence often accounts for snipers getting into trouble. How would you like it if you were looked to as the person in your office who knew most of the answers and then found out someone else was coming to town to take over that role? Snipers have large egos and are easily threatened in this type of situation. Unfortunately for snipers, times change and procedures change, and it is often the role of the presenter to come out and deliver this message. So what is the answer? I assure you, I fear no trainee and am in no way a coward. However, in this situation I recommend one simple, time-tested approach. If you can't beat 'em, let them join you!

Let's assume you have a one-week training seminar. That really means you are going to be running that seminar for approximately 40 hours. Would it be so bad to give up a little piece of the show? One of the best approaches to working with snipers is to prepare yourself to give up a piece of the show. If possible, try meeting with the individual before the seminar and map out a strategy for his assistance. Your discussion may sound something like this:

PRESENTER: Hi, Rob. Thanks for coming. Listen, if it isn't too much trouble, I was wondering if I could count on your assistance in this training. I am well aware of your expertise in _____ [fill in the appropriate topic] and wanted to know if you could give me about 10 minutes on Thursday getting the rest of the class up to speed. I will then go over the new procedures. Can I count on your assistance?

For those of you who are a little squeamish about giving your sniper the floor, notice how you can carefully map out what, where, and for how long your sniper will speak. This should settle any feelings about losing control. If your trainee has no abilities whatsoever to offer the seminar, try "Counting on their help" in passing out handouts and setting up break stations. The magic of this approach is that it often creates a model trainee from what once may have appeared to be a potentially volatile trainee. The responsibility of training now falls on both of your shoulders, and given an opportunity, the sniper will rarely fail you.

In reminiscing back to my early training days, I can honestly say that this approach may actually have provided me with one of my biggest career breaks. The government contract that I was working on called for some important training in Tampa. What we did not know was that there was a sniper laying in wait for one of our top trainers. The two-day training session became so disrupted by the sniper and trainer battles that the training was halted after the first day. Our trainer angrily flew home while the letters began to fly. The government monitor demanded we send someone down to Tampa and "Do the training right!" When the pool of trainers I belonged to was asked for another victim, I volunteered to go underfire. My goal was a simple one. Meet with the sniper beforehand, involve that individual in the training, and try and stroke his ego at the same time. Not only did this solution work, but letters were again generated, this time positively by, you guessed it, the sniper. I was given my first significant promotion, and needless to say, I have been a fan of this method of working with snipers ever since.

One irony that seems to be rather consistent with snipers is that they tend to be either really bad or really good. There is not a whole lot in between. When they do behave and write commendatory letters or what not, it is almost as if they are saying to those who are listening, "See, it isn't me. I have been telling you all along that given a good trainer I will more than behave!"

What to Do If You're Blind-Sided by a Sniper

The second, and more difficult scenario, involves the same type of sniper as mentioned earlier, but this time, you have no warning about his behavior. There you are, happily going through your introduction to the module, when your sniper rears his ugly head with a shot right between your eyes. In the training world, we call this getting blind-sided.

First, let's look at what *not* to do. The first instinct a lot of presenters have is to shoot back. How dare this trainee be so rude! How dare they take such an obvious cheap shot at you! Normally I preach to presenters to trust their instincts in most of the decisions they are faced with, but not this time. The critical point to remember here is that the sniper's behavioral pattern is not a secret to those around them. Other trainees know when a student takes a cheap shot at the presenter. If you felt it, most likely, so did the rest of the class. At this point, even if the other trainees were equally hostile coming into the seminar, they too will be somewhat appalled at the sniper's behavior. Most trainees know it takes guts to stand up in front of a class and will not support inappropriate behavior. That is, unless the presenter fires back. Once a presenter allows himself to get sucked into a confrontation in front of the class, all bets are off. The other trainees then get subjected to inappropriate behavior from the presenter as well and the battle lines are drawn. It now becomes a question of which knucklehead they should support.

This leads to my first recommended tactic, which may be somewhat of a disappointment to you. Look the other way. It is from years of experience that I say you will be much better off if you develop a motto that says "The first one is free." To begin with, you run absolutely no risk of overreacting and alienating the rest of the class. The fact of the matter is that, occasionally, trainees make rude comments inadvertently. As I used to tell my parents, every now and then I'm going to put a ball through a window accidentally. I'm still a good kid. Often trainees will test a presenter they are unfamiliar with. Granted, I would prefer a different test such as patting my stomach and head at the same time (I practice that one just in case), but in the real world some trainees want to see just how well that presenter reacts underfire. On many occasions, these snipers will come up at the first break and apologize for their behavior. In a sense what they are really saying is that you passed the first test. You did not blink.

Flushing a Sniper Out

Now, let's just say that after turning the other way and muttering to yourself about the first one being free, your sniper does not go away. One of the most frustrating aspects of dealing with snipers is that they often make their nasty comments hidden securely behind the rest of the class. Sometimes, only their slightly sarcastic grin gives them away, confirming that you are not paranoid and that the comment you just heard was meant to embarrass you. This next recommendation may sound a little bit risky, but in some situations it may just do the trick. When the sniper is attempting to mask the hostile comments you are absorbing with an air of innocence, you may want to ask your sniper one simple innocent question in return.

PRESENTER: You know Rob, that sounded like an aggressive remark. Was it intended that way?

What I particularly like about the technique is that it forces the
sniper to put his or her cards on the table and 'fess up to what is going
on. Nine times out of ten, the sniper will back off and choose his words
a little more carefully. While staying professional, and without being
drawn into a confrontation in front of the class, you may very well have
passed test number two.

Despite your attempts to handle yourself professionally, without
overly embarrassing your sniper, there are still those rare individuals
who want to have it out in front of the class. You absorbed the first inappropriate remark, and attempted to flush out the sniper with the second
remark, but the negative comments just keep coming. It is now time to
move to the third and final tactic. If you have ever wondered what it
might be like to fly without a net, here comes your big chance. The approach I am going to outline for you may seem risky, but it has never
failed me, or the presenters I teach. The single most effective approach
I know of (and have used on numerous occasions) requires relaying the
sniper's comment back to the rest of the class. The exchange will most
likely sound something like this:

SNIPER: Excuse me. I think I speak for all of us here when
I say that what you are presenting to us today is
really a waste of our time. We have been through
this garbage over and over again with no results to
show for it. When is the home office going to wise
up and leave us alone?

PRESENTER: So your concern is over the value of the training
that is being presented. Fair enough, you make an
interesting point. How do the rest of you feel
about the value of the training you are in town to
receive?

TRAINEE NO. 2: Well, I—for one—am interested in the training
and am willing to at least give it a chance.

This strategy is based on the belief that people do not want to see
another person publicly humiliated and even if they concur with the
comments that the sniper has made, they will not support them. It is

vital to maintain your composure and allow the other trainees to side with you, if for no other reason than to maintain your professionalism. In my years of teaching new presenters, I have ended every class by handing out a business card and asking the students to write me if this strategy ever failed them. To date, I have never received such a letter. I am more than happy to make that same offer to you.

Once Trainee No. 2 (whoever that wonderful person may be) comes to your rescue, you are not out of the woods yet. You need no other confirmation; you have a real live sniper in your midst. It is doubtful that the sniper will now just go away. What really needs to happen now is a conversation off line between the two of you to iron this situation out. The only problem is you may have another 30 minutes until you can take a break and get to the bottom of this. There is no sense making this situation any worse than it is, so stay away. If you feel it is absolutely necessary to involve your sniper in the presentation, try to stick to close probe questions that deal with facts and not feelings. Once you have made it to a break, subtly try to have a private conversation with the trainee. Maintain your composure and try handling the conversation the same way you would work with the snippety snit trainee. That is, probe around and see if you can figure out what is disturbing the sniper before you jump down his throat. Assuming this sniper is not going to make your job an easy one, and is offering no real reason for their actions, here is a six-step process for confronting the trainee and putting this problem behind you:

1. "I need your help."
   Sometimes the most difficult part about confronting an individual is that it is difficult to find the words to get started. No one wants to be standing there, looking at the ground hemming and hawing, searching for a way to begin. Beginning your conversation this way sends out a message that you are serious and about to have a frank discussion.

2. "The situation is . . ."
   The second step of this process, in my mind, is the most crucial. Starting out by describing the situation really forces both parties to deal with facts, and not feelings. This has the potential to be a highly emotional moment. It is easy to disagree with another person's feelings but far more difficult to disagree with facts. State

the problem clearly, and discipline yourself to avoid using the word "you." This will also help the individual you are confronting to look at the situation for what it is, and help reduce its emotional aspects.

3. "The difficulties this creates . . ."
   Now you can begin to shift gears and let the individual you are confronting see the results or ramifications of his behavior. A couple of reminders. Once again, avoid using the word "you" and stick to facts, not feelings. One other recommendation. Try to avoid using the word "problem." It is a very confrontational word and can emotionally charge your sniper. Try replacing this word with other adjectives such as "difficulties," "concerns," "barriers," or "limitations."

4. "In the future . . ."
   At this time, begin outlining the solution, or possibly a suggestion to eliminate the behavior you are correcting. Remember, although you are in charge and running the show, you are also in a negotiating position. Allowing the person you are confronting a token piece of the pie is good for all concerned. In other words, try to make your solution a fair and reasonable one for both parties, and then stick to it.

5. "If this situation were to occur again . . ."
   I am highly opposed to making threats within a training environment. In this situation, however, you must map out the consequences if the inappropriate behavior continues. This brings me to an important conversation that every presenter must have with his immediate supervisor. Before anyone starts training, there must be a clear understanding of the procedures in a worse case scenario trainee behavioral problem situation. This is no time to be a hero or go out on a limb. Most training departments institute a "send home" policy to aid presenters with trainees who just will not cooperate. This policy empowers the presenter with a tremendous responsibility and obviously should be used in only the most drastic situations. In my years as a trainer, I have never sent home a student for bad behavior. The real benefit of such a policy is that it provides presenters with the confidence that they will have management support and regardless of the situation, they will win in the end.

6. Gain agreement.

During the conversation that has now been outlined, many trainees will not have a lot to say. As a matter of fact, many will be gazing at the floor or around your office avoiding eye contact all together. Gaining agreement not only allows you to see if the problem has been solved in the trainee's eyes, it psychologically makes it more difficult for the trainee to create the problem again. There can be no misunderstandings.

Remember, this technique is recommended when all other options have failed. The realistic outcome of this type of conversation is that the problem will almost certainly go away. That is the good news. The bad news is that your confronted trainee might feel humiliated and may withdraw from the rest of the seminar. I would like to tell you otherwise, but this is the reality of a confrontation of this nature; therefore, use it wisely.

In most courses that teach people how to react to feelings of anger, the instructor tells the students to count to 10. Well, when underfire, you do not have the luxury to count off in front of a class, so often turning the other cheek is the next best thing. You have the support of the other trainees, management, and anyone else who has ever had to step into the pit. Maintain your composure and professionalism, treat confrontation as a challenge, and you will do just fine.

SOME CLOSING THOUGHTS

When looking at trainees' personality types it is important to remember a couple of basic rules. To begin with, you are not a licensed psychologist. Therefore, in no way does any strategy that may be implemented involve "curing" this trainee of the particular problem. Your basic strategy throughout is survival, yours and the seminar's. Do not be so naive as to think that your solution will undo years of deviant weird behavior. It will not! These trainees have had years of practice. Your goal is not to *fix* any of them, only to *manage* them while they are in your seminar. What your work with these trainees will do is allow you to take a diverse group of individuals who have been thrown together for a period of time, and allow them to move from point "A" to point "B" as painlessly as possible.

The rule to remember deals with identifying the various personality traits. It is rare for me to lecture on this topic without trainees cornering me after class and asking me what type of personality they or the rest of the class represent. With all due respect, they have somewhat missed the point of this entire topic. In no way am I suggesting that you immediately psychoanalyze every student in your seminar. The key to keep in mind is that you are on the lookout for extremes. I like having someone with a sense of humor in my class. I do not necessarily label him a joker. Some people really do know certain pieces of information regarding your topic and want to share it with the class. Fantastic! Your job is to keep an eye out for extremes and attempt to pull these trainees back from their extreme postures.

As far as your reaction to the extremes in personalities being displayed by your trainees, I have one final point that needs to be made. I have saved it for last in fear that if I wrote this in the beginning of the chapter, you might not feel a need to read on. If you discipline yourself not to overreact to any of the personality traits that have been discussed, and show just a little patience, often the other trainees will take care of the deviant behavior for you. On many occasions, I have either been told about the message or have overheard trainees telling others to lighten up, quit talking so much, or lay off the instructor. It is when the trainees cannot or will not react that you will have to react for them.

Avoid the "Squirrel Mentality" of Reaction

Behold the squirrel, one of Mother Nature's true treasures. The squirrel possesses amazing physical traits; speed, agility, power, and strength to name a few. Yes sir, the squirrel is truly one amazing creature. Unfortunately, the squirrel is also saddled with one tragic flaw. It cannot make up its mind. Just look in the street if you need a sad reminder. The real tragedy is that as you come speeding around the corner, bearing down on my little friend, he has the ability to easily avoid the inevitable. As he spots you, his keen sense of vision and hearing make many options immediately available to him. He can go left, and he does a few steps. He can go right, and he will a few steps. He can go forward, and he can go back. Unfortunately, at this critical moment of truth, the only thing he cannot do is make up his mind. He does not commit to a decision. Therefore, despite his motions, the squirrel winds up right back in the middle of the road.

You must also avoid the "squirrel mentality." You can decide to react, and if you do, then damn it, be committed and react! You can choose not to react and allow the trainees more time to react for you. Stick with that decision. The worse thing you can do, however, is to make a weak reaction, back off, react again and appear undecided. You are now looking up at a 2,500 pound car bearing down on you at 50 miles per hour, and you are going to wind up being flattened. Learn from your successes with your trainees and failures as well. No two trainees are exactly alike and neither are their reactions to your solutions. Try not to second-guess yourself; stand by the decisions that you make and you will live to fight another day!

Chapter 4

The Pace Race: How to Train Groups with Diverse Needs

One of the most emotional areas that often affects a presenter's performance involves training pace. It is a potentially emotional issue because of the impact the right or wrong decisions can have on a seminar.

When conducting your training, although you may feel your product knowledge is sound and your command of the logistics of the curriculum is good, the next task has to be determining the knowledge level of your audience. This information will better allow you to adapt to a speed tailored to that knowledge. Now, in a perfect world, you will know the experience of your group ahead of time, and they will all be at roughly the same level. Unfortunately, this is not a perfect world and training rarely cooperates so reasonably.

The good news is finding out the pace you may need to communicate is usually not much of a problem. Depending on the size of the seminar, you should run an icebreaker exercise designed to give you the information you need regarding the background and experience level of your audience. Even with larger crowds, or in shorter training time frames when the background of your audience is still necessary, there is still hope. All you need to do is poll your audience as to their experience with your chosen topic. The bad news is that sometimes you may not like what you find out in your poll.

HOW TO PACE A COURSE FOR A LARGE GROUP WITH WILDLY DIVERSE NEEDS

Years ago I was giving a pilot workshop for the National Flood Insurance Program in Los Angeles. This 3½-hour workshop attracted an audience of approximately 140 participants. Add to that number another 15 to 20 government monitors from the Federal Emergency Management Agency (FEMA). Looking back on this experience, I remember with a smile that I had conducted this same pilot one week earlier in Red Bank, New Jersey, and one government monitor showed up. When we moved the show to Los Angeles, the world decided to travel out of National Airport to take a peek. There I was with just a "little bit" of pressure on me teaching a flood workshop to a mountain of people I knew nothing about. I began to poll the audience to get a sense of what speed I would be working at and received the shock of my young training life. I asked the audience how many of them had written less than 5 flood policies in the past year and about 70 hands went up. I then asked them how many had written 5 to 10 policies, and no hands went up. 11 to 25 policies? No hands went up. 26 to 50 policies in the last year? No hands went up. My voice let out an adolescent type crack as I asked about 51 to 100 policies and no hands went up. Finally, in a stunned, somewhat apologetic manner, I asked how many of them had written over 100 policies in the year and about 70 hands went up. I am proud to tell you that I did not pass out, but I will tell you I was damn close.

With a large group like that, there was really only one alternative. I told the group that I was probably going to be covering the material at a slightly quicker pace than some of the individuals in the room would prefer. I also told them that I would be more than happy to address questions during the two breaks and stay after the conclusion of the workshop and answer questions for as long as it took. I then told the group that, for some in the audience, the pace might seem a little slow. I told them to bear with me, there were some changes to the program they might not be aware of and they could use this workshop as an opportunity to brush up on the basics. The off-line questions offer stood for them as well, offering them time to have their more advanced questions answered. Once again, you see the realities of training and a presenter underfire. The result of the seminar? Of the 140 evaluations received, about 70 of them rated the seminar highly but mentioned the pace was a little fast, and about 70 of them rated the seminar highly but mentioned the pace was a little slow. I, in turn, felt like a gymnast who had just stuck a difficult landing without even a little hop. I could have done no better.

Now you may be saying to yourself, well now wait a minute, how could he be so pleased with such mediocre results? The answer is simple. There is really only one other alternative to the situation outlined, and that is to pick one half of an audience and abandon the other half. This solution simply will not work. The result will be that half the audience will love the work you have done, and the other half will revolt. With a large group, there are no perfect answers. It becomes a case of selecting the lesser of two evils.

With smaller groups, your success rate with split experience levels can actually improve. You have a greater ability to offer individual attention. The rule of thumb that is generally followed is gearing your pace about two-thirds below your quicker students.

WHAT *NOT* TO DO WHEN TRAINING DIVERSE GROUPS

When conducting technical training, the issue of pace once again grows to monstrous proportions. While teaching automation to the government, I have witnessed tremendously emotional situations regarding training pace. Once, while conducting training in a contracted facility, I was one of three trainers teaching the same curriculum to three different classes. Fortunately, I was lucky that week and was working with a group of trainees with fairly similar experience levels.

The trainer next door to me was not as lucky. As the story was relayed to me, when the trainer polled his audience he found out that of the 16 trainees in the room, 12 had their computers in their field offices and were actively using them. Since only about 5 percent of the offices in the country had their computers, that level of experience within the room was unusually high. To make matters worse, the other four trainees in the room not only had no experience level with the computers, they were from a minority of offices that had not even received the computers yet. Well, the trainer must have tried using the "eanie, meanie, miney, mo" method of selection because he selected the fast group without compromise. As a result of this decision, the group of four trainees banded together and began to steadily become more and more abusive to the trainer, culminating with one trainee actually picking up her notebook and slamming it into the wall. The trainer in turn was devastated, ran out of the room in tears, and never taught another class again.

In retrospect, I certainly felt for the trainer, but I felt for the abandoned trainees as well. Especially with technical training, an almost indescribable frustration can surround a lost trainee. Have you ever been lost or stuck while working with a computer? The funny thing about computers is they are not real compassionate with a trainee who is close to the right answer. It either is correct, or it is not. If it is not, equipment can be merciless. Nothing is more frustrating to sit with a locked-up piece of equipment, hearing the trainer calling out commands and seeing your classmates merrily pecking away, while you drift farther and farther behind. As the trainer, you must empathize with that frustration and do what it takes to catch trainees up.

HOW TO TRAIN THE "SLOW POKE"

Let's now shift our attention to two new trainee roles and look at some methods designed to work with individual trainees who are slipping behind the class or possibly even easing ahead. First we will look at the potential trouble this may cause, and then we will look at some recommendations to cope with the situation.

The *slow poke* is a trainee role that most presenters become accustomed to working with. The slow poke is a trainee who, for whatever reasons, simply cannot keep up with the pace of the rest of the class. This trainee may also suffer from low self-esteem and should be watched closely. The reason I say to watch slow pokes carefully is that they are often embarrassed about their need for assistance and would often like nothing better than to simply go unnoticed.

Sadly, some presenters would be more than happy to comply with the slow pokes' wishes to be left floundering alone. Hey, as long as they do not slow the rest of the class down what could be the harm? Well, your week may in fact seem to run a little smoother turning the other way, but we both know that just cannot be done. Good presenters can reach most of the trainees, and great presenters can reach all of the trainees. Your job as a presenter is to attempt to reach all of the trainees with every breath you possess. This attempt to work with the slow poke must not be to the detriment of the rest of the trainees, so let's look at some ideas that may help.

To begin with, remember that the slow poke may be somewhat sensitive to the way you offer him assistance. There is certainly no need to grandstand and publicize that the class must stop to wait for the slow poke to catch up. Some of the best ways to work with these trainees require proactive thinking. You might as well face the facts right now that you are going to get slow pokes in your training room, and you are going to have to work with them. One approach I have found helpful is to prepare for this type of trainee by always adding backup exercises for the material I teach. If it is a technical course, try mirroring whatever exercise you have the class doing, but without notes, or with different criteria. It is far more difficult working with slow poke trainees in a technical environment because their inabilities are usually a little more obvious and you, the presenter, often cannot move ahead without these trainees being on board. By laying out these extra activities, you can buy some extra time to work your way toward the slow poke and quietly offer your help.

With nontechnical training, you can often just make yourself available during breaks, lunch, and before and after the seminar. Sounds like fun, huh? The reward of seeing a slow poke succeed makes it all worthwhile.

HOW TO TRAIN THE "WHIZ KID"

In their own bizarre way, the *whiz kid* trainee can cause enormous difficulties in the delivery of your curriculum. The whiz kid is a trainee who not only knows a lot about your topic, but is so confident he constantly insists on moving ahead of the rest of the class.

The whiz kid has the potential to cause two difficulties. To begin with, these trainees have a strange habit of intimidating the rest of the class. As luck will usually have it, the whiz kid will offer some inappropriate, confusing question just as you are attempting to nurse the rest of the class in learning a difficult concept. While the class is precariously teetering between understanding and confusion, your whiz kid will give his fellow trainees a rather unfriendly push causing an overload and resignation. The problem is, you the presenter are also balancing on a thin line of wanting to not answer the question while assuring the class the question was not as difficult as it sounded. Sometimes you can accomplish both as illustrated in the following exchange:

TRAINEE: Can you give us a better idea of the PC6300's ability to send and or receive information using the 9600 baud modem system?

CLASS: (Nervous murmur and puzzled expressions)

PRESENTER: I believe Simon's question was in reference to the computer's ability to communicate. Is that right Simon?

TRAINEE: Uh . . . well . . . uh . . . yes. I guess so.

PRESENTER: Well, as I mentioned earlier, I am in town to teach only the information outlined in your course agenda. I would be more than happy, assuming we have the time, to answer off-line any questions that we are not scheduled to discuss in class. Are there any other questions?

Addressing the whiz kid's response this way gets two things accomplished. First, it simplifies the question in an attempt to rebuild the rest of the class's confidence. Second, it reminds the trainee in a fair and nonaggressive way that questions of that nature are inappropriate in your seminar. This example should also serve as a warning as to the importance of carefully setting up-front expectations in your training. This subject will be covered fully in Chapter 12.

The second problem a whiz kid can present in your training involves his own pacing. Whiz kids are notorious for attempting to move ahead of the rest of the class—and for missing out on important information. As you know, I would never advocate lying to any students at any time . . . exactly. In the event you are faced with a whiz kid who just cannot stay put, try this idea. Tell him that although he may be comfortable with the material you are covering or has been through it before, there have been some changes made (this could mean the presenter who is teaching it to them), and you suggest staying with the rest of the class so he can be apprised of these changes. See what a good, well-placed lie can do?

Sometimes you can even pair up your whiz kid and your slow poke in team exercises. I am all for this technique but strongly recommend you keep a watchful eye out that both trainees are involved in the exercise.

Remember, the slow poke would like nothing more than to have some-one do his work for him and the whiz kid would be happy to oblige.

The pace of your training can have serious effects positively as well as negatively on the success of your training. Poll your audiences as to their knowledge level and adapt your message to fit their speed. Addi-tionally, keep a watchful eye out for the slow poke and the whiz kid and act quickly if needed.

Chapter 5

Anatomy of an 8:00 A.M. Start: Finalizing On-Site Preparations

At last, the preparation is behind you and it is time for your training to begin. What I would like to do now is take a rather simplistic look at what your morning may look like before you deliver any real curriculum. Sometimes, this is the most difficult time for inexperienced presenters who are finally facing the moment of truth and preparing to go underfire for the first time. The strange thing about training is that, regardless of a presenter's tenure, to some degree, all presenters feel that same moment of truth right before training is set to begin. The degree of anxiety is often related to a presenter's experience, but it is there just the same. Most anxiety is caused by a fear of the unknown, so let's look at a typical start to training. If you do not usually start your training in the morning, plug in your own times and come along for the ride.

7:20 A.M.: ARRIVE EARLY TO ENSURE EVERYTHING IS READY

It does not matter how many times I have taught a seminar; arriving a full 40 minutes ahead of time is a necessity for me. No matter what potential problem may have cropped up since the Friday afternoon when I left the room, 40 minutes should be enough time to fix it. I will admit, usually all I do is pace off a little bit of nervous energy, but it is time well spent just the same.

Arriving at 7:20 also gives you some quiet time to run a few necessary checks before the trainees arrive. To begin with, you will be able to check your visual aids. I like my trainees to see the visuals I have prepared only when it is show time. You are much better off checking your focus and equipment well before the trainees enter the room. Especially when using visual aids, you are probably going to need to call somebody if you have a problem more serious than a light bulb. Believe me, these somebodies have a tendency to take their time in arriving.

At 7:20 A.M., you can also take one last look over the morning's events. At the very least, you can make sure you feel comfortable getting to that first break. When looking over notes, most presenters spend more of their time studying the logistics of the morning than their actual notes. By logistics, I am referring to the coordination of exercises, activities, and technique. Truth be known, when learning a new course, the logistics usually are more difficult to master than the curriculum itself. Most presenters have some experience in the subject matter they present, so the words themselves do not usually give them much difficulty. Unfortunately, the words do not offer a lot of support in coordinating the actual delivery of the curriculum.

The perceptions of most trainees, regarding the competence of the presenter, are often based on the *comfort* the presenter shows in delivering the material. That comfort comes from having a firm grip on what comes next. Being able to transition smoothly from one area to another can make a presenter look a lot more comfortable than he may actually be. The funny thing is, knowing that you have the logistics part of your presentation under control can give that impression and reduce anxiety. Time well spent indeed.

7:30 A.M.: ARRANGE WHO SITS WHERE

It may seem like a trivial point, but let's turn our attention at this time to seating arrangements. Who sits where? In the "real world" of training, it is rare to know much about your audience until they walk in the room. One thing we do typically know about them, however, is where they come from and their names. In reality, that is all I would choose to know. Sometimes, other co-workers or managers will approach me to give me the "inside scoop" regarding a trainee who will be attending a future seminar. Why not get in the habit right now of giving everyone who walks into your room a fair and equal chance? Frankly, I couldn't care less what has happened in the past. If they are ready and willing to get to work, let the chips fall where they may. You do not need any help in prejudicing their performance in your seminar. Trust your instincts that you will be ready to take action if there is any hint of trouble from a trainee. Innocent until proven guilty.

Now some controversy. To assign seats or not to assign seats, that is the question. Not to disappoint anyone, I of course have a rather strong recommendation. *Assign seats!* Some presenters will tell you that it is hard to predict who will get along with whom, so why not start immediately to create that relaxed atmosphere we so desperately desire, and treat trainees like adults. In all honesty, that is the best argument I have ever heard for sitting anywhere, and I made it up. From what I have seen, it is usually stubbornness and laziness that keep presenters from putting name tags on seats.

Once again, the two pieces of information that are usually readily available to me are the student's names and location of origin. Two strategies here. Use this information to separate the locations, and mixing the sexes. Separating the locations will help reduce the risk of cliques. Also, it will force your trainees to work harder at meeting the other trainees in the room. Finally, it will help reduce the chances of frequent side conversations that can occur when two good buddies spend a week sitting next to each other in your seminar.

Mixing the sexes will pay off a little more subtly. When splitting the seminar into small groups, at least early on, it is far easier to section off the seminar room where the students are sitting than going through a count-off procedure. The real benefit is that you will be assured a good cross section of men and women in each group, which will probably make their discussions a lot more interesting and productive.

As far as name tags are concerned, if you want interaction, please do yourself a favor and do not conduct a seminar without having them in front of the trainees' desks. If you do not receive that information ahead of time, have the trainees fill out tags when they arrive. It is amazing how much more comfortable a trainee feels when you call him by name. After a day or two you cannot help but have memorized it after seeing it all day long. In an interactive seminar, some trainees will shy away from addressing others if they do not know each other's name. Using name tags on desks not only will promote this type of interaction but will promote more of a family atmosphere within your training room among all the participants.

7:45 A.M.: IT'S TIME FOR MUSIC TO CREATE A RELAXED ATMOSPHERE

Fifteen minutes before the seminar begins is usually the earliest time your first trainees will arrive. Assuming you want to create a relaxed atmosphere within your training room, you may want to consider playing some music. As with everything else, it is a good idea if you take just a moment to consider the choices that lie before you.

I do not want to create problems where none exist, but you can play correct or incorrect music. Most likely, your favorite kind of music is incorrect. Sorry. The idea behind playing music in your seminar is to try and create a relaxed atmosphere. Therefore, an appropriate music selection consists of music that is basically indistinguishable. If you select rock music, it will probably distract those who do not prefer that type of music. Those who like rock music will probably listen to it too attentively. These disadvantages apply to just about any stylized piece of music. That also means, no words.

The rule of thumb is to make a selection that neither attracts or distracts anyone. What I find to be the best choices are more progressive jazz or classical arrangements. I am not particularly attracted to this music, and I do not listen to classical music in my car. I have simply found that such arrangements can blend into the background better than any other music I know. I offer no endorsements regarding music, but I have become a fan of both Earl Klugh and Stanly Turrentine.

An additional benefit to having a music collection is that you can play it not only in the morning as the trainees arrive, but during breaks, after lunch, and while the trainees are working on small group exercises. Sometimes, when break-out rooms (additional rooms set aside for smaller group meetings) are not available, the music will assist in keeping your small groups from overhearing each other's work.

7:50 A.M.: GREETING YOUR TRAINEES

Most presenters are really not sure what to do with themselves while the trainees are coming into the room. There is an awkward period of time, right as the majority of the trainees are entering the room that can give presenters a little trouble. If the training that you will be conducting is to be shorter than two hours, or your audience consists of a large enough number that you do not feel you will be able to spend time with them individually, I would certainly recommend that you plant yourself at the door, put a big smile on your face, and greet your new family. There is not a lot of time, and this could be an excellent opportunity to begin to warm up your audience. Be prepared to make idle conversation, and if that discussion turns toward training, be on your best behavior and display a model attitude.

Now let's assume that your seminar is more typical of corporate training in its structure. The seminar lasts for five days, and you are dealing with anywhere between 6 and 16 trainees. Here, my approach may be unique. Most presenters will position themselves at their doors or in front of the room, making conversation with whatever moves. What's more, many trainees will come into the room with questions for that ready-and-willing presenter to answer before the room gets too full. I happen to feel this is a terrible misuse of time by the presenter for a couple of reasons.

First, what the presenter is unwittingly doing is actually stifling the learning environment. Trainees typically come in a little nervous. The presenter who stations himself in the room cannot help but give off an authoritative presence. What usually happens is that the trainees either end up sitting quietly waiting for the seminar to begin or safely and softly speak with the person next to them.

The second concern that I have with the accepted practice of waiting in your room for trainees involves the questions that are quietly being directed to the presenter. A question from a trainee usually represents the "tip of the iceberg." If one trainee has a question, chances are a couple others have the same question, too. It would be more beneficial to answer that question in front of the entire seminar not only so all the trainees can benefit from the answer, but so you can use the question to show how safe it is to participate in your seminar.

My recommendation is a simple one. Get lost! You will have more than enough time to demonstrate your enormous talents. While the trainees are entering your seminar, mill around outside or possibly even a few doors down the hallway. I like to be in sight to make sure there are not any problems I should be taking care of. In your seminar room, a wonderful event is occurring. Trainees are meeting and greeting each other uninhibited by your presence. The more curious trainees are probably looking around the room trying to anticipate what they will learn and what you will be like as a presenter. Usually, the room will be alive with laughter and conversation when you make your grand entrance. In terms of warming up a room, what could be more perfect?

My goal in any training situation is to warm the trainees up, as quickly as possible, so we can get past our "first date jitters" and get some work done.

8:00 A.M.: LET'S GET READY TO RUMBLE!

Assume that the visual aids are ready to go, the curriculum is in place, an overview and objectives are set to kick off the training, and the trainees are in their seats. What are the first brilliant words going to be that escape your lips? I do not want to disappoint you, but reality says, they will probably have a lot to do with housekeeping.

If you are not familiar with the term housekeeping, it refers to just about everything except your curriculum. You will get to your curriculum all in good time, but for now, you had better take care of a few more basic pieces of information. These questions are on your trainees' minds so it is wise to remove these distractions by providing answers:

Approximately when are the breaks?

When is lunch?

What arrangements, if any, are being made for dinner?

Where are the restrooms?

Where are the pay phones?

How do we get our messages?

Are there any evening activities?

What sort of recreational activities are available?

When does the seminar end each day?

When does the seminar end on the last day of training? (Travel arrangements)

What transportation procedures have been arranged?

When is checkout?

Depending on the logistics of your training, questions certainly could be added or deleted. The list does give you an idea of the housekeeping issues that you need to deal with before you attempt to begin your curriculum.

8:10 A.M.: TIME TO BREAK THE ICE

At this point, I hope I am not frustrating you too much, but you are still not ready to jump into your curriculum. Depending on the length of your training, the next 15 minutes to an hour could be the most important time segment within your training. It is time to begin transforming your room full of trainees into a cohesive team that is eager to learn, and covering housekeeping issues will not accomplish this, nor will jumping into your curriculum. The good news is that it is time to spend an enjoyable couple of minutes learning about your trainees and allowing them to learn about you. It is time for the famous "icebreaker"!

Icebreakers

You now need to turn your attention to an artful task conducted by just about every presenter under the sun. These next few minutes could set a tone for the duration of the training; good or bad. The problem is that although just about all presenters use icebreakers, they do not really understand what they should be accomplishing and therefore begin to lose faith in the value of such an exercise. Let's look at the knock against icebreaker exercises, illustrate some sample icebreakers, and then outline their less obvious and unappreciated benefits.

Icebreaker Misconceptions

One of the biggest knocks against using icebreaker exercises in training is the time required to run them. Make no mistake, icebreaker exercises can take a while to conduct properly. In a two-week training seminar, I have seen icebreakers last as long as four hours. As the length of training is shortened, often, so too is the allotted time for icebreakers. Relative to the time you have to deliver your training, the time issue can create a misunderstanding. Certainly, if you have three days to teach your seminar, taking half a day for icebreakers may seem a little excessive. I tend to agree. I do not think it would be excessive to take one to two hours though.

To understand the value of an icebreaker, it may be helpful to visualize what most presenters feel when they first walk into the room. That is the presence of "The Wall." "The Wall" is the imaginary border that separates the trainees from the presenter. This barrier also often separates the trainees from each other. Behind "The Wall," trainees are safe. There is no real interaction, or free sharing of ideas or trust, but sadly there is safety. If any type of interaction is desired (and I cannot think of many times when it is not), that wall must be broken down. That is what most presenters use an icebreaker for.

As far as time is concerned, the misunderstanding is that some people believe they can save time by shortening an icebreaker or doing away with it altogether. This simply is not true. No alarm goes off if you jump into your curriculum, and initially your training will shoot way ahead of similar training by presenters who use an icebreaker to warm up their audiences. The problem this creates, though, is twofold. First, interaction is down, often causing boredom among the trainees and resentment toward the presenter. Second, the presenter must constantly backtrack to learn about issues that should have come out earlier, and he must react to situations that could have been avoided by warming up the trainees with an icebreaker.

Time saved without an icebreaker to start a seminar is more fact than fiction. What really happens regarding time can be related to the story of the tortoise and the hare. The icebreaker starts a seminar out slowly and steadily, whereas without an icebreaker, the seminar sprints out to a faster start but ultimately loses the race.

The second, and more tragic reason why icebreakers are not used within training is more a developmental misunderstanding than a presenter misunderstanding. Many misguided developers, consultants, and customers argue that icebreakers are perceived as silly and frivolous. I call this a developer misunderstanding mainly because any presenter who has actually been in the pit, underfire, would never support such a statement. Icebreakers form trainees into a supportive, cohesive team. Bypassing the icebreaker exercise slows down the development of the team significantly. Capable presenters can pull off the icebreaker exercise professionally to guard against any perceptions that the trainees are wasting time.

Icebreaker Considerations and Examples

Different icebreakers are effective in different situations. Various factors have to be taken into consideration, such as size of the audience. Many icebreakers involve talking to each trainee. When the seminar size begins to creep over 20, this can be a long and tedious process.

Large groups are not without icebreakers, however, as illustrated by the following example.

Large Group Icebreaker

First, ask participants to pair up with anyone they wish to in the room excluding people they already know. Emphasize that the participants be bold and seek out someone they would like to get to know better who is not in their immediate vicinity. Their task, once they have found a person to pair up with, is to spend a set amount of time (10 minutes is suggested) learning something significant about each other. You may set up desired questions or intentionally be vague. The idea is for the pairs to meet and begin to feel comfortable with each other. Watch to make sure nobody is left out. If there is an uneven number of students, create a threesome.

Next, ask your pairs of participants to seek out another pair of participants. They may select any pair they want except for pairs with a member that one of them knows. Once they have settled into their foursomes, they are given 10 more minutes to introduce themselves and come up with a list of criteria to use in grouping up with another foursome. The only criteria that they should not use in making their selections is familiarity. They may select any criteria—from a group with at least one lefthanded participant to a group with all participants wearing black shoes.

I usually stop the combining process with groups of eight, but you can certainly keep combining. Once the groups have reached the desired size, you can assign a small task such as outlining group expectations for or benefits of the topic you are in town to discuss. Your groups' tasks will become clearer to you depending on your topic.

The strength in using this icebreaker exercise is its *flexibility* and *speed*. I have used it with groups as large as 500 and completed it in less than 45 minutes. I guarantee the group will be buzzing after the completion of this exercise and will be a lot more receptive toward what some presenters consider to be an impossibility—large group active participation and interaction.

The time allocated for training will affect your choice of icebreaker technique. If the scheduled training is expected to be shorter than one hour, an icebreaker may be impractical. There are certainly quick techniques to use in these situations, but their effectiveness is questionable. If you must conduct training that is scheduled to last less than an hour, you usually will not have time for a lot of interaction among the trainees. There is still an opportunity to warm the group up with a story, analogy, or questions pertaining to your topic. Moving toward the next step of examining the group's expectations may also do the trick when there is not a lot of time. Expectations will be covered in the next phase of the Anatomy of an 8:00 A.M. start.

Your choice of icebreaker may depend on the familiarity of the students with each other and you. Certainly, if the trainees all work together in the same office, they would have little need to familiarize themselves with each other. The same applies if the trainees know you. This familiarity tells you nothing about a host full of questions that still need to be answered and understood by the presenter. Again, the mistake many make is they do not understand the other treasured information being collected from an icebreaker.

A final consideration that would affect your choice of icebreakers to use in training involves the level of interaction your curriculum requires. A goal for most seminars is to create an environment that allows the opportunity for anyone who wants to be involved to get involved. If there is a question, feel free to ask it. If you are lost, feel confident to seek help. This type of interaction is a far cry from the type of interaction I am accustomed to, but in some forms of training, it is a reality. For example, some share the belief that there is no necessity in technical training for the students to freely exchange ideas. It is hard for me even to write this because in the technical training I have conducted, I welcomed this form of interaction with open arms. The rule of thumb is, however, for highly interactive seminars, the need is greater for lengthier icebreakers.

My Favorite Icebreaker (Old Faithful)

First, pair trainees off. Hopefully, you were able to separate the trainees who came to town already knowing each other, but if this was impossible, try to pair the trainees off with people they did not previously know.

Next, ask the students to take about 15 minutes to interview the trainee they have been paired off with. Use a visual aid or a handout to provide a series of questions for their interviews. They may ask additional questions, but must use the questions provided as a minimum. Tell the students to listen carefully and take good notes because after the 15 minutes are up, they will use the information collected to introduce their partner to the seminar. Here are some suggested questions:

What is your name?

How long have you been with your current employer?

What is your position title?

Have you taken other training courses similar to this one?

Why are you attending this training program?

What are your hobbies and outside interests?

Each of these questions has an essential purpose. Let's look at them one by one starting with the trainee's name. Most name cards are printed up by taking the trainee's name off some sort of official registration. Looking around your room early on a Monday morning you may see many Arthurs, Reginalds, Williams, Steffanies, Margarets, and Cassandras. By the time this icebreaker is over, you could just as easily be looking at several Arts, Reggies, Buzzes, Steffs, Maggies, and Caseys. One of the first ways to warm up a new trainee is to find out what name they prefer to be called, adjust their name cards, and learn it.

The next two recommended questions refer to length of time with their employer and job title. These questions can often provide early clues for detecting opinion leaders and amiable trainees.

The question about previous experience is one I have really grown to appreciate. If a trainee has experience or taken other courses in the corresponding subject matter, there is a good chance you may have an enlightener trainee in your midst. Remember, this is not necessarily a troublesome trainee, and may actually be a diamond in the rough when it comes to warming up the rest of the seminar. If you need a war story or someone you can count on to help break the ice and join in on the conversation, your enlightener is ready and waiting.

Asking trainees about their reason for attending accomplishes two things. First, it provides you with clues for tailoring your message to satisfy particular needs, depending on the subject matter you are working with. The more diverse the subject matter, the more necessary this question becomes. When I teach a Train-The-Trainer course, this becomes a critical question because of all the different types of training that may be represented in my seminars. It helps me a great deal to know where the technical presenters are as opposed to the presenters of more subjective material.

The second benefit of asking a trainee his or her reason for attending a course relates to another potential personality indicator. For example, snippety snit trainees will tend to use this question to let you know of their unfair situation. The message will usually be tempered by the trainee who is doing the introduction to the rest of the seminar, which allows you to begin the work necessary to turn this trainee around.

The final question dealing with hobbies also serves two purposes. The first and most obvious reason, is that it gives the trainees an opportunity to talk about a topic that is not job related. This in turn provides the greatest opportunity to allow the trainees to relax and calm down. The faster this happens, the more effective the seminar will become. There are those who oppose asking this question thinking it is nothing more than a throwaway question and a waste of time. I do not agree, especially when you consider these presenters rarely utilize the other less obvious benefits of this question.

The real benefit of asking about hobbies relates back to the theories discussed in Chapter 1 on working with adults. One of the key principles was to relate the subject matter to adult experiences. As mentioned earlier, adults have an enormous number of experiences to draw on. The presenter can relate these experiences to key subject matter and often can allow adults to make key connections to important material. Learning an individual's hobbies and outside interests often provides you with all the experiences you will need to maximize the use of this technique.

In addition to allowing you to better work with adults, hobbies and outside interests also allow you to work better with quiet trainees. These trainees often need a little extra support to build up their confidence. Relating information to something they know about and feel comfortable talking about may be just the ticket to getting them a few successes they so badly need. What a coincidence you made an analogy to their hobbies . . . or was it!

The trainee personalities already outlined are not the only ones you can detect with this icebreaker. You will be able to identify the quiet trainee and the clown trainee merely by listening to their introductions. Neither of these personalities does a very good job of hiding who he is.

The Presenter's Role in the Icebreaker Process

Probably one of the biggest mistakes most presenters make during their training stems from the missed opportunities within the opening icebreaker in their seminars. Most presenters are just not active enough. This is your first opportunity not only to warm up the group, but to let them learn about you and your style as a presenter.

To begin with, take notes! By taking notes, you can begin to put together some of the valuable information that you should be retrieving now that you are aware no throwaway questions are being asked. It also is one of the best ways to demonstrate to trainees that what they say is important and that you value the information you are learning about them. Truth be known, on many more occasions than I choose to count, I have taken down absolutely useless information for no other reason than that the trainee's eye contact indicated he felt the information was important.

I also feel that, given time, it is imperative that you strike up some sort of conversation with each trainee. This technique shows a personal touch and does wonders at warming up a new group of trainees. Some presenters find this difficult because they have to make conversation in front of the seminar with what may be 10 to 20 trainees, one at a time. Guess where a lot of the information you may need will be coming from? The notes you are taking. It is truly amazing what a couple of simple questions to the trainees can do to help make trainees in a seminar feel more relaxed.

The final task of the icebreaker process is an introduction by the presenter. If you have given the trainees a set list of questions, it is only fair that you use that list to introduce yourself. However, you are better off not pairing off with another trainee; do your introduction yourself. If there is an odd number of trainees, just triple up one of the interviews. Separating yourself ensures you do not contribute to the creation of a loner trainee and allows you to walk around during the icebreaker and visit with the trainees.

8:30 A.M.: EXPECTATION TIME

One of the many reasons I view training as a position underfire has to do with the trainees' expectations. Managers can send trainees to attend training for any number of reasons. Once these trainees set foot into the seminar room, these expectations become the presenter's responsibility. In real world terms, whatever misconceptions or problems the trainee may bring to town are inherited by the presenter.

One of the biggest problems that can confront presenters, regardless of their experience, is a trainee attending a seminar with unrealistic expectations. This can be caused by a number of different factors. Misconceptions by the field is just one example. Most managers have never attended the basic training they send their employees to. They do not take the seminar; they do not audit the seminar. Sadly, it is not uncommon to receive calls from managers who do not understand some of the terms used on the evaluations presenters mail to them. Let's forget, for a moment, the implications that they are in absolutely no position to offer any support or follow-up to the training. They do not even understand what the words mean. Those who have distanced themselves from the training can often inadvertently give trainees the wrong impression of what to expect from the training you are about to conduct.

In addition to a lack of support from the trainee's manager, claims by course promoters can distort expectations. Often, those who teach the seminar never interact with those who promote the seminar. Poetic license takes on a whole new meaning when you read how a seminar will be written up to attract attendees. I am not in favor of misrepresenting a course, which often happens in the world of training. Those who attend the seminar are giving their time and money and deserve to get what they have been promised. If you ever want to get a firsthand glimpse at a presenter truly underfire, watch what happens when a trainee shows up expecting information that has been promised but will not be delivered.

For example, once I taught a seminar that combined educational techniques with sales techniques, entitled "Educating the Customer." The main thrust of the course was to teach people that combining good solid training techniques helped ensure a customer who not only understood what he was buying but was less likely to be confused by another salesperson into giving up what he had purchased. I was asked to design a write-up explaining the intent of the course. The company I was doing this for was to print my write-up, advertise the course, provide the facility, and basically take about 80 percent of the tuition. (Young training consultants sometimes get desperate for contacts!)

It was only after the seminar trainees began to arrive in three-piece suits with Mont Blanc pens that I began to suspect there might be a problem. On a hunch, I asked if anyone had a brochure on the seminar, and as luck would have it, one person did. My jaw dropped as I read about "Selling in the 80's, from Cold Call to Close." The write-up was just as foreign as the title. The only piece of information they did not get wrong was my name and the seminar address. Needless to say, my audience was not thrilled with the topic they were about to receive that night. It is the presenter who takes the heat, and it is the presenter who must learn to survive in this situation.

One sure way to survive faulty expectations by the trainees is to condition yourself as a salesperson does. In short, check for objections before unveiling your product. Get in the habit of always being suspicious of trainees' expectations and prepare for some misunderstandings. The mistake so many good presenters make is telling trainees what their course is about and then trying to convince those with different expectations why they still can benefit. Not bad logic, just bad results.

When a salesperson wheels in his product or brochure and tells you why you need it, you usually resist. One of the first questions people often ask themselves is who is this person and why does he assume I need his product? This situation can give customers the impression that yet another salesperson is trying to sell something they do not need. One of the best techniques in selling is still simply listening and asking questions. The customer will tell you all you need to know and like you better if you just listen and ask questions. Customers perceive salespeople as more trustworthy and empathetic when they follow those two basic rules. Trainees perceive their presenters as more credible and interesting when the presenter adheres to these rules as well.

How to Set Expectations

The most successful approach that I can recommend is to, from this day forth, hide all course maps, put away schedules, and listen to your trainees. Basically, keep your product out of sight until you find out what your trainees are looking for. This approach can benefit a presenter in three ways. To begin with, the exercise itself can act as an icebreaker. If the program you are teaching is very short, and there is not a lot of time for an icebreaker, just use the act of gathering expectations as a warm-up. Even if there is sufficient time, finish your icebreaker portion of the program by collecting expectations.

The second benefit of collecting expectations is the up-front information from your trainees of what they are looking for from your seminar. As mentioned earlier, you are in a much better position to convince a trainee of the benefits of your material before you tell them what you are going to cover in the seminar. If the trainees' expectations match your material, terrific, no problem. If the trainees' expectations are unrealistic, or do not match your curriculum, you can probe further and discuss it without looking defensive. In short, you are still holding your cards!

Another benefit to collecting trainees' expectations before you go over your own expectations involves the value of the responses. When some trainees, particularly new hires, hear what you intend to teach, they will often parrot back what you have already gone over. It is impossible to get a feel for what they were really expecting. With an honest list of expectations, a presenter gets a good indication of what information may need to be covered more carefully or added. Without changing the curriculum, the presenter can actually somewhat tailor the message to fit the trainees.

Collecting expectations before addressing them is a necessity. I would even go so far as to recommend if you post nothing else during the duration of your training, post the expectations. This sends a message to the trainees that you are serious about your desires to see their expectations fulfilled. Tacking these expectations to the wall allows you to keep a watchful eye out for what needs to be covered. If you choose to place the trainee's name by his respective expectation, you can even include the individual who requested it in your discussion. This increases participation and again sells the message that the trainees' expectations are important to you.

Once you have collected these expectations you can go over the course map and an overview of what you have planned for the training. At this point in your training, you walk a tightrope between not telling too much and telling enough to generate interest within the seminar. Next, you must create a lesson plan sequence to address many unanswered questions as well as various adult learning characteristics. Take your time and stay enthusiastic because the best is yet to come! It is now time to learn the secret of successful training . . .

II

DELIVERY:
THE ART OF
MAKING GREAT
PRESENTATIONS

Chapter 6

The Secret of Success: Selling Your Presentation

Through the years, many people have asked me if I ever look back on my private consulting days. Those were the days when I ran my own business, worked when I wanted to, and somewhat lived the American dream. I was a sole proprietor. What in the world would possess any successful entrepreneur to ditch it all and come to work for a massive corporation? Most people work the other way around. First you work for the massive corporation, then you work for yourself. But I was looking for something more to teach people when it came to actual training technique. I wanted something tangible, something process driven that could be taught to anyone incorporating any topic.

There were only about three different companies I would have left my business for, and Xerox was one of them. One reason for my fascination and respect for Xerox was their *commitment to training*. A corporation that builds a training facility that sleeps 980 students on 2,300 acres obviously takes training seriously. My second and equally important criterion for selecting Xerox was their reputation for being *process driven*. By process driven, I am referring to working with concepts that teach predictable and repeatable steps.

As a consultant, I could demonstrate effective training techniques to you at the drop of a hat. I could analyze your own speaking style and curriculum and make delivery recommendations. I could even make creative suggestions regarding some approaches to getting people interested in your presentation. The problem with me and most consultants is we offer no real process. Before learning the process I will be teaching you in this chapter, I would tell trainees about appealing to adult learners, and to address the concerns outlined. The problem was I never really told them how. This is where a process is critical. Forget statements such as, "The first thing you want to accomplish is clearing the air with your audience." I want to know how! When you learn from a process you basically learn, "Do this, this, this, and then this, and you will have cleared the air with your audience."

It has been said, "You only have one chance to make a first impression." In this chapter, I want to offer the most critical piece of information I can give to any presenter. I want to *systematically*, within a process that is *repeatable* and *predictable*, show you the most effective approach for addressing basic adult learning needs, selling your information better, and establishing credibility as a presenter. I do not want this to be subjective in any way. What I offer you is a process that you can see, measure, and use no matter what the circumstance, no matter what the topic.

One of the largest presentations I ever conducted was for a Hostage Negotiation Seminar put on by the Baltimore County Police. Police officers came from all over the country to hear about how Xerox negotiates with its customers. The thinking was that the hostage negotiators could pick up some tips from the top sales training organization in the world. What does a copier salesperson from Silver Spring, Maryland, know about hostage negotiation? The truth is, in my selling I had a few people who were unhappy with my products, but I never had one customer take any of my machines hostage! OK, I might have been a little out of my league, but I know about selling, and I believe negotiation is negotiation. The trick was, I had to figure out a way of getting that point over to my police friends quickly or my message, no matter how good, would fall on deaf ears. In a sense, this situation is a microcosm of what all presenters face at the beginning of their presentations.

I plugged in the process I am about to show you, and within 10 minutes I had the audience excited about my material; they gave the presentation the highest rating in the 12-year history of this annual seminar. With the former guest speakers including Ted Koppel and Ronald Reagan, and an audience that I had been told was skeptical as to my very presence, I was more than satisfied. I was elated, and I had my process to thank.

The nature of seminar delivery and the realities of going underfire demand a process. Learning the process I am about to teach you will benefit you personally by making you feel a lot more confident about whatever training assignments you have. Corporate training burns many people out quickly. If I had no way of knowing what I was doing that was contributing to my success or failure, I would not last long either. This process will answer those questions, making you feel much better about the seminars you conduct.

A second benefit you can derive from following a process within your seminars is the change you will notice in how you perform your job. Following the process will assist your trainees in learning more effectively, thus making for smoother seminars and better evaluations from the trainees. This is not merely an indicator of satisfied customers, it is also an indicator of a good presenter doing great work in one of the most public positions within the company.

Your company benefits also from the process you are about to learn. No profession I know touches as many internal and external customers as training. When a presenter performs effectively, it is the company that is looked on favorably, and ultimately benefits.

In this chapter, I want to teach you how to build your presentation. I want to provide you with a process that will, step by step, lay out what it takes to deliver training seminars effectively. I want you to feel that it is a process that you can use regardless of the topic or nature of your presentation, and I want you to use it within the seminars you conduct.

To accomplish this, I will walk you through the critical overview process. We will then look at some approaches for constructing the body of your presentation and a process for concluding your presentation. The plan will be to start and finish strongly.

We will do this by breaking down the steps of the process. This will give you a solid foundation on which to build your own presentations. I will also provide you with a sample of the process outlining the various steps. This sample is designed to act as a model you can go back to and use for quick brushups when necessary. Finally, I will provide you with a three-page worksheet that will help you in constructing your own presentations. I would suggest you make copies of this worksheet for future presentations.

When this chapter is complete, I hope that those of you who use the process outlined within this chapter in its entirety, will fill out the reply card in the back of this book and mail it to me. This will let me know how the process is working for you. It is my firm belief that of the reply cards received, at least 95 percent of you will respond favorably, enjoying the immediate success this process can offer.

The information for most of this chapter comes from a source I have come to know well. That source is Xerox. When I first came to the Xerox training center, I was asked to rewrite the Train-The-Trainer being delivered to Xerox personnel. There were 10 modules and I conducted major rewrites of 9. The only module that remains untouched to this day is the module that lays out the process you will now be learning. It was written in 1972, is a timeless piece that needs no adjustment, and to this day remains one of the most significant lessons I have ever learned in training.

Perhaps one of the most telling events that I can recall involving this subject occurred with a close friend of mine. They say that opposites attract in relationships and, in my opinion, this certainly holds true for friendships as well. I have a friend named Claude who illustrates this point well. At first glance, we do not appear to have much in common. To begin with, Claude is about 10 years older than I am. He is somewhat quiet, while I am, uh, well to put it nicely, not. Even our occupations are dramatically different. Claude is a computer science major from the late 1960s and has worked with computers for more than 20 years. I, on the other hand, am more of a people person. For years, Claude and I have conducted a mutual teasing of each other's careers.

The one thing Claude and I do have in common is a quiet, common belief in friendship and loyalty. Claude, quite simply, is a friend for life. Well, one day this friend for life showed up at my doorstep somewhat pale. It turns out that my friend Claude had been interviewing with another company and had successfully completed three phases of interviewing. Only one more phase to go, but this is where the lack of color came in. You see, Claude informed me that night he would be giving a 20-minute presentation in the morning that would determine whether or not he got the job. Talk about the power of a presentation!

There was no career teasing in his eyes that night, only fear. I asked him what he had prepared, and like a good computer whiz (sorry Claude), he produced a 20-page document. Remember, this was supposed to be for a 20-minute presentation. I will not belabor the point. To make a long story short, we threw out the mess he walked in with, took 30 minutes to reconstruct the presentation using the process you are about to learn, and the next day Claude delivered the presentation of his life. He not only got the job, he has become a fan of the process, and he is not what I call a man blessed with natural training abilities.

So, get comfortable, curl up, and let me show you some ideas on how to bring your presentations to life. I hope not only that you will return the reply card after using the method within your seminars, but that you will find the success I have found in working with a process that makes presentations a breeze.

INTRODUCING THE "UPPOPPR"
(pronounced "you-pop-er") PROCESS

Let me ask you a few questions. Are you curious about what I have to show you? Have I gotten your attention? Are you interested in what you are about to learn? I believe you are. I believe you answered yes to all three questions because I have already performed the UPPOPPR process on you in the introduction you read in the preceding pages of this chapter. Maybe some of you were already excited and ready to learn. Maybe, just maybe some of you were not. This is what a presenter faces every time he approaches a new group of trainees or even a new topic. Trainees have many questions that they may or may not ask. You read in Chapter 1 about working with adult learners and the fundamental needs these adults have. You have also heard me say over and over again that a presenter is guilty until proven innocent. Well, we are now going to take care of those adult learning needs, clear the air of any misunderstandings, and start more powerfully than you could ever imagine. We are going to do all this with the help of an acronym called a UPPOPPR, and all within the first 10 minutes of your presentation! Here is what UPPOPPR stands for:

Utility
Product/Goal
Process
Objective
Process Justification
Proof of Ability
Review

UPPOPPR

Utility: Conveying the Benefit of the Training Program

The "U" stands for the utility of the subject you are prepared to teach your trainees. It attempts to provide benefits to your trainees that show them *why* it is *necessary* to learn the subject you are about to teach. There is no accident as to the order of this acronym. If a trainee sees no *benefits* to learning what you are about to teach, you have no audience! So many trainers and speakers go into their topic without ever really knowing whether their audience sees any importance in what they are about to learn. You read in Chapter 3 about all the different types of personalities that may appear in your training room and recommendations for handling them. One of the best ways to avoid personality problems is to not allow the situation to occur in the first place. Establishing some utility for what you are about to teach goes a long way toward making trainees *want* to learn!

In Chapter 1, you read that adults must have a need to learn. Establishing utilities does just that. Once again, you have to approach every training situation understanding the basic fact that your audience is selfish. We are all selfish to a degree. Trainees unconsciously apply a universal thought to every training topic the presenter brings up: "What's in it for me?" Every trainee who will ever walk into your training room will listen to you with that thought on his mind. Some will verbalize it; some will stew about it; others will remain silent. All will think about it.

The single biggest problem that trainers face is the trainee who does not want to be in class. If you felt there was nothing you could get out of a class, would you want to be there? Again, it becomes critical for a trainer to appeal to the sense of greed by letting trainees know what is in it for them; but let's talk about how. One approach is to get expectations of the trainees up front; this information tells you exactly what the trainees want to learn. If you commit to addressing these needs and take that list seriously, you at least have a head start. Unfortunately, you cannot list expectations for larger audiences but an overhead question that samples the audience's interest or a prepolling might help.

Now let's get back to the UPPOPPR and the approach within the process itself. As you begin your presentation, you must address the utility of what you have to say. You can do this one of two ways. The first, and more traditional way is to show consequence. As children, most of us were brought up by learning to do certain things based on consequence. "Finish your peas or no dessert" was one of the earliest lessons I can recall. Funny thing is, I never learned to like peas! As we grew, so did the consequences. Bad grades, bad jobs, bad lives. Unfortunately, the only real lesson learned from most subjects motivated by consequence is rebellion. This is not to say that utilities supported by consequences are all bad, it is simply a reminder that you should carefully examine your topic and choose to motivate adults by consequence when there are no other options.

Examining another option brings me to the second approach to establishing utility. That approach is by showing value. If at all possible, I like to show value, or how the material will help the trainee. This tends to be a more positive, motivating technique and appeals to most adults more favorably. Whether you establish utility through consequence or value, you need to address three questions:

"How will it affect me personally?"

"How will it affect me on the job?"

"How will it affect the organization I work for?"

In examining each of these questions, you can now look at how I addressed these issues in the beginning of this chapter. (As I mentioned, I have modeled the entire process in overviewing this topic.) Let's start with the utility addressing this topic's value to you personally.

Here's an example of what you might say to your audience:

The nature of seminar delivery and the realities of going under-fire demand a process. Learning the process I am about to teach you will benefit you personally by making you feel a lot more confident about whatever training assignments you have. Corporate training burns many people out quickly. If I had no way of knowing what I was doing that was contributing to my success or failure, I would not last long either. This process will answer those questions making you feel much better about the training you conduct.

Simply stated, by learning this information, you will benefit personally. That is what is meant by *a personal utility.*

The second question that needs to be addressed is how the topic will affect the trainee on the job. Here's an example of what you might say:

A second benefit that can be derived from following a process within your seminars is the change you will notice in how you perform your job. Following the process will assist your trainees in learning more effectively, making for smoother seminars and better evaluations from the trainees. This is not merely an indicator of satisfied customers, it is also an indicator of a good presenter doing great work in one of the most public positions within the company.

Most trainees will become more interested in your topic when they see how it may benefit them on the job.

Finally, you need to answer the question of how your topic will benefit the trainee's company or organization. It is the last small piece that will ensure an effective utility. Here's an example of how to convince them:

Your company benefits also from the process you are about to learn. No profession I know touches as many internal and external customers as training. When a presenter performs effectively, it is the company that is looked on favorably, and ultimately benefits.

If the members of your audience are demotivated and disgruntled with the company they work for, I would not necessarily recommend this third part of the utility. I will say that establishing organizational utilities gives a certain polish to a very critical part of your presentation.

When establishing a utility, there are a couple of different styles that can be used. Often presenters will deliver their utilities in a lecture type format. Sometimes these utilities will be initiated by questions to the trainees. The third approach, and my personal favorite, is to begin to establish utilities by telling a story that involves your topic. If you noticed in the beginning of this chapter, that is exactly how I started the utility for this topic. I gave you not just one story, I gave you two. Here they are again:

Through the years, many people have asked me if I ever look back on my private consulting days. Those were the days when I ran my own business, worked when I wanted to, and somewhat lived the American dream. I was a sole proprietor. What in the world would possess any successful entrepreneur to ditch it all and come to work for a massive corporation . . .

One of the largest presentations I ever conducted was for a Hostage Negotiation Seminar put on by the Baltimore County Police. Police officers came from all over the country to hear about how Xerox negotiates with its customers. The thinking was that the hostage negotiators could pick up some tips from the top sales training organization in the world . . .

The bottom line to establishing a utility is summed up with this humble Jolles motto:

"Don't tell 'em, sell 'em!"

By this, I mean a lot can be learned from selling our idea to an audience the same way a salesperson sells an idea to a customer. Effective salespeople will not approach a client with a product and tell them why they need it. Just the opposite is true. The top salespeople will get a customer to want their product and then show them their product. Creating utilities for a presenter does just that. The idea behind establishing utility for your topic is that it puts you in a position to create interest and literally get your trainees to want your topic before you show them your product. Utilities are not only the most *difficult* aspect of the UP-POPPR; they are the most *critical* as well. If you now have an audience that cannot wait to hear what it is you have to talk to them about, you are in a most envious position.

U**P**POPPR

Product: Setting a Goal for the Training Program

The first "P" of the UPPOPPR acronym stands for *product* or *goal*. As mentioned in Chapter 1, adults want to know what the big picture is. Understanding this may clear up any questions or doubts the trainees may have. It is a lot easier for adults to learn when they can see what the goal of the seminar is. Typically, the product is the shortest part of the UPPOPPR and can often be stated in one or two sentences. In some situations, after being tantalized with some crafty utilities, this is the first time the trainees are actually told what it is they are about to learn. Here's an example:

> *In this chapter, I want to teach you how to build your presentation. I want to provide you with a process that will, step by step, lay out what it takes to deliver training seminars effectively. I want you to feel that it is a process that you can use regardless of the topic or nature of your presentation, and I want you to use it within the seminars you conduct.*

Allowing your trainees to see the big picture about what you are preparing to teach them helps adults learn and allows your trainees to see the goals of your program. Keep it short and to the point. More detail regarding the subject you are introducing is right around the corner.

UP**P**OPPR

Process: Describing the Approach to Training

The second "P" of the UPPOPPR acronym stands for *process*. With the product that preceded it, the intention was to provide the trainees with the big picture or goal of your seminar. Now, quite naturally, it is time to give the trainees a better idea of how you expect to *achieve* this goal.

The process portion of the UPPOPPR can be broken into two parts. What you need to cover in this part of your overview is not only *more detail* on what you are going to be talking about, but *how* you intend to talk about it as well. When describing "what" you are about to talk about, there is no need to get into too much detail. A light touch on the major points of your presentation will do. For example:

> *To accomplish this, I will walk you through the critical overview process. We will then look at some approaches for constructing the body of your presentation and a process for concluding your presentation. The plan will be to start and finish strongly.*

Most modules are comprised of three to five major points. A pitfall to avoid in this section of the UPPOPPR is to discipline yourself from giving up too much information. The intent is to *overview* the material, not to teach it.

The second part of the process portion of the UPPOPPR begins to deal with the method or "how" you are going to teach the material. Most presenters will unconsciously address the content or "what" they are about to speak about, but rarely will they address "how." This is a mistake. Once again, and not to sound like a broken record, you are guilty until proven innocent. This means, if a trainee came to town a year ago and was bored to tears during his seminar, he will assume your seminar will be boring as well. As a matter of fact, the realities of being a presenter are that whatever negative experience the trainee has suffered in the past is expected in the future. Nobody said training was fair. It is my hope that this book will inspire you to think out of the box and be more creative. Why keep this a secret? Tell the trainees how they will be learning this information. By addressing this key point of the process, you also begin to address a host of adult learning characteristics.

Here is an example of a presenter communicating *how* the material will be taught:

> *We will do this by breaking down the steps of the process. This will give you a solid foundation on which to build your own presentations. I will also provide you with a sample of the process outlining the various steps. This sample is designed to act as a model*

you can go back to and use for quick brushups when necessary. Finally, I will provide you with a three-page worksheet that will help you in constructing your own presentations. I would suggest you make copies of this worksheet for future presentations.

Remember, you must address the major adult learning characteristics:

- Adults learn more effectively when they are motivated.
- Adults learn more effectively when they are kept interested.
- Adults learn more effectively when they are involved in activity.

Here, they begin to take form! Have you ever sat in a seminar, frantically taking notes, only to find out that there was a handout at the end of the seminar with all the notes in it? This is your opportunity as a presenter not only to reduce any fears the trainees may have, but to influence the way *you* want them to learn. Do you want questions throughout? *Tell* the trainees how you want them to participate. Are you walking into a hostile situation? Tell the trainees to hold all questions until the end. The key is that you make the rules here when you tell them "how" the module will be taught.

For challenging modules that are difficult to learn, this is your opportunity to keep the trainees from getting frustrated too early. The process in this module is a classic example. I know the UPPOPPR is challenging. One of the goals within the UPPOPPR process I laid out for you was to give you confidence in your ability to master the technique by letting you know up front that I would be providing you with a sample and a worksheet. If you are not careful to lay out "how" you are going to teach something, you may sometimes lose a significant number of trainees who become too frustrated and give up.

UPP**O**PPR

Objective: Write Specific Training Goals

The fourth step in the UPPOPPR approach to training is to focus on training objectives. Numerous books and courses have been devoted solely to the "art of writing objectives." This is a topic that has been made much more difficult than it needs to be. The problem and confusion stems from the fact that developers attempt to include far too much in their objectives. This may be a result of trying to package too much of their overview in the objective. One thing is for certain. Most trainees, and presenters for that matter, are completely confused by the term "objective." Let me make a few suggestions to keep you from acquiring any of the bad habits associated with objective writing.

One bad habit to avoid is becoming intimidated by the subject of objectives, causing you to not want to get involved with writing them. I would love to be able to tell you to look the other way when it comes to objective writing, but that just is not possible. Objectives are just too valuable to a presenter, and although many presenters are not asked to create them, you often will have no choice. You see, if you are in the pit, and trainees are unclear as to what is expected of them once the training is complete, it is you who will be receiving the sniper fire, not the developer. An important adult learning characteristic previously discussed is that adults want to know what is required of them before the seminar begins.

Instead of avoiding objectives, look at the tremendous value a well-written objective can offer you. To begin with, an objective allows both the trainee and the presenter to evaluate how well they are doing. If an objective has been established, and some trainees could not meet the objective, they begin to see where they are in relationship to where they should be. You also have the ability to see how well you are doing as a presenter. If 50 percent of the seminar participants could not meet the established objective, you are the one who needs to do some reevaluation. It is not a time to panic or become upset. It is simply a time to take that 15-minute review you had planned in the morning and make it 30 minutes instead.

The first terrific benefit of training with objectives is that you will be providing a gauge for you and the trainee as to how well you are doing. An exciting indicator as to the success of your objectives can often be found in simply watching the participant guides. When the trainees are meeting your objectives, they will usually leave their participant guides on their desks at the end of the day. When they are unable to meet the established objective, the participant guides mysteriously vanish for the night.

Another strength behind writing objectives lies in your ability to influence what you want the trainees to learn. There is "nice to know," and "need to know." A good objective deals with the "need to know" areas. If I tell you that you will be using a particular portion of the material at the end of the module, you will probably listen harder when that point is covered. Carefully crafted objectives will even assist you in your selection of visual aids. Adults learn through their sense of sight, but adults will not learn as effectively if everything is visual. Therefore, you can plan your key visual aids around your objectives. This, in turn, will help your trainees to retain and achieve more. So what is the secret to writing a good objective? Four simple steps:

1. Action.
2. Requirement.
3. Degree.
4. Benchmark.

Step 1: Include action in the objective. The first step, "action," is probably the most misunderstood step. Typical objectives read, "At the end of this module, you will have a greater appreciation for . . ." or "When this module is complete, you will be able to . . ." I want to be somewhat delicate here so let me just say I think these objectives are a bunch of bunk! How does a trainee know if he is able to do something unless he does it? Most objectives look more like recipes than real live objectives.

Therefore, the first step that I would recommend is an actual "action" or activity: "At the end of this module, you *will* demonstrate [role play, participate, show, etc.]." The most classic example of "action" that most of us were raised on is testing. In fact, it is an accurate objective "action." The only problem is that it lacks creativity. It may sound corny, but I have a dream that trainees will actually look forward to an objective rather than fear it. One way to accomplish this is to get more "action" in the objective. Try to have your trainees actually do what it is you are teaching. If you are training someone how to answer a phone, do not give him a written test on the skills taught. Have him actually do it!

Step 2: State the Requirements of the Training Program. Stating the requirements of your objective up front is another way to reduce the fear behind objectives. What are the rules? For some reason, these are kept as a closely guarded secret in many schools. Isn't the intent behind education to teach rather than terrify? You study your notes and are tested from your book. You study your book and are tested from your notes. Sorry folks, I just do not accept this form of education. One of my goals as a trainer is to have my trainees be able to accomplish more, using what they have learned, than they have achieved from any other seminar. "Pop quizzes" and other such mysteries on a corporate level do not help people learn; they intimidate.

I would rather *motivate* you to learn than frighten you to learn. As a student, when I heard we were going to be tested, I wanted to know the "requirements." I was the obnoxious voice in the back asking if it was an open book test or a take home. I had no idea that I was asking such a reasonable question! It certainly would have changed my approach to learning. If a student knows that he will be tested from his notes, it makes sense that he will take good notes. What is so wrong about teaching the objective? Not word for word, but heavily focused. Explain the "requirements"; for example:

■ Tell trainees they will be asked to volunteer.
■ Tell them there is a time requirement.
■ Tell them they will be selected at random.
■ Tell them they will all participate, or some will participate.

Whatever your requirements are, clear up any misunderstandings and let trainees know what those requirements will be.

Step 3:   Explain the "Degree" of Accomplishment Expected. How well should the trainee be expected to accomplish the "action" you have created? Once again, you were conditioned during testing. You were told that you would need to get a certain number of questions right in order to pass. You do not have to ask trainees to perform perfectly the activity you are planning. Perhaps you will give them three opportunities, or maybe assist them once. The intent here is to provide the trainees a yardstick as to how well they are doing versus how well they should be doing.

Step 4:   "Benchmark" the Performance of Trainees. You must give the trainees a standard for the activity they are performing. If you were teaching someone how to hit a baseball, you could tell them that they will each hit three baseballs at the conclusion of your presentation (that is your "action" and "requirement"). They are to hit at least one baseball down the right field line (there is your "degree"). The problem is, if you do not provide the trainees with a benchmark, they can try to accomplish this any way they want to. Since you are teaching a seminar on hitting, I would assume you want them to use the techniques provided in your lecture. Therefore, that fact becomes your benchmark. It could be an author, a visual aid, or even yourself, but there must be a benchmark for the trainees to measure their results against.

Example

So, do these four steps look difficult? As with anything else, they take a little practice. Now let's look at the objective established for this module and see if you can distinguish between the four parts that have been outlined:

> *When this chapter is complete, I hope that those of you who use the process outlined within this chapter in its entirety fill out the reply card in the back of this book and mail it to me. This will let me know how the process is working for you. It is my firm belief that of the reply cards received, at least 95 percent of you will respond favorably, enjoying the immediate success this process can offer.*

■ Action: *. . . fill out the reply card and mail it to me. This will let me know how the process is working for you.*

■ Requirement: *When this chapter is complete . . . those of you who use the process . . .*

■ Degree: *. . . 95 percent of you will respond favorably . . .*

■ Benchmark: *. . . outlined within this chapter in its entirety . . .*

It all boils down to one key question: Did you meet your objective? The irony is that your success does not in fact depend on whether or not you actually meet your objective. Success lies in whether or not you can answer the question. With the four steps you have just seen, trainees will know, without question, what is expected of them. What's more, with a little creativity on your part, they will be anxiously awaiting their opportunity to show you just how much they have learned!

UPPO**P**PR

Process Justification: Identifying the Source of Information Presented

A logical question that is often asked during a presentation involves where the information that you are using came from. It is no coincidence that "process justification" follows your objective. Chances are you have just given the trainees a benchmark within their objective. It is now time to finish that thought for the trainees. Where did the information that you are using come from and why did you choose that particular source? Sometimes, this source may be you. Sometimes, it could be an author you chose to select. Here's an example:

The information for most of this chapter comes from a source I have come to know well. That source is Xerox. When I first came to the Xerox training center, I was asked to rewrite the Train-The-Trainer being delivered to Xerox personnel. There were 10 modules and I conducted major rewrites of 9. The only module that remains untouched to this day is the module that lays out the process you will now be learning. It was written in 1972, is a timeless piece that needs no adjustment, and to this day remains one of the most significant lessons I have ever learned in training.

The importance of including the process justification is often dependent on your material and your audience. Guilty until proven innocent. Why take chances? Trainees have a right to know where the information you are using came from and why it was selected. It is a good idea to head off any potential conflicts and offer this information to your trainees.

UPPOP**P**R

Proof of Ability: Demonstrating the Success of the Training Approach

As you are preparing to deliver your curriculum to your trainees, there is only one other point that needs to be covered. Is there a proof source? Has what you are about to teach ever really helped someone in the past? Does it really work? At this time, you have systematically attempted to get people to see what is in it for them, and told them the goals for your seminar. You have explained what you will be doing and how you will be doing it. Additionally, you have told them what is expected out of them, where the information came from, and why you selected that information. The only question that may be left unanswered by the trainees is, "Will it work for me?"

The intent behind stating a "proof of ability" is to provide the trainees with some sort of proof source designed to build confidence in the trainees' minds. This proof source could be how what you are teaching helped you personally. It could, just as easily, be how what you are teaching helped someone else. For example, I cited this experience earlier in this chapter:

> *Perhaps one of the most telling events that I can recall involving this subject occurred with a close friend of mine. They say that opposites attract in relationships and, in my opinion, this certainly holds true for friendships. I have a friend named Claude who illustrates this point well. At first glance, we do not appear to have much in common . . .*
>
> *. . . He not only got the job; he has become a fan of the process, and, he is not what I call a man blessed with natural training abilities.*

When putting together a proof of ability, you can use a story or an analogy. The idea is to provide one last push to fire up your trainees and instill confidence in the fact that they *can* accomplish whatever it is you are teaching.

UPPOPPR

Review: Emphasizing the Critical Information

I know what you are probably asking yourself: "What can we review? We haven't entered the body of our presentation yet." When you start using the UPPOPPR overview, you will find that this entire process can last anywhere between 5 to 15 minutes, depending on your timing and the length of the module. It is a good idea to lightly, very lightly, touch on three critical areas. Those areas are the process, objective, and utility. The idea is not to rehash exact "what" and "how"; the intent is to net out the critical pieces of these three areas. For example, I do it this way:

> *So, get comfortable, curl up, and let me show you some ideas on how to bring your presentations to life. I hope not only that you will return the reply card after using the method within your seminars, but that you will find the success I have found in working with a process that makes presentations a breeze.*

Try to avoid transitions into your review such as "In conclusion . . ." or "To summarize . . ." Gently remind the trainees of the "need to knows" of the process, objective, and utility, and jump on it. You are now ready to rumble!

MASTERING THE UPPOPPR

Well, what do you think? Mastering the UPPOPPR is challenging. The rewards, however, will make it all worthwhile. One of the most important lessons that can be learned from working with this process comes from the art of *selling*. Think back on the teachers or presenters who really made a difference in your life. Did they just dispense information or did they touch you in some way? Salespeople do not just tell: they sell! That should be your motto as well, regardless of the curriculum.

Some presenters will look at it and assume it is too time consuming to deliver. In reality, using the UPPOPPR can be equated to the case of the tortoise and the hare. Rather than jumping into your topic and constantly going back addressing issues that should have been already explained, you will slow your entry into the body of your presentation a bit by using this process. In return, you will methodically move into your presentation without having to stop and clear the air answering questions that should have already been addressed.

With regards to actually writing a UPPOPPR, try using the UPPOPPR worksheets (at the end of this chapter), to guide you in addressing the critical points. As with anything else that is worthwhile, the rest is up to you. Practice, practice, practice, and use the reply card to let me know how it is working for you!

The Body

The actual body of the presentation is the easy part. Typically, the body of the presentation is that lifeless creature sent down from the home office developer's desk. If you are writing your own curriculum stylistically, you can choose one of three methods.

One method of writing your curriculum is the "manuscript" method, which means writing out every word of the presentation you are to deliver. It works well for TV anchorpeople who are reading off teleprompters, but it can be a nightmare for a presenter. Nothing will be more embarrassing for you, as a presenter, than to pathetically fumble about, looking for your place in your script. It is often a good idea to manuscript a UPPOPPR, but only to make sure you are confident that it is complete before you begin to synopsize it.

Another approach to writing the body of your presentation is to use a sentence outline. This technique provides the presenter with bulletized information in broken sentence form. Sentence outline may be helpful for capturing transitions and a well rehearsed UPPOPPR.

Finally, there is a word outline. As the title suggests, this is an approach that forces you to capture key areas of your presentation in a single word. Recommended for presenters who know their material extremely well, the idea is to use the outline only as a guide to make sure you do not skip over an important point.

What often happens is that presenters will mix and match the techniques depending on their familiarity with their topic and curriculum. It often becomes a question of style.

The Final Review

I happen to believe that there is a common link between presenters who consistently dazzle their audiences. Although each has his own unique style, one similarity can be found time after time. They start their presentations strongly and they finish their presentations strongly. If you adhere to the structure of the UPPOPPR, I can assure you that your presentations will start strongly. If you remember to incorporate these next three steps, you will finish strongly as well.

The first step in finishing your presentation is to review the major points from the body of your curriculum. To find these major points, you will probably have to look no further than the "Process" portion of the UPPOPPR. It is difficult to say just how much time you will need to spend reviewing the material. Factors such as nonverbal cues, participation, difficulty of the material, and time allocation will help you decide. The goal, however, is not to review everything, but just the most important points. Once again, depending on timing, this can be done using questioning techniques, or just a presenter's summary. One technique that I use when I review with questions is to make this deal with the trainees. I tell them (without necessarily using these training terms) that I will promise to ask them overhead questions, if they will promise not to look at their notes. This way no one is put on the spot not knowing an answer, and I am able to determine what information has actually stuck.

The second step is really more of a reminder. During the UPPOPPR you have carefully created an objective for the seminar. It is time now to test your objective and evaluate performance.

The third and final step should be logical as well. You started your presentation generating interest and answering the question, "What's in it for me?" It is only appropriate to now tie the presentation back to that utility. Now, I am not suggesting that you rehash all of the benefits. This could start to sound a bit redundant. I think it is effective to end on a positive, reassuring note and that means briefly explaining the basic utility once again. That is the intent, and that will allow you to finish strongly with confidence.

UPPOPPR Worksheet
Page 1

Utility

Story, analogy, lecture _____

_____

_____

_____

_____

_____

_____

What's in it for them: _____

1) Personal _____

2) Job _____

3) Corp. _____

_____

_____

_____

_____

_____

Product/Goal

The big picture _____

_____

_____

_____

_____

_____

_____

UPPOPPR Worksheet
Page 2

Process

Content: "what" _____

_____

_____

Method: "how" _____

_____

_____

Objective

Action _____

_____

_____

_____

Requirement _____

_____

_____

_____

Degree _____

_____

_____

_____

Benchmark _____

_____

_____

_____

_____

UPPOPPR Worksheet
Page 3

_____
_____
_____
_____
_____
_____
_____

Process Justification

Where info. came from _____

_____

_____

Why this source _____

_____

Proof of Ability

Build confidence _____

_____

_____

_____

Review

Touch on process, objective, utility _____

_____

_____

_____

Chapter 7

Twenty Tips on Maintaining Interest

One of the hottest issues in training involves the topic of this chapter. How do you maintain interest? Whether it is 10 minutes, 10 hours, or 10 days, the reality most presenters face is that a great deal of their success or failure will most likely be judged by how well they keep their trainees interested. Through my years in the pit, I have tried many creative, and sometimes bizarre, ideas to try and maintain interest throughout my presentations. Over the years, I have developed a fascination for this topic.

Do not forget the intended message behind this topic—maintaining interest. It is my hope that two key points have already stuck from your readings thus far. First, no presenter is immediately interesting when he appears in front of a seminar for the first time. Oh yes, I must admit that I have walked into new classes that have neither seen nor heard of me, and have been greeted by thunderous applause. Unfortunately, that is about the exact moment the alarm clock goes off and it is time to start a new day! The art of creating interest is employed gradually and, at least early on, subtly. The second point from the preceding chapters is that the UPPOPPR overview is designed to initiate interest, not sustain it. My hopes are that once a group is properly prepared for a topic using the overview, the ideas within this chapter will keep the momentum going in your favor.

In putting this chapter together, I think it is only fair to warn you that maintaining interest is a never-ending brainstorm. What is right for some may be totally inappropriate for others. It is therefore my intent to shower you with as many ideas as possible with the hope that a handful will find their way into your presentation.

1. Use Your Voice Effectively

One of the biggest fears most people have when they are asked to speak publicly involves their voice. The worry often involves how our voices sound. There is an easy way not to worry about that problem, because there is nothing you can do about it. Almost no one likes his own voice when he hears it played back. It sounds different from the way we hear it when we are speaking and that tends to bother people. What you should focus on is avoiding any hints of monotone.

An example of this involves a story I once heard about Mark Twain. It was written that Mark Twain had a terrible habit of cursing, which bothered his wife a great deal. She would try to correct him, but it was no use. As the story goes, once while shaving, Mark Twain cut himself and let out a long string of curse words. His wife, who was in the other room listening, was so upset at his language, she wrote down every word he said. When he finished shaving, she marched into the bathroom and read back every word—to which Mark Twain patiently replied, "That's very good, honey. You've got the words; you just don't know the tune." Now you need to think about the tune. How you say it is as important as what you say.

2. Tell Anecdotes

Anecdotes or stories that relate to your topic are another way to keep adults interested in your presentation. As with most of the ideas presented in this chapter, too much of anything becomes a waste. Used selectively within your presentation, these stories not only create interest, they often help to relax you as well. A prime example of an anecdote is the story you just read about Mark Twain. Certainly while telling a story that relates to your topic, there is no need to be stuck behind a lectern at the mercy of your notes. Often when presenters launch into an anecdotal story that involves their subject, you will observe a noticeable change in their facial expressions and body language.

The biggest trick to using anecdotes within your presentation is to remember to actually tell the story. A recommendation here would be to put a word or title in the margin of your notes to remind you to tell the story. When you are underfire, things happen very quickly. There is nothing more frustrating than finishing your training only to realize that you forgot to tell a couple of key anecdotal stories! With reminders clearly visible in your notes, the only reason you will forget to tell a story is because you made a conscious decision to skip over it.

3. Keep Moving While You Talk

In my mind, movement is one of the easiest and surest ways to keep trainees interested in a presentation. Perhaps you can tell an anecdotal story that relates to your subject and move around as you tell it. There is something truly wonderful about a presenter who moves around as he speaks. It communicates comfort with the subject matter, credibility, and most important of all, interest.

In corporate training, a horseshoe style seating arrangement benefits a presenter for two reasons. First, it helps the trainees by allowing the trainees to see each other, learn each other's names, and get comfortable around each other. Second, it creates an open area (I have been referring to as the pit) that presenters can move around in to generate interest.

4. Vary the Pace of Your Presentation

The rate at which you speak, or your pace, can also add to the interest you are creating within your seminars. There are some presenters who speak quickly and others who speak slowly. Each is successful in his own way.

So, which is correct, fast or slow? The answer is both and neither. The key is not to necessarily adapt a speaking style that is fast or slow. The key is to adapt to your own style and vary the pace. We can hear at about 325 words a minute and generally speak at about 170 words per minute. Our minds can receive as quickly or as slowly as someone wants to speak. To maintain interest, all we need to do is vary the pace. If you naturally speak quickly, force yourself to slow down at times. If your pace is naturally slower, give yourself an occasional kick in the pants and speed up. The actual words per minute is not the trick: the *variance* of the pace is.

5. Distribute Handouts

Most presenters do not like to hand out materials because they are afraid they will lose the attention of the trainees. I happen to agree with that philosophy, but I would like to offer a benefit to waiting on certain materials. If timed properly, handouts can actually help create a little interest within your training room. The obvious plus in holding handouts until you are ready is that you can focus the trainees' attention at the proper time.

What most presenters fail to realize, however, is that there is another plus as well. You can incorporate movement and pass out the handouts to each trainee yourself. Next time you take a seminar, notice that when the presenter passes out any handouts, he will most likely drop a pile on one trainee's desk and ask that the stack be passed around to the rest of the seminar. Instead, you can make it a wonderful opportunity to get in each trainee's face a little bit. You can incorporate some movement and get a little more benefit out of an easy interest-sustaining idea.

6. Incorporate Trainees' Names into Your Discussion

Name involvement is a technique that is subtle but effective. To incorporate name involvement, all you have to do is use some of your trainees' names in a rhetorical sense. This approach is especially useful when you are delivering a lecture or slower curriculum. An example of the approach would sound like this:

PRESENTER: Now John may not agree with what I have just shown you and Tom might. The key is that they have both formed opinions that are valid and strong.

The intent behind name involvement is not to *embarrass,* but to *refocus.* No one should be put on the spot. Trainees' names are only used within your conversation. Gone are the days when presenters pounce on a poor, defenseless trainee with questions they know their trainee cannot answer. This is a dangerous technique still used with the intent to shock trainees back to reality. In the real world of working with adults, not only will this approach cause anger and defensiveness from the trainee, it can also act as a catalyst for a sniper attack down the road.

7. Use Visual Aids

Visual aids are a natural for kicking life into even the dullest curriculums. Visual aids can be used to appeal to any of the five senses. A well-timed presentation aid can break up a difficult module. Be selective, watch your timing and remember the motto from before: "If you emphasize everything, you emphasize nothing." Also, look over Chapter 9 on visual aids!

8. Ask Questions

One of the best ways to keep generating interest throughout your training is to keep a steady flow of creative questions going between you and your trainees. One of the most common mistakes that I observe from presenters is the positioning of questions. Often the questions from the presenter come in bunches. Twenty minutes will go by, and then the presenter will begin to ask questions as if trying to fill a quota. The idea is to maintain the interest level of the trainees throughout the presentation.

Try mixing up the types of questions that you ask the trainees to fit the appropriate part of the curriculum. For instance, you might want to begin a module with opinion-based questions, develop the topic with case study and comparison questions, and review at the end with factual-based questions. The key is to keep a somewhat steady flow of questions throughout and to vary your questioning techniques as well.

9. Conduct Small Group Activities

One of my favorite techniques to maintain trainees' interest and improve learning retention is to use small group activities. This technique can take on many forms, such as case studies, participating activities, or even exercises created for as few as two participants.

One of the biggest shocks I received before I rewrote Xerox's Train-The-Trainer was in the area of participating activities. Here was a course designed to teach new trainers how to teach. During the four days of lecture before the individual presentations, there was plenty of talk about the need for small group activity. The problem was, we did not practice what we preached. There were *no* participating activities. We also averaged about three deliveries a year.

When I rewrote the curriculum, I updated and added some information in almost all the modules, but these changes were not drastic. The major change took place within the delivery side. There is now not a morning or afternoon that goes by without some sort of group activity reinforcing the curriculum being taught. These activities total 14 in four days. As a footnote, for the past two years, Xerox's Train-The-Trainer is now averaging about 18 deliveries a year with a healthy 6- to 9-month waiting list of trainees from all over the country trying to get in. Amazing what small group activities can do for a course!

10. Personalize Your Presentation

A simple and fun idea, personalization can add some real sizzle to your presentation. Personalization techniques involve taking whatever your topic happens to be and creatively personalizing some of the key areas. This can often involve unique signs or slogans involving you or your participants.

The first time I ever taught a Train-The-Trainer course, I stumbled on this idea. I had a couple of important sayings that I wanted the trainees to remember. Right before the training was to begin, I wrote these slogans down on large poster boards. I then personalized the ideas by writing across the top of each poster, "Rob's Rule" and an appropriate number. I suppose I could have just told the trainees these were important rules, but it is funny how personalizing them made it a little more interesting and a little more fun. As I introduced each rule to the trainees, I attached the poster to the wall, working my way across the room as the class went on. I believe that it ultimately allowed my trainees to learn the information a little more effectively. When I see some of the people I trained eight or nine years ago, one of the first things they will start reciting is "Rob's Rules!"

The other classic personalization technique that I relied on heavily throughout the early stages of my training career involved my name. At that stage in my life, I was tasked with delivering two-day, 16-hour, flood insurance seminars. These lectures were mandatory for many insurance underwriters, claim adjustors, and agents on an annual basis. These people were also accustomed to being bored to tears on an annual basis as well. I felt that implementing certain interest-generating ideas would help, but not if I was unable to get this audience's attention from the beginning. That was when (with the help of my artistic wife) I decided to create a unique name tag and incorporate the personalization idea. This name tag was actually metallic paint on a canvas scroll, attached to dowels.

My technique involved a short speech about how this year's seminar was going to be different from last year's seminar. As I finished my attempt to convince them with words, I would complete my speech by saying to the audience, "You can believe this is true, if my name isn't Rob 'The Thriller' Jolles!" I would then rather dramatically let the scroll drop over the lectern. As a footnote, and a piece of training trivia, the author of this book had the distinction of being known across the country by all who knew flood insurance as the original "Thriller." It was a full two years before Michael Jackson came out with his famous album. I wonder to this day if he might have slipped into the back of one of my larger flood seminars and taken the name for himself. I wonder . . .

11. Show a Sense of Humor

This is a valued tool to some presenters that can come in handy during some of the dryer sections of curriculum. It certainly makes the list of interest devices but in no way is it a necessity. I have seen some extremely good presenters who did not incorporate a sense of humor within their style. Sadly, there are still those who believe the only way to succeed as a trainer or a public speaker is to incorporate a sense of humor. Please do not get me wrong. I think a sense of humor is helpful to a presenter, as long as it is natural.

One of the most frustrating aspects of being a consultant involved this very topic. Often I was asked to help work with fairly prominent individuals within various organizations to assist them in their public speaking duties. One of the first requests from many of them was often for me to write them a joke to start their presentation off with. Most of the time, I would literally beg them not to do it, but it was no use. The jokes were told, the polite laughter followed, and the message was sent out loud and clear to the audience. "This person is not funny."

There is one other recommendation I would like to make when incorporating humor within your training. *Do not overdo it.* Presenters who display a large amount of humor within their seminars can run the risk of losing control of the seminar. In any seminar, the goal is to create a relaxed and open learning environment. It is not a carnival. I, too, have been down this road. In my zest to get my trainees to loosen up, I used to be guilty of loosening up the trainees too much. This would create a lack of control and discipline. Unfortunately, this happens to be one of those situations where it is much easier to give slack than take it away. Once a presenter encourages trainees to relax and have fun, it is difficult to all of a sudden change the rules. Presenters can be perceived as phony and inflexible. This happens to be one of those situations where you, as a presenter, must walk a very narrow tightrope.

12. Use Nonverbal Communication

If I may quote a lesson learned early in most of our lives, "It is not what you say, but how you say it." This holds true with this next interest device, nonverbal communication. This form of communication can include facial expressions, hand movements, body movements, or any type of gestures. Much has been written on the subject of nonverbal communication with some of it being quite fascinating. Personally, I think you can overdo it a bit. For a presenter, the key to incorporating nonverbal communication is to try and pay attention to just a few things. First, make sure if you are using a lectern that you do not hold on to the sides of it. This is a noticeable indicator of anxiety. It also destroys a major portion of your nonverbal communicators. If you free your hands up, the rest will come naturally. In a sense, nonverbal communication is a little bit like breathing. It is only difficult to do if you think about it.

Once you free yourself up to let your nonverbal communication take over, there is only one other tip I would recommend. Try to keep your gestures as open as possible. It is somewhat contradictory to be asking trainees for questions and strolling around the pit while your arms are crossed tightly in front of you. Loosen up! Generate some excitement through your nonverbal communication and keep those palms extended out!

13. Mix Up Your Techniques

One simple and effective approach to maintaining interest can be accomplished by mixing up your techniques. Some presenters are comfortable acting as facilitators while others prefer more of a lecture style. Still others prefer a take-charge authority role. Each can be effective at different times for different presenters with different curricula. The key to creating interest, regardless of which approach you prefer, is to change techniques throughout your training.

It is important here to emphasize that I am in no way suggesting any deviation from the curriculum that is written. I am recommending that you use the available delivery techniques creatively to keep the trainees' interest with multiple approaches.

14. Use a Team-Training Approach

Another solid technique that can be used to spice up your training may be to attempt to use a team-training approach. Team training refers to more than one presenter within the seminar. Sometimes presenters develop what I call "vocal rapture," which is a deep affection for their own voices. This affliction can cause presenters to overlecture. It can also cause presenters to be a little short sighted in looking beyond the resources that may be available.

No matter how talented a presenter is in delivering material, a second speaker, strategically placed, can only add to the interest the first presenter has created. In reality, I am talking about the potential of 39 hours and 45 minutes for the presenter, and 15 minutes for another speaker. That is not exactly a huge risk or loss of control on the presenter's part. With this in mind, let's look at three possible areas where you might be able to find the help you are looking for.

The first, and most common, is another presenter. Perhaps you are in the process of cross-training a new presenter. This might be an excellent opportunity to allow this individual to get his feet wet by teaching a module, conducting a feedback session, or even role-playing a character for the seminar participants depending on the subject matter. Maybe another presenter is floating without a seminar that week. Typically presenters are off for a reason. That reason is to clear their minds, and take care of other areas that may be backing up. We are, however, talking about a limited period of time to give your seminar a shot in the arm. With a promise of reciprocation, you may find a more-than-willing partner. Given that the teaming of presenters is still considered a luxury by many training departments, let's look at two more areas that usually are available to everyone and may be right under your nose.

Peer training is one approach that is a natural, utilizing the team-training concept. Often members of your seminar have isolated experiences that may be pertinent to your topic. What a wonderful opportunity to tap into this experience and create a little interest within your seminar at the same time. You can even use some of your more talkative trainees or sniper trainees to assist you using this approach. Now, you have not only stroked their egos allowing you to get a lot of these types of trainees under control, you have generated some additional interest as well. The only other important recommendation that I would make here is to make sure you lay out the parameters of how these trainees are contributing. The most important rule of all is to be very up front and clear regarding time. Emphasize that you are going to give them 10 or 15 minutes, and whatever time you arrive at, stick to it. This should help to reduce any worries about losing control of your seminar.

A final recommendation for team training involves the use of a possible guest speaker. Now I know what you are saying, "Guest speakers do not grow on trees. I'll never find one!" Well, that is where you might just be wrong. I am not necessarily talking about finding the type of speaker you would find at a high school graduation. I am referring to the less obvious, the often overlooked. Let me provide you with an example of just such a case.

Years ago, I was conducting a five-day class in Nebraska. The topic was automation training and I was forewarned that the employees there were famous for their lack of energy and interest. As I was setting up for the class, I was racking my brains as to how I could make this class more interesting. It was then I noticed a custodian cleaning up the day's office debris. It hit me like a flash! I asked him if he could come in later in the week and talk for 15 minutes or so about how the automation of the office I was teaching in had changed his job. I did not have to ask this individual twice: He was very excited about being a speaker within the training that was scheduled. For three days, I tantalized the class with the promise of a guest speaker who specialized on the effects of office automation. When the day finally did arrive, this custodian truly delivered a presentation that would have made many presenters I know somewhat envious. The trainees loved it, the custodian loved it, and the class was a success. What more could I have asked for?

15. Encourage Competition among Trainees

Everybody has their own favorites when it comes to trying to create and maintain interest. Competition happens to be one of mine. It is astounding what a little friendly competition can do to an otherwise dull curriculum. I have seen presenters use all sorts of prizes and awards to create a competitive situation. Unfortunately, those who focus on the prize too much are missing the whole point behind the strategic use of competition. It is not the actual prize that so many of us crave, but rather the thrill of winning. Ironically, when the prize exceeds the event, trainees lose their focus toward learning, and become blinded by winning the prize.

In my career as a trainer, I have seen others give away items ranging from $50 bills to company merchandise. I have also witnessed in those seminars trainees who were at each other's throats trying to win these valuable prizes. There is no sense of teamwork, and even a sense of professional jealousy often transpires. If the winner's answer is at all subjective, there can be resentment by other trainees not only toward the winner but toward the presenter as well. Some trainees can become somewhat hyper while others will simply shut down. In this situation, the emphasis is too much on the prize and not enough on the event.

The prizes that I would recommend should be far more symbolic. Let me give you a couple of examples. When I taught for the National Flood Insurance Program, one of the worst courses to teach was traditionally a seminar that required trainees to actually rate premiums for insurance policies. Not only was the course a bit boring, the trainees themselves were not exactly the most lively bunch. Getting them to rate 20 individual policy examples was like pulling teeth. Without making any changes to the curriculum, I started to pair up trainees (also utilizing idea 8 for maintaining interest), and have them compete for "valuable" prizes. The valuable prizes turned out to be certificates that read "Oh Boy, Can I Rate a Policy" and the all important Baby Ruth candy bars that accompanied the certificates! Funny thing was, the trainees learned the material, had fun, and no one got too worked up over the prizes.

Now to be perfectly honest with you, I should confess and tell you that I have, in fact, given money out in some of my seminars. The only difference is that I will give somewhere between a nickel and a quarter. Once again, it is more the thrill of winning than the actual prize.

One last point about competition. You do not have to look too hard for areas in your curriculum to introduce this technique. A trick I like to use in some of the seminars I teach is to work competition into answers to questions. For example, if I have a study that I am bringing into the seminar to show a statistical breakdown of some sort, I will merely take a couple of volunteers to take their best shot at guessing what the results are. Of course, I do not get much of a response until I tell them there is a prize on the line. Then my only worry is to limit the number of volunteers I will accept. Great participation and interest is immediately created the moment I introduce competition.

As far as prizes are concerned, keep them simple. To this day, one of my most successful prizes happens to sound a little arrogant, but it works like a charm. For winning a contest, or even answering a tough question correctly, I give out an 8½" × 14" poster. Of what you ask? Me! As a matter of fact, I have about three or four of the most obnoxious, arrogant poses you'd ever want to see. Depending on the course and the timing of the award, I usually put some sort of caption across the top. Of course, no Rob Jolles poster is complete without an autograph slashing across the middle. A couple of reminders if you are interested in this particular idea. Wait a while before distributing these prizes until the trainees get to know you and understand you are poking fun at yourself. Also, this idea is not recommended in potentially hostile environments. Talk about adding grease to the fire!

16. Try an Offbeat Approach

Now this is not necessarily an area that I would dabble in . . . exactly. If I did, however, I would probably recommend a number of ideas that I have used.

One of my favorite unique "finds" actually came to me as a result of a trip to the supermarket. At the time, I was battling a boredom problem at work. My trainees were writing papers every night, and every morning I would read them and return them with my comments. I began to get creative and put symbols like checks and smiley faces on the homework, but that still just did not seem to be motivating the trainees one way or another. Then, I found them. It happened to me harmlessly enough. I slipped away from my wife at the grocery store, promising to pick up a couple of items. One item I usually volunteer for is the cereal. I do this because for some strange reason, I still like to see what is being offered on the back of those cereal boxes. As a kid growing up, I used to send away for many of the strange little items and then anxiously wait for their arrival in my mailbox. I have never really gotten over this thrill. Well, on this fateful day at the supermarket my perseverance payed off. As I quietly began turning cereal boxes around I became transfixed at the Cheerios box. For a whopping $1.00 (and a couple of proofs of purchase), they were offering to take a photo you sent them and make a rubber stamp out of it. With four boxes of Cheerios in tow, I ran home and put my plan into operation. No more smiley faces, now I could be using my face! I immediately shot two pictures, one of me happy and one of me not so happy. Cheerios was kind enough to make good on *this* kid's request and provide me with a stamp of each. The great thing about these stamps is that my trainees become seriously concerned when they see the "unhappy Rob" and will vow to do what is necessary to get the "happy Rob" next time.

Another idea that borders on the unique and the bizarre is one that I refer to as the "Bob Jolies Doll." Carefully designed and handmade as a birthday gift from my wife (an artist), Bob is quite a work of art. The idea behind Bob was to provide me with a sort of alter ego that I could use strategically, depending on the seminar. The expression given to Bob was probably the most difficult part of the creation. The idea was to create a look that was not well defined, making it useful in a variety of situations. The expression can be read as sarcastic when used as a customer who is put off by a salesperson trying to sell features instead of needs. The expression can be interpreted as embarrassment when perched behind a lectern as a presenter being sniped. The doll was created with the intention of generating interest within the presentation.

As a footnote, I have rehearsed with "Bob" much like a performer would with a prop. The main point to remember is that as a presenter you have to be careful not to cross the line of unique into distracting and silly. The "Bob Jolies Doll" is used sparingly and presented on rare occasions for that same reason. The goal behind appealing to the unique is to add interest to the presentation and not detract from it.

17. Deviate from Your Topic

This idea is probably one of the most misunderstood in the list. Simply put, topic deviation is nothing more than allowing trainees to stray off the current topic you are covering and letting them go for a few moments. This particular phenomenon happens in most seminars. The reason I say it is misunderstood stems from the average presenter's reaction. What most presenters do is immediately assume an authoritative role and wrestle the conversation away from the trainees and back on to the topic at hand. What a waste!

The idea is to try and create a training environment that is *conducive* to discussion. With that expectation comes the probability that the discussion that may break out will not always be exactly what you want them to be. So what! You should be flattered that trainees feel comfortable enough to discuss issues openly in your training room. Often the role of the presenter is to slip back out of the pit and let nature take its course. Watch for nonverbals from the trainees, and they will typically signal you when the discussion has gone on long enough. On the average, these conversations will last between two or three minutes. Once some of the trainees begin to look at you instead of those who are speaking, it is time to enter with a closed probe and bring the seminar back on target. Your reentry may sound something like this:

TRAINEE No. 1:   (after a few minutes) . . . that is how we do it in our area.

TRAINEE No. 2:   Well, in our district we have been known to tell people.

PRESENTER: (Breaking in) So it sounds like there have been a variety of approaches used in the field. Well, if you look at some of the tactics that we have been discussing, you will see a variety there as well. To begin with . . .

Sometimes, when breaking in or waiting to break in, you may hear a trainee slyly comment about you losing control of the seminar. Do not get defensive or feel obligated to explain your conscious decision. What they don't know won't hurt them!

18. Music

As mentioned in Chapter 5, music can be used in training not only to create a mood, but to create interest as well. Playing conservative music when trainees are entering the seminar helps to set a certain tone for the rest of the training. The idea behind this recommendation is not to stop here. Look carefully at some of the small group exercises or activities and see if you can mix in some quiet music while they are working. Many of my musical selections are based entirely on the type of exercise the trainees are working on.

For example, in a Quality class that I teach, the trainees participate in a culminating simulation. The entire class works together, using all the skills they have learned, to complete one final task as a team. During that simulation, I will play the theme from "Rocky" and other similar motivational songs. The bottom line is that music can often make a good small group exercise or activity just a little better.

19. Take Breaks

So far we have looked at a number of creative approaches for maintaining interest within your training. Now let's look at an interest-sustaining device that tends to be taken for granted. Breaks are often a presenter's best friend. Similar to topic deviation, this technique is also often misunderstood. Let's take a look at some of the misunderstandings and then at some suggested solutions surrounding the idea behind breaks.

The first misunderstanding surrounding the idea of a break is that it should be carefully tied to a particular spot within the curriculum. Often a presenter will open an instructor guide only to be greeted by the developer's references to where to take breaks. The intent behind these references is legitimate and typically corresponds to shifts in curriculum. The mistake so often made by presenters is to misinterpret these suggestions as fact. The developer may want you to break on page 25 and the book may say to break on page 25, but if the trainees are drifting away on page 20, you had better think again!

A second misunderstanding that preys on many presenters centers around the preset timing of seminar breaks. A preset break refers to seminars where breaks are scheduled out at the same time every day. For example, you may be conducting a seminar that starts at 8:00 A.M. with a planned break at 9:30 A.M. That is all well and good, but once again I am left with one question: What if the trainees are falling asleep at 9:00 A.M.?

The solution regarding breaks? Watch your trainees. *Read their non-verbals.* You usually will not have to look too hard to pick up on when trainees need a break. If you are pressured into breaks that are far apart, work in short five-minute breaks. Insist that the trainees stick to the five minutes and start back up on time. This conditions the trainees to learn you mean business. What usually happens is that those who need to run to the bathroom do, and the others will just stretch and mill around. Ironically, that five minutes will probably allow you to teach more in a day rather than less because the trainees will be better able to focus on your topic.

One other technique you can use with breaks is what I call foreshadowing. Sometimes trainees come back from a break, and within 20 minutes begin nonverbally signaling for another. You may want to say something like, "We'll be taking a break in a couple of minutes, so hang in there." It does not sound like much, but you would be shocked at how many trainees snap back just from hearing the word break. OK, it's a cheap trick. All's fair when you're working that pit!

20. Show Enthusiasm!

Last, but by no means least, is enthusiasm. I have attempted to show no preference or order to the list of interest-maintaining devices because each is appropriate in its own way, depending on the audience and style of the presenter. I would like to break from that rule at this time, however, and present you with my number one interest device: *enthusiasm.*

When presenters ask about maintaining interest (and it is the most-often-asked question during a Train-The-Trainer), I tell them to sit through the course for a week and I guarantee, if they keep their eyes open, they will get plenty of ideas. It all starts with enthusiasm. Think of it this way. You've misplaced an overhead? Trainees will forgive you. You stumbled over an extension cord? It could happen to anybody. You're fairly new to the curriculum and are forced to read more than you would like to? That's OK. Drop a stack of handouts on the floor? Pick them up; it could happen to anybody. You see, the bottom line is that when delivering seminars, workshops, or corporate training, audiences will forgive just about anything. Anything . . . but a lack of enthusiasm. It is no coincidence that if you look over the performance of most presenters, you will find that usually, each time they taught a new course, there was a strong trainee reaction. By that, I mean the trainees usually bond closely with the presenter and each other. Often, the presenter will be given a card or gift by the trainees. This is not etiquette, but for some strange reason, it usually happens . . . or is it so unusual? You see, the first time a presenter teaches a new seminar, regardless of tenure, there is a feeling of *eagerness* and *challenge*. This often translates to added enthusiasm and thus satisfied trainees. As the presenter becomes more accustomed to the new curriculum, the enthusiasm dwindles.

Perhaps the single most challenging aspect of corporate training revolves around the maintaining of enthusiasm. This maintenance takes a tremendous amount of *discipline*. The fact of the matter is that some days it is extremely difficult to find the enthusiasm necessary to do the job you know you are capable of doing. I suggest you keep a couple of reminders in your head. Lesson number one comes from an article I read about a fighter named Marvin Hagler. Hagler was said to view his own physical training with an intriguing attitude. On days he felt up to conditioning himself for an upcoming fight, he worked very hard. On days he did not feel up to doing the things he knew were necessary to prepare, he worked twice as hard! Pound for pound, Marvin Hagler was considered one of the greatest fighters of all time. His reign as champion stretched over a long period of time. Few fighters won more: Few worked harder. That attitude needs to take place within your training.

With respect to maintaining enthusiasm for your training, lesson number two comes from the attitude adopted by an actor. If an actor had to recite the same lines to the same audience each night, it would not take long for boredom to set in. Fortunately, the audiences change nightly. It also should be pointed out that although the presenter may feel as if he has told a story or an analogy one too many times, it is being heard for the very first time by the trainees.

As for me, I put a tremendous amount of importance on the enthusiasm I demand out of myself. I will continue to be enthusiastic teaching my seminars, workshops, and training classes. When I can no longer muster up that enthusiasm, do not feel sorry for me. There will not be enough time. I have vowed that when I can no longer put the enthusiasm necessary to conduct corporate training on the level that I feel is appropriate, I will learn to do something else very well and move on. Presenters must take responsibility for maintaining their own enthusiasm. It is just too important to do without.

WHAT TO DO ABOUT SLEEPY TRAINEES

Up to now, you have been presented a list of ideas designed to help trainees stay awake and interested in your training. No matter how skilled you are as a presenter and how many interest-maintaining ideas you implement, some trainees are still going to get sleepy in your seminars. How are you going to react? The first point you should consider is why it is happening. Try to remember that the average time an adult learner can go without a break is somewhere between 45 and 55 minutes. Class segments in school are usually 45 minutes, with lectures in college averaging about 50 minutes. For whatever reasons, most corporate training curriculum schedules break every 90 to 120 minutes. This is not good and tends to put a lot of pressure on the presenter.

A second reason that trainees may be falling asleep in your seminar is the plain and simple fact that they may be tired. Too often presenters' egos get hurt from working hard in the pit only to look up and see the whites of the eyes of one or two trainees. It can be demoralizing as well as debilitating. What you need to remember is that some people may absolutely love what it is you are talking about and how you are presenting it. Unfortunately, they are tired. This could be due to time change adjustments, sleeping problems due to stress or unfamiliar surroundings, or any number of other reasons. Think back on your own experiences as a trainee. Were you ever fascinated with the topic you were learning and the presenter teaching it, but you had trouble staying awake?

The real issue becomes how you are going to react. Hopefully, from your own experiences, you will be empathetic to those who are having trouble staying awake. It is not an insult, and it is not a signal to speed up. It is reality. You are not dealing with children. Gone are the days when a sleepy student was pelted by a piece of chalk or an eraser. This form of humiliation will most likely result in aggressive behavior from the trainee and rightfully so. My hope is that sleepy trainees will inspire you to work even harder.

Now let's turn our attention to how to strategically work harder with trainees who are dozing off on you. To begin with, one of the most classic techniques is to move toward the sleepy trainee. It is important to note that I am not suggesting you call on him with the intent to embarrass. I am merely recommending you move near him and perhaps increase your volume just a little bit as you continue your conversation.

Movement is effective in some situations with sleepy trainees; unfortunately, in other instances, it is not enough. When trainees are very sleepy, they will tend to snap to it as we brush by in the pit only to succumb to sleep again once we move away. When I was teaching flood insurance, this was a chronic problem for most of the trainers on staff.

A solution that I came up with then and still use to this day was the invention of the "Thriller Chiller." The intent behind this idea was to assist those who were overly tired. In the event that my moving toward these trainees was not enough to keep them awake, I would move to "phase two." I would return to the lectern where I kept the "Thriller Chiller," a pitcher loaded with ice water, pour some out in one of the paper cups I kept with it, and return to the pit. This time, however, I would not only brush by the offending trainees seat, I would subtly drop off the cup of water. The trick was never to break from the conversation I was having and to call absolutely no attention to what I was doing. The effort was and always is appreciated.

SUMMARY

No presenter typically starts a seminar by making it instantly interesting. The good presenters aim to build interest throughout and generate excitement as they go. Alone, few of the ideas you have just read through will provide you with the level of interest most presenters desire, but in combinations, four, five, six of the ideas in a module begin to add up and create interest. Before you know it, your trainees will be referring to you as the "Thriller III"!

Chapter 8

The Art of Effective Questioning: Getting Trainees Involved

What is it that often makes one seminar jump while the one across the hall bumps? What is it that transforms ordinary curriculum into dynamic text? Finally, what is it that often separates the great presenters from the good presenters? The answer lies in the presenter's ability to get the trainees *participating* and *involved*.

The best way of accomplishing this can be stated in one word: *questioning*. The title of this chapter suggests that becoming skilled in this area is the equivalent to mastering an art form. That is because effective questioning can transform even the most difficult text to life the same way an artist brings a blank canvas to life. As mentioned earlier, I am a firm believer that most conflict arising between a presenter and trainee is initiated by the presenter. Additionally, I feel one of the biggest culprits that contributes to this problem involves questioning.

TYPES OF QUESTIONS

When first examining the art of questioning, it is important to understand that, as a presenter, you can ask your trainees many kinds of questions. Each kind can be effective depending on various criteria. So many presenters make the mistake of seldom using more than one kind of question within their training sessions. As you will see, there is a whole world of questions out there that will not only get people involved in the material being taught but will help to promote the kind of stimulating training environment that so many presenters search for.

Fact-Based Questions

Let's start with the kind of question that is most often used in training today. A fact-based question is a question posed by the presenter that has a right-and-wrong answer. A fact-based question is the kind of question that most people associate with a learning environment. As a matter of fact, because once again the only teaching models most of us have are schoolteachers, most presenters will use fact-based questions within their training. This lesson learned early in life becomes perhaps the single biggest mistake presenters make when attempting to use questioning within their presentations. Guess which kind of question is the most dangerous to ask in a training environment? Murphy's Law strikes again! There are pros and cons to using this kind of question within your training, and I will be more than happy to examine both, but right now I want to emphasize that fact-based questions can often do more bad than good when used improperly . . . and they are often used improperly. Here are a couple of examples of fact-based questions:

PRESENTER: Which of the techniques are most commonly used?

or

PRESENTER: What are the proper steps, in sequence, to logging on to your personal workstation?

One of the key goals any presenter must work toward is to create a stimulating training environment that is both participative and alive. You are attempting to conduct your training using adult learning principles to create such an environment. As a matter of fact, about 90 percent of this book is dedicated to allowing you, the presenter, to use proven techniques to assist you in putting on the most informative and fun training programs imaginable. Fact-based questions can undo a lot that has already been done. Why? Because fact-based questions have a habit of putting trainees on the spot in front of the rest of the class. One thing you do not want to create within your training is a threatening environment. When trainees feel threatened, they tend either to stop participating or become aggressive toward the presenter. Remember the last time you did not know an answer in front of the rest of the class? The reaction to being put on the spot and possibly embarrassed will vary depending on the personality of the trainee. It is hard to predict exactly what this reaction might be, but chances are it will not be positive.

Up to now, it may appear as though I am not much of a fan of fact-based questions. The fact of the matter is, there are times within training and types of courses taught where fact-based questions are necessary. Technical courses, for instance, require trainees to learn definite right-and-wrong responses. The funny thing about a computer is that a computer is not interested in how you feel or your opinion. A computer is also not interested in the fact that your answer was close. In addition to this, fact-based questions are often quite effective during review sessions at the end of modules taught. My only concerns about fact-based questions are that they are often overused and can intimidate. Also remember, if you are going to use fact-based questions effectively, you should study up on some of the techniques recommended later in this chapter.

Opinion-Based Questions

The second most frequent kind of question asked within training is opinion-based. As the title suggests, this type of question does not have a right or wrong response. It is a safer kind of question to ask a group of trainees whom you do not know because of the decreased chances of putting anyone on the spot. Sometimes this type of question can be a little frustrating for the presenter because you must remember the basic principle that states, "Everyone is entitled to his own opinion." Clearly stated, you are not allowed to tell someone their opinion is wrong! Some examples would be:

PRESENTER: What is your opinion of this technique?

or

PRESENTER: How do you feel about this type of training?

The only disadvantage to using opinion-based questions within your training is that often the trainees' responses will lack substance. By this, I mean you are often simply asking trainees how they feel. They are not necessarily using any of the information that you have given them to formulate a response. I often think of opinion-based questions as a way to take a temperature reading within the seminar. This type of question will allow you a small peek at what the trainee is thinking, but it defeats the whole purpose of this kind of question to probe for too much more. Additional information can be gathered by using a couple of other kinds of questions yet to be discussed.

The advantages of opinion-based questions are simple. First, and foremost, they help reduce anxiety within the training room. Once a presenter demonstrates the fact that no opinions will be openly challenged, trainees begin to participate. The old saying, "Walk before you run," certainly pertains to this situation. I am in no way suggesting that throughout your training, you ask nothing but opinion-based questions. I am saying, however, that early on in your training (used strategically like an icebreaker exercise), opinion-based questions are terrific for preparing a seminar for active participation.

Another advantage to opinion-based questions centers around the personalities in your training room. The faster you can figure out the types of trainees you are working with, the better you will be able to appeal to their learning styles. Opinion-based questions allow trainees to express themselves freely. That gives you the opportunity to determine attitudes, interest, and personality types within your training room.

Comparison-Based Questions

Now that you have reviewed the two most common kinds of questions, let's look at some types of questions that are not used as often. As the name might indicate, a comparison question asks the trainees to examine the similarities and differences of the topic in question. Comparison-based questions are similar to opinion-based questions but require more of a response from the trainee. Typically, the response is somewhat opinion based, but it is often lengthier and more substantial. A couple of examples of this type of question are as follows:

PRESENTER: Based on what you have learned so far, how would you compare the educational approaches used in your schooling days with some of the approaches recommended in this course?

or

PRESENTER: Given the current method of accessing information for the customer and the automated method that has

> been demonstrated for you today, how would you compare the two?

This kind of question is more challenging to the trainee and rarely can be answered in a word or two. Once you have asked a comparison-based question, you can often count on some sort of discussion within the seminar. The only danger in asking a comparison-based question would once again involve your timing. I would not recommend asking a question of this complexity until the trainees have settled in and gotten to know you. Once this has been accomplished, this kind of question begins to create a nice bridge between "feel good" opinion-based questions, and "work harder" case-history-based questions.

Case-History-Based Questions

Perhaps my favorite of all questions that can be asked within a training environment is what is referred to as a case-history-based question. The disappointing reality is that it is also the most seldom used of the kinds of questions recommended. A case-history-based question requires the trainees to think on their own by providing a scenario without out a conclusion. The trainees are then asked to provide a solution based on the information that has been taught so far. Let me give you a couple of examples:

PRESENTER: Let's say you were set to give your first training seminar. Everything appeared in order until you noticed that on the schedule, the time committed to your training had been increased from one hour to two hours. Given the points we have covered so far, what strategy would you use to lengthen your training without wasting trainees' time with unimportant filler?

or

PRESENTER: Aren't interactive skills wonderful? Suppose the next phone call you received came from an irate customer whose first words to you were to suggest you not use any damn interactive skills or other such foolishness, and solve their problem . . . now! What approach would you take with this type of customer, and why?

As you can see, case-history-based questions require a lot more work from the trainee. Picking up where the comparison-based question leaves off, now the trainee must use not only the skills that you have taught him, but some of his own intuition as well. This is a tremendous kind of question to use when trainees are riding along taking in what is said without question.

The only real danger in using case-history-based questions is the risk that is once again involved in working with a trainee who has no idea of an answer. At this point, you have come full circle from a one-dimensional, fact-based question that requires regurgitating memorized information, to a trainee who is thinking and breathing on his own two feet. As far as suggestions for working out some of the negatives to asking questions, these factors can be suitably addressed in techniques for asking questions.

PREPARING AND COACHING TRAINEES TO ANSWER QUESTIONS

In deciding what kinds of questions you may want to use within your training, you may want to consider a few suggestions. First, as far as your *timing* is concerned, try and spend some time learning the various personalities within your room. Until you do, try and hold back on asking the fact-based questions. For example, Monday morning is not a good time to begin firing these high-pressure questions at your trainees. Give the class some time; learn which types of trainees you have in your room, and then you can more carefully introduce the kinds of questions that are most appropriate for the personality types you are training.

The second preparation you must make when preparing to use fact-based questions within your training involves *coaching*. Take a proactive position right now, and anticipate some trainees are not going to know the correct answer. Do not wait for this to happen in front of the entire class. Take my word for it, it will. What are you as the presenter going to do?

Remember, when a trainee is stuck, or having difficulty with your question, it is not only the trainee who is uncomfortable. The other trainees in the seminar feel it as well. Once I took a course (a Train-The-Trainer of all courses), where a trainee was asked a question he did not know the answer to. The presenter waited and waited and waited. The other trainees, sensing the embarrassment of the trainee who could not answer the question, began raising their hands in an effort to help out. The presenter insisted they put their hands down and allow the trainee in question to respond. After at least two agonizing minutes, the presenter finally moved on. This one situation created an air of anxiety and tension that never did leave the seminar. It was apparent that the only result that was accomplished by putting this trainee on the spot was to limit the flow of further questions or responses. As with most seminars, trainees began nervously to second-guess themselves and shut themselves out from active participation.

Forcing responses out of students may work in television dramas, but it does not work when training adults. It would be unfair to say that you will no longer get participation from the trainees in front of the class because you probably will. You may not like the form of participation you receive. Unfortunately, the reaction will probably come in the form of an attack somewhere down the road.

When a presenter embarrasses a trainee in front of a class, retaliation often comes from the trainee much later. Trainees do not want to appear argumentative or negative so they will often wait for the right opportunity, and when they see it, the presenter gets it right between the eyes. Maybe it is a controversial point. Maybe it is an unpopular stance that you the presenter must take. Maybe you simply misplace a handout. Rest assured, this sniper you have created is waiting to pounce. Often we as presenters are left pondering, "Gee, what got into him?" It could very well be that our own insensitivity and rudeness created this situation.

I cannot emphasize enough how important your sensitivity to your trainees is. With questions, you have a rare opportunity to prove to the class what you have been preaching all along: This is a safe environment where your input is taken seriously and highly regarded.

Knowing that despite the disadvantages, you will still need to ask fact-based questions, prepare yourself to coach all responses that are necessary. Try to keep rewording and subtly feeding more of the answer you are looking for. Your conversation may sound something like this:

PRESENTER: What kind of question do you use more often in your technical training type courses . . . Danny?

TRAINEE: Uh . . . um . . .

PRESENTER: Remember, it was the type of question that had a right and wrong response.

TRAINEE: Oh, well that would be . . . uh . . .

PRESENTER: Based on . . .

TRAINEE: Facts! Fact-based questions.

PRESENTER: Excellent!

In addition to this technique, it is by no means inappropriate to move the question to another volunteer. This approach may be helpful depending on the personality of the trainee being questioned and the cohesiveness of the class.

Sometimes, trainees will not hesitate at all. As a matter of fact, they will proudly and confidently give you the wrong answer with a big smile. Here too, the subtle approach can spare a trainee from unnecessary embarrassment. Try to find something, anything that may be close to your answer, and then simply fix the rest of the response. Here is an example:

PRESENTER: What kind of question do you use more often in your technical training type courses . . . Jessie?

TRAINEE: Definitely the opinion-based questions.

PRESENTER: What is your reasoning behind this answer?

TRAINEE: Simple. Everyone has an opinion, and in this type of training, finding out their opinions would be very helpful.

PRESENTER: You make a good point. We certainly cannot go wrong finding out an individual's opinion in any type of training we conduct. You may also want to consider fact-based questions to assure the trainees have the correct processes learned. Good answer.

Another example of the compassion I am referring to can be borrowed from an old sales technique. When a customer has misunderstood a point the salesperson has made and is objecting to it, rather than risk egos being hurt, the salesperson may simply use a process called, "Feel, felt, found." The idea is to gently nudge the person from the misunderstanding without making him feel foolish. The "feel" portion of your answer does just that. The "felt" portion of your answer adds empathy, and the "found" portion gently provides your trainee with the correct information. Putting it all together would sound something like this:

PRESENTER: What kind of question do you use more often in your technical training type courses . . . Jessie?

TRAINEE: Definitely the opinion-based questions.

PRESENTER: You know, that's kind of interesting you say that. A lot of people *feel* the same way you do. If they are going to ask questions, they want to start slowly with those opinion-based questions and work their way up. I *felt* the same way myself when I first started to conduct technical training courses. Strangely, what we *found* was that for technical training, often the best approach centers around fact-based questions to assure the trainees have the correct processes learned.

With either of these two examples, do not worry that you may not be clearly communicating the exact, textbook response in this particular case. As mentioned earlier, adults learn by repetition, and this is a prime candidate to not only be repeated but cleaned up as well. In some cases, it is also a classic example of maybe not quite winning the battle, but eventually winning the war.

TECHNIQUES FOR ASKING QUESTIONS

So far we have looked at different kinds of questions that you can use within your training sessions and ideas involving participation and coaching. Now I would like to turn your attention to various techniques for actually delivering or using these questions. It would seem logical to learn more about who is in your training room and try to figure out the best kinds of questions to ask of your seminar, but the question that still needs to be answered is "How." The truth of the matter is that although a lot of consideration should be given to the kinds of questions used within your training, just as much, if not more, should be given in planning how to ask them.

Guided Technique

One of the most common techniques used by presenters in asking questions is a guided question. Guided questions are aimed directly at a trainee, giving you complete control over who is going to answer the question. A key strength to using guided questions lies in the control it gives the presenter when working with the seminar participants. Many individuals simply will not participate unless a question is guided directly at them. In addition to this, there are other trainees who will attempt to answer *every* question unless the question is guided away from them. Guided questions allow you to choose who will answer the question.

Unfortunately, guided questions are not without risk. This approach can be viewed as somewhat threatening if overused and can also inhibit the potential for spontaneous participation. The good news is that the biggest problem with this questioning approach can be easily avoided with a little discipline on your part. You see, what almost all presenters do when they ask a guided question is start off by addressing the trainee who will be asked the question. Sounds somewhat logical. The question may sound something like this:

PRESENTER: *Danny,* given the skills you have just learned, and the text provided, what would you do if there was no system administrator to help you through the process just taught and an irate customer called wanting immediate action?

Here you have a rather classic case history question using a guided technique. Looks harmless enough, doesn't it? The problem is that the moment the trainee's name was introduced in this question, the trainee tuned in . . . and the rest of the trainees tuned out. In this example, the typical trainee most likely heard, "Danny, given the skills," and left sometime soon after to dream about the next scheduled break. Seems like kind of a waste for such a well-thought-out question. A much more effective approach would be as follows:

PRESENTER: Given the skills you have just learned, and the text provided, what would you do if there was no system administrator to help you through the process just taught and an irate customer called wanting immediate action, [pause], *Danny?*

Formulating the question and then pausing will allow all the trainees to mentally work toward an answer. Then guide the question to the student you select. Also, the pause lets you look at the group and choose someone who shows a sign of recognition. This may very well help you to avoid the embarrassment of choosing someone who is without a clue!

Look easy? The next seminar you attend, watch how often this technique is used. I will give you fair warning; you will seldom see it. The only thing easy about this technique is how easy it is to forget. Using this approach will allow you to involve all your trainees in the questions you ask. With some practice, it becomes a snap.

Overhead Technique

Just as common as the guided technique in delivering questions is the overhead approach. When asking questions with the overhead approach, you are basically allowing anyone in the seminar to take a shot at answering them. One key advantage to using this approach is called Monday. Monday represents the beginning of any training that you may conduct. The trainees are typically a little tense, and it is your job to begin to create the type of environment that is conducive to learning. Icebreaker activities help, and so does the demonstration of a non-threatening environment. Overhead questions also allow you to begin to learn about the various personality types within your seminar. Overheads allow those who want to talk, a chance to talk, and those who need a little more time, a little more time. You will begin to get an insight as to the nature of some of your trainees simply by observing how they react to the overhead, allowing you to carefully strategize the kinds of questions you intend to use. As you begin to demonstrate the safety of participation, the room begins to thaw.

The actual delivery approach for overhead questions can be done a couple of ways. Sometimes if you just ask the question and extend your arms out, trainees will assume the question is aimed at anyone who wishes to respond. Of course, you may wish to not be quite so cute, and try asking a question similar to the following example:

PRESENTER: Can anyone tell me at least two of the four behavioral styles that were discussed earlier?

or

PRESENTER: What are at least two of the four behavioral styles that were discussed earlier today (pause), anyone?

The second approach is recommended once the class has had a chance to warm up, allowing all of the trainees to once again begin to work out a solution not knowing if you will guide the question at them.

The only real disadvantage to the overhead approach to questioning arises around total participation. Some trainees just will not volunteer an answer unless a question is guided directly toward them. Just remember to be patient: Often, the trainees who do not appear to be involved, may just need a little more time. There is no law that says everyone must participate on day one by 9:00 A.M. If you give these trainees some time, you may find that they too will participate and get involved with questions delivered overhead to the class.

Relay Technique

Another technique that you can use when working with questions is the relay technique. This approach involves the presenter asking a question of the class and then simply moving that same question around the room getting input from other trainees. This technique is particularly effective when combined with case history or opinion-based questions. Here is an example:

PRESENTER: Let's say for a moment that you are approaching a training situation where you know there are going to be some unhappy trainees. What are some of your thoughts regarding your initial participation (pause), Jessie?

JESSIE: Well, I think I would probably make an attempt to figure out, before the training is to begin, what their particular grievances are.

PRESENTER: Good idea. How would you approach this situation (pause), Artie?

With the relay technique, you can ask the same question of each trainee. You benefit by getting to know the trainees and by keeping them involved. The trainees benefit by being exposed to a variety of opinions and solutions to a given question.

Reverse Technique

The final technique that you can use when questioning trainees is called a reverse. The reverse technique is actually initiated by the trainees. Often, many presenters are totally unaware of the opportunity at hand. This is what happens. A trainee asks the presenter a question, and before you can say, "Bob's your uncle," the presenter has answered it. The question is often gobbled up by newer presenters, because of their desire to achieve some credibility. What a wasted opportunity! Here is this chance to really get one of your trainees thinking about an issue relating to your curriculum, and it is gone. Add to that the fact that there are many shrewd trainees out there who will pick up on this weakness and literally try to get the presenter to do their job for them. A reverse approach solves all of these problems by putting the question right back into the trainee's lap. Here is an example of how it may sound:

TRAINEE: Uh, excuse me. What do you think is the best approach for us to use in our role plays tomorrow morning?

PRESENTER: That is a good question. What approach do you most strongly favor?

TRAINEE: Well . . I . . . uh, thought maybe the strategic tactical approach.

PRESENTER: What benefits do you think could be gained by that tactic?

TRAINEE: I could use both processes taught and still be in a position to think on my feet if I was not receiving the kind of information anticipated.

PRESENTER: Excellent! I could not agree more. Allowing yourself the flexibility to react in the role play should in fact be a major factor in the approach you select. Good job.

This response could have just as easily been relayed to another in the seminar. The key is that the presenter should not waste chances like these to get trainees more involved in the curriculum. You will also notice something else that is important when using this technique. In the example, you will notice the presenter adds support to the response where it is necessary and in a way puts the finishing touches on the trainee's answer. Some presenters will argue that they do not want to appear as if they do not know the correct answer. They probably get that feeling from watching some other poor presenter nervously try and get at a response from the class to a question they obviously do not know the answer to. Once a response has been given, they nervously nod and move on to another topic. I will not lie to you and tell you that I have been 100 percent sure of the answer to every question I have relayed or reversed back to the trainees. I will tell you that I will use the resources available to me in the room, which is often other trainees, and offer my opinion in support of their responses.

Reversing a question is a wonderful approach to helping a trainee to think on his own. Many trainees have strong opinions about questions they pose to the presenter, and it is simply safer and easier to have the presenter answer the questions for them. Certainly not for every question, but in many situations, it is a gold mine of an opportunity for you to gain participation within the seminar and help trainees to think for themselves.

DO'S AND DON'TS OF QUESTIONING

Whether it is asking questions of or receiving questions from your trainees, there are some definite do's and don'ts. Let me finish our discussion about the art of questioning by presenting you with an outline of each, starting with the do's.

Have a Positive Attitude Toward Questioners

For starters, do maintain a positive attitude when addressing questions generated by your trainees. Too many presenters make the mistake of appearing defensive when handling questions from the class. Unfortunately, questions are often viewed as something bad when just the opposite is true. To begin with, questions from the trainees demonstrate a show of interest in the material taught as well as an environment conducive to a discussion. This type of atmosphere should be cherished by the presenter and not feared. Truth be known, in my years of delivery underfire, I have seen just about everything. With these experiences behind me, I can honestly say there is not much that will rattle me . . . except the absence of questions. Nothing is worse than talking and talking and talking and then being faced with dead silence when searching for questions from the class. That makes even Rob a little uncomfortable. Remember also that usually when one trainee has a question regarding something that is being covered in the seminar, other trainees have the same question. Often the question posed to the presenter is more the tip of the iceberg than the exception to the rule. With this in mind, you should be flattered to get the questions you do, and carefully explain those areas of information that are unclear for the benefit of the kind soul who asked the question, as well as for the rest of the class.

Know Your Material

Do try and know your material as well as you can. The reality of corporate training is that there is always going to be a first time, a new seminar, or an unrealistic time schedule. Do the best you can within reason, and try to anticipate the more difficult areas by looking over your notes. This will give you added confidence and credibility.

An example of this comes from my insurance days. When I sold insurance for the New York Life Insurance Company, I was considered a pretty good group health insurance agent. I must admit, I do not think I knew that much more than my competition, but I was conscious of one subtle difference. When I was learning about health insurance, I became totally confused (along with the rest of the public), with an area of the policy called "preexisting conditions." This part of the policy dealt with what would and would not be covered in the event the insured switched policies and had already received treatment for an illness. Within this provision, there were rules dealing with 30, 60, and 90 days that dramatically affected coverages and liabilities. Now do not worry, I have no intention to try explaining this to you any further, but it was a critical issue in the eyes of the insured. I studied and studied this provision, anticipating questions in that area, and I was not disappointed. I was one of the few agents who had a clear understanding of this area, and I was able to explain it to others. This ability translated to increased credibility and, in that profession, increased income.

Understand the Question

Make sure you understand the question being asked of you. With the typical presenter's mind moving at a highly accelerated pace, it is quite easy to misinterpret the question being asked. Occasionally, I have been guilty of this error in judgment. You see, when a presenter is attempting to control the training room, many issues are swirling around in his mind: What is being said, what key points need to be made, what is coming up, personalities and timing, to mention just a few. Therefore, it is extremely easy to hear a question and mentally jump to a point that you have been wanting to make. To complicate matters a little more, it is not uncommon for trainees to ask rather vague questions. Underfire, in the pit, it is the presenter's responsibility to make sense of what has been asked, not the trainee. It is rather embarrassing to answer a question, see a confused expression on the trainee's face, ask if that answered his question, and hear: "No, not really." Oops! Here is an example demonstrating how easy it is for a situation like this to occur:

TRAINEE: What is a good way to apply this technique?

PRESENTER: That is a good question, I'm glad you asked. This technique can be applied on just about any customer as long as you are working with the decision maker. That is a topic I want to discuss now. Does that answer your question?

TRAINEE: Uh, no, not really. All I wanted to know was how you get started in learning the technique itself.

A recommended technique to avoid this embarrassment is called restating. Restating simply involves repeating the question asked by the questioner to confirm your understanding of what was asked. Once the trainee agrees to the restated question, you have the green light to go with an answer. An example of restating would look like this:

TRAINEE: What is a good way to apply this technique?

PRESENTER: OK, the question has been asked, What is a good way to apply the technique that has been taught? I assume you are referring to customer applications, is that correct?

TRAINEE: No, just some ideas to help us learn the concept.

Another benefit to restating the question is to assure that all the trainees were able to hear what was asked. It can be frustrating to be sitting in a training room, hear a trainee from the other side of the room mumble a question that cannot be made out, and hear the presenter say, "Boy, I'm glad you asked that one! Tuesdays and Thursdays without fail." Many trainees will not ask what was said; they will simply sit back and stew. A few minutes, an hour, a day later the presenter gets sniped by the trainee who could not hear and wonders, "What's that guy's problem?"

Making sure you understand the question may appear obvious, but it is well worth your time. In a small seminar, with a trainee who speaks clearly and loudly, and words his question so that there can be no confusion, do not worry about the formality of restating and clarification. Make that decision the exception to the rule, however, and remember, in a large training environment, or where the acoustics are bad, there really is no choice. Consider this technique an insurance policy to handling questions effectively.

Ask Questions if None Have Been Asked

It always amazes me to sit around a table of trainers at lunchtime after the first day of training and hear some of the stories: "I've got the dullest group of slugs you have ever seen," or "Boy, you could hear a pin drop in my classroom this week." Not wanting to disturb the slightly large ego of most trainers, I will usually quietly ask these trainers if they are asking questions of their trainees, to which I get the standard answer, in stereo, "Of course!"

Earlier in this chapter, you read about the different kinds of questions that you can ask and the techniques for asking them. What I failed to mention is that sometimes trainees are not ready for even the simplest opinion question. Oh, they will certainly answer it, but there still may be an air of apprehension hanging over the room. Your job as a presenter is to get rid of that uneasiness felt by the trainees and promote interaction. In this case, you do need to ask questions of the trainees if none have been asked. The difference now is that, as with other issues relating to training, you may have to take on the attitude that you will crawl before you walk, and walk before you run.

Let me give you an example. You have a group of trainees who, as fate would have it, are all rather quiet. There are a couple of trainees who would normally talk, but not until a couple of others were speaking first. There you have it, a standoff. Many presenters will ask a few simple overhead opinion questions, get no takers, direct a question at someone, and try a couple more times. Eventually, the presenter will resign himself to the fact that there will not be much interaction, so here comes the lecture, full steam ahead. Why not back up one step and ask questions that really do not require answers? Here are examples of some questions designed to warm up the trainees slowly:

PRESENTER: This concept was difficult for me the first time I saw it, how about you?

TRAINEES: (Grumbling, mumbling, and nodding collectively).

Not exactly a word, but I'll take it! That is what I call crawling. Now let me show you what walking might look like:

PRESENTER: Of the three items you see before you, which do you think will be most helpful in assisting you in your everyday duties?

TRAINEE: (Eyes averted, looking down or away) Number two.

Now you have them walking, by giving you real words. A few more questions like these, and you should have them dancing with sentences in no time. Then it is more appropriate to ask the more involved opinion questions.

Bad combinations of trainees? There really is no such thing. The presenter may need to work harder, however, to bring some of these trainees out of their shells. The results you witness within your training rooms will certainly be rewarding.

Handling questions from your trainees properly provides many rewards: increased credibility, opportunities to involve other trainees, and the creation of a training climate conducive to the sharing of ideas are just a few. There are some pitfalls that must be avoided however. Let's now turn our attention to some of the negative approaches to handling questions.

Don't Discount or Discourage Questions

Perhaps the single most destructive act a presenter can inflict on a seminar is to discount questions that are asked. Discouraging trainees from asking questions is not something most presenters actually plan, but nevertheless they are often guilty of it.

One of the most blatant examples I can provide occurred when I was a student attending a technical writing class at a local university. There was little to no interaction in a class of 20 that met once a week. Now there are those who would say that there is not a lot of need for interaction in a technical writing class, but I would strongly disagree. The class was three hours long, with most of the students remaining conscious for about the first two hours. I guess you could say that it was the responsibility of the student to stay awake or risk a failing grade, but as you know, I come from the school of thought that believes you motivate students in other ways. I would also have loved to have heard what the other students were working on and the obstacles they were facing, but without any interaction, the class remained full of strangers.

On one magic night, about eight weeks into the class, a strange thing happened. At first, I did not know exactly what it was, and then I recognized it. A student was raising his hand. We looked back and forth from the teacher to the student, nervously waiting for the teacher to turn around. Finally, in mid-sentence, the teacher turned around and, with an indignant leer, stopped talking and stared at the student for what seemed like an eternity. Mercifully, the teacher then asked my fellow student what his question was. As the student anxiously began to ask his question, the teacher's face began to register a kind of disgust (I quickly decided I like the leer better). Once the student finished his question, the teacher started her response with "I can't believe you asked that question. We just went over that a couple of minutes ago. Were you listening or just daydreaming again? The answer is . . ."

To this day, I still do not know the answer that was given. I was too mortified with the teacher's response to care. I do remember that when the teacher finished answering the question, she then asked if there were any other questions. There were no more questions that night, nor were there any more for the remaining eight weeks of the course.

The ramifications of discounting student questions are very real. You run the risk of creating a potential sniper trainee, alienating a class, and destroying your chances for group interaction. I am one who does not like to dwell on the negatives, so let me relate a story that deals more with the positive aspects of not discouraging questions.

When I was a training consultant, I once assisted in a listening seminar that an acquaintance was giving. I did not know much about the seminar, but for a waiver of the $100 admittance fee, I agreed to help with registration at the door. I also knew that my friend had a good reputation as a presenter. The one characteristic I had been told to look for was his ability to relax his audiences and get them to participate. As I helped to seat the last of the 175 participants, a sly smile appeared on my face. "So in less than seven hours, this guy is going to get this mass participating? Fat chance," I thought. Sure enough, as he began his presentation, he mentioned his desire for the audience to feel comfortable, ask questions, and participate. Sure! Twelve people maybe, 175, forget it. Then, after a rather quiet first half hour, it happened. It started innocently enough with one hand being raised in a sea of humanity. The presenter quickly finished what he was saying, smiled warmly, and asked the trainee for his question. What happened next is something I will never forget.

TRAINEE: When you mention sound and different noises, is it kind of like a butterfly and a train?

The rest of the audience found this question strange and a confused murmur filled the room. My sharp trainer eye caught a subtle leg buckle of the presenter as he reached to pull on his chin in thought. Within a split second, the presenter's smile reappeared, as he remarked:

PRESENTER: Well, when you consider that a butterfly makes a quiet sound, much like our own communication, and the train makes a loud sound, much like many of the day-to-day distractions we are all faced with, then in fact, they are very much related. I guess it becomes a matter of which will be most likely to win. I am rooting for the butterfly and maybe some of the ideas we discuss today may help us all to deal with the trains in our lives. Excellent question, thank you!

The trainee who asked the question, smugly nodded to the answer that was given to his question, and rather arrogantly sat back down in his seat. I looked around the room. Many of the trainees were peering off in a confused kind of daze, but this soon changed. The glazed expression was replaced with almost universal understanding. The message sent from the presenter was clear. No question would be rejected. At that moment in the seminar, you could literally see the trainees thinking, "If he got away with that one, then I have a question."

A transformation had occurred. The seminar continued with active participation from a crowd most presenters would consider impossible to warm up. To this day, I have given serious consideration in my larger seminars to actually slipping in a planted trainee to ask one or two questions that are off the wall. Fortunately, when the numbers are that large, chances are a plant will not be necessary. You should have the real McCoy. You see, the last time you taught a course and someone strange appeared out of nowhere, you may have been lucky. You just did not know it!

The skill demonstrated in the following example is a technique every presenter should practice. Many times, you will be in a position where you are not receiving the question or response you are looking for. It is critical that the questioner be made to feel his participation was worthwhile. It therefore becomes necessary for you to find value in whatever the trainee is offering. Sometimes, as in the example just illustrated, this can be quite a challenge. The rewards make it all worthwhile. Trainees know when you show empathy to them or their fellow trainees. Sometimes it almost becomes a question of whether the glass is half full or half empty.

A good illustration of this type of exchange recently came up in a quality course I was teaching for Xerox. The question I asked related to a customer service issue the trainees were discussing. They had just watched a tape showing a rental car clerk being somewhat rude to a customer. I asked the class if they felt the problem they had just witnessed was a people problem or a process problem. The response that I was looking for was a process problem. The point I wanted to bring out was that 85 percent of the problems of this nature are process problems, and 15 percent are due to people. Here was our exchange:

PRESENTER: From the video you just watched, do you think this problem was a people problem or a process problem?

TRAINEE: A people problem, for sure!

PRESENTER: I see. Well, you are in good company because a lot of people feel the same way you do. Fifteen percent of the time you are right. What's really surprising is that 85 percent of the time it is a process problem.

To me, it is most challenging to turn a response around when it is so emphatically stated incorrectly. Try not to put yourself in that type of position and avoid catch questions altogether. Let me illustrate this point to you with another example from that same quality class. I used to ask students to finish this statement. "If it ain't broke . . ." The response that I was looking for was really "fix it better," but that is not what I received. Often, I would get trainees who would not only finish the statement with the immortal "don't fix it," they would go on to sing the praises of this statement's wisdom. Why put yourself in that position? I still ask that question in the quality class I teach, only I changed it a bit. I now say, "Finish this statement, but let me warn you now to be careful. 'If it ain't broke . . .'" With this fair warning to the class, I have not had a problem since. The trainees do not feel tricked, and the question becomes a fair one.

Finally, you may receive questions from trainees that are so far off the wall, that you cannot even relate them to anything that you have talked about. In that instance, the best statement I can recommend is to look at the questioner, pause purposefully, and tell him, "That is an excellent question. One I haven't even considered before. Let me work on it a bit and get back to you." It has not failed me yet, but make sure they have not read this book before using it!

Don't Rush to Fill in Those Moments of Silence

They say that time flies when you're having fun. Well, that can be true when conducting training as well. This feeling of speed can make a presenter susceptible to another problem that needs to be avoided. Do not become uncomfortable with moments of silence.

To begin with, these moments (due to all the fun you are having) are really shorter than you think. It is quite common to hear a presenter ask a class, "Are there any questions?" and about one one-hundredth of a second later say, "Good, let's move on." To the presenter, it seems as if he has taken a long pause, but to the trainees, that pause went by in a flash.

Often, when a presenter asks a class if there are any questions, initially, the trainees will not offer any. The reason for this is simple. When the presenter is conducting training properly, most trainees are left thinking about what was just said. It takes a few seconds for them to digest the information and then pose a possible question. When a presenter moves on quickly without slowing to see what questions the trainees may have, the presenter is wasting a wonderful opportunity for interaction. By the way, this slowing down and listening for questions is easier said than done. I will usually either force myself to count (using my fingers behind the lectern) to eight. Another technique I will use with a smaller class of 5 to 10 trainees, is to point to each student in about one-second intervals.

If you need one more piece of evidence to slow you down, consider this little experiment I run in my Train-The-Trainer programs. I will tell trainees of my recommendation to slow down. I will then tell them that within the course of the week they are in town to take Train-The-Trainer, I will model what I am teaching and wait for questions. I tell them that I will ring a bell every time I receive a question after at least five seconds of waiting, reminding them that these are questions and discussions they would never normally hear. I bet them that the bell will ring at least 10 times within the week. That is one bet I have not lost yet!

Don't Worry about Questions without Answers

One of the biggest fears many newer presenters experience is of not knowing the answer to a question asked in a seminar. Although this fear may be somewhat illogical, it needs to be addressed just the same. I say it is somewhat illogical because when you consider the idea that one individual should know everything there is to know about another topic, it does seem rather ridiculous. We do not necessarily expect this from someone who is training us, but we do expect it of ourselves. Hogwash! Repeat after me:

> I do not have to know everything about my topic. What I do know will be much more than what the vast majority of my students know.

When you are teaching a course, especially for the first couple of times, you may want to take a proactive approach to this issue. Rather than waiting to be stumped in a topic that is fairly new to you, try clearing the air while still in your overview with a statement similar to this one:

PRESENTER:　. . . and as for the material that we will be covering, I am certain that I will be able to answer the vast majority of your questions. Of course, no one knows all the answers including me, but I do know where I can get the answers. Therefore, what I do not know I will write down on this pad (or flipchart), and I will get you the answers by ＿＿＿＿＿＿.

Before you start your training, make sure there is a contingency plan in place that will allow you to get answers to questions you cannot answer. This may mean someone you can call, a place you can go for the answers, or even another presenter who may have more experience in the subject matter in question. Whatever the solution, make sure you communicate this process to your trainees. This may mean answers by a certain time in the week. It could also mean a memo to all attendees clarifying issues that could not be addressed in the seminar.

By discussing this point at the beginning of training, before there are any problems, you will feel a tremendous weight lifted from your shoulders. You are not expected to know everything. Get rid of some potential anxiety and get that issue out in the open early. If a trainee is asking for your opinion, then make sure you emphasize it is just that, your opinion. If someone asks a question that requires a factual response, then answer the question just that way, factually. The critical point here is to *never,* under any circumstance, *make up an answer* to a question you are unsure of. This is the quickest way to destroy credibility that I know of.

Now, I believe I have made my point regarding this issue, but be forewarned. It is easier to violate the trainees' trust than you may think. Recently, a colleague told me about his experience teaching a course that he had taught many times before. A trainee asked a question in an area that the trainer had not been questioned about before. What's more, he did not really know the answer. Before he could stop himself, he heard a voice take a guess at the answer. The voice did not indicate that this was a guess or an opinion, the voice stated the answer as a fact. The voice was his own! He told me it happened so fast that he almost threw a hand over his mouth, but it was too late and, besides, survival instincts began to take over. The major problem he was now faced with was attempting to sell this answer to the class while he thought of a way out of this mess.

Unfortunately, the saying "Oh what a wicked web we weave, when first we venture to deceive," was far too real: My friend believes that some of the trainees sensed his discomfort, as well as less than his usual conviction when speaking on an issue, because every time he attempted to move on, he got another question from a trainee, and another puzzled expression to go along with his new response. Apparently, he was in too deep to reverse his answer, so he did what any red-blooded presenter would do: He conveniently shut down further questions due to time, promised to revisit the issue later, and moved on with a nauseous feeling in the pit of his stomach. He told me he did, in fact, revisit the issue the next day after getting the correct answer, and he told the students that they could consider the new response as a viable alternative (he never exactly told the whole truth).

His story gave me a new respect for not making up answers. As a presenter, your guesses will be interpreted as fact unless you state otherwise. It takes self-discipline to continuously tell the trainees what you do know and what you do not know.

When you really stop and think about it, are you not even a little skeptical spending 5 or 10 days with one presenter who knows *every* answer? I can understand that a presenter might know *most* of the answers, but *every* answer? I personally would begin to wonder. As strange as this may sound, there is one time I will not tell the truth within the training I conduct. On some occasions I will actually tell trainees I am unsure of a response to a question I know the answer to. I will then go through the motions of confirming the answer through the designated channels and follow the process that the trainees and I established from the outset. This not only inspires *more* trust from the trainees in the answers they will be receiving but solidifies a lot of the responses already given. Remember, this is an acceptable lie in the name of good, honest training!

Thank Trainees for Their Questions

One last minor point I would like to make regarding handling questions from your trainees is a friendly reminder. Do not forget to thank the trainees for their questions. As emphasized throughout this chapter, receiving questions from participants benefits a seminar in many wonderful ways:

- It demonstrates a show of interest from the trainees.
- It allows you, the presenter, some insight as to the clarity of your message.
- It assists in keeping people interested in your topic.

To receive this type of participation is flattering, and you should continue to encourage it. One of the best ways I know to accomplish this is to get in the habit of thanking the trainees for their questions before major breaks such as lunch and the end of the day. This little "thank you" should aid in allowing you to pick up where you left off in terms of predicted levels of participation.

SUMMARY

It is hard to tell you in quantifiable terms exactly what makes a good presenter, and what makes a great presenter. If I were forced to choose a couple of skills, however, questioning would certainly be one of them. Challenge yourself to ask more thought-provoking questions and use these techniques to better manage the personalities within your seminars. I firmly believe that if you can master the key areas outlined in this chapter, you too will find the art of questioning a pivotal tool for your own personal success.

Chapter 9

Using Visual Aids

Years ago, when I decided to hang up my insurance sales shoes and become a trainer, I attended my very first Train-The-Trainer course. As I nervously entered the room, I began searching for my name tag. The trainees' list read more like a who's who from various Fortune 500 companies. With little to no training experience behind me, I was a walking sponge. The room was fairly quiet, with trainees fidgeting nervously with the training materials when the trainer entered the room. The room immediately fell silent. I was struck by the fact that he made little to no eye contact as he headed for the overhead. Without a smile, without an acknowledgment, he flicked on the overhead. There was a newspaper article that had been copied onto a transparency. The headline read, "Expectations for Trainers in the Workplace to Decrease 75% by 1994." There was a moment of uneasy silence, which was soon broken by nervous laughter and finally conversation from all in the class. It seemed as if everyone was discussing the article and the ridiculousness of it when the trainer again moved into the pit, turned the overhead off, and began to speak. "Now that I have your attention," he said, "I want to start talking about the wonders of training." The four-day class was not yet 30 seconds old, and I already knew I was going to like the course and the trainer who was teaching it! That is an example of the potential of a well-thought-out visual aid.

Do your presentations *jump?* Up to now, we have spent a great deal of time talking about the *words* you are going to use in your training presentations. Now we will talk about how you can *enhance* those words with *visual aids.* Ask a trainer about the importance of a well-prepared visual aid and he will sing its praises. Remember, 75 percent of what you learn comes from your sense of sight. The more visual aids you use, the more your trainees can retain.

So why are they so often poorly used or not used at all? One reason is fear. There are risks you must take when using a visual aid. Fortunately, the rewards far outweigh the risks. The second reason comes more from our previous learning experiences. All of us, at some time in our lives, have witnessed a presenter who has had problems with the visual aids he intended to use. We swear to ourselves that it is not worth it.

Visual aids are just too vital to your training to avoid. You must use them to strengthen not only your trainees' retention but your own presentation as well. With that in mind, the intent of this chapter is to explore the weaknesses, strengths, and ultimately the proper use of some of the most commonly used visual aids.

THE OVERHEAD PROJECTOR

I would like to start with the overhead projector. It is the visual aid that is most commonly used in corporate training. It is also the visual aid that is most commonly *misused* in corporate training.

One of the first problems that contributes to the overhead projector's misuse is the fact that transparencies are so easily made with copiers. This could certainly be considered a strength, but in reality, I believe the copier actually does more harm than good (and I work for Xerox). How many times have you sat through a presentation that was made up of pages copied straight out of a book onto a transparency? The realities of being a presenter are that each time you get up in front of a group, an enormous number of assumptions are made about you based on the way you handle yourself. When a speaker puts up an overhead that shows no imagination or thought, he is sending out some pretty negative messages.

Another problem the copier can create is overuse of transparencies. Making transparencies is so easy that it paves the way for presentations that abuse our visual senses. Remember, "If you emphasize everything, you emphasize nothing." That message especially holds true when audiences are subjected to massive stacks of overheads.

Conducting your training on the road is the next point we need to address. When you conduct training on the road, you will usually be renting the equipment. Projectors require extension cords. Most hotels do not have their own equipment and contract through local vendors, creating the potential for the extension cord to be forgotten by all parties. Unfortunately, *you* are the one who is ultimately responsible for this situation. You will face an unsympathetic audience that expects this problem to have been taken care of.

The same situation applies to the overhead bulb. Some presenters view the cost of the bulb as a disadvantage in itself. Depending on where you go, and the number of bulbs you purchase, you can expect to pay anywhere from $28 to $40. Although it is a high-intensity bulb, my only guess as to why vendors charge that rate is . . . because they can. They may be expensive, but you must make sure there is an extra one. Bulbs do burn out, and the show must go on.

There certainly must be some key strengths to counterbalance some of the weaknesses that have been mentioned, or nobody would use the overhead projector. Here are some advantages:

- Overhead projectors are commonly associated with adult learning and professional training. It is very much an accepted and often expected aid in corporate training.
- The overhead projector is versatile. Overheads can be prepared in advance or created spontaneously depending on the need.
- Overheads are also easy to transport, making them a preferred aid for presenters who teach on the road. In short, depending on the need, overheads can often come through in even the toughest situations.
- The overhead projector can accommodate a variety of audience sizes (and most other visual aids cannot). I have used overheads with audiences as small as three and as large as 900. As long as you stick to the principles explained in the proper use of the overhead, audience size will never be a factor.

With the various strengths and weaknesses identified, let's take a look at how to use the overhead projector properly. To compensate for the possibility of missing extension cords and blown bulbs, get in the habit of not leaving home without them. Almost any overhead bulb will work, and any three-pronged extension cord should do the trick as well. Think of these belongings as you would the jumper cables in your car. Chances are you will not need them, but boy, are they nice to have just in case. If you are permanently assigned to the same training room with the same projector, try taping the spare bulb right inside the unit. This way, you will not have to fumble around looking for it if the bulb blows.

Regarding the creation of overheads, try a few of these tips. First, do not cram too much on one overhead. No more than seven to nine lines of information should appear. Use large type and net out what is needed. Try bulletizing your information as opposed to writing it in standard paragraph format. Finally, try to make the transparencies as visually stimulating as possible. You may want to use multiple colors or clip some artwork to the transparency.

Once you have created the overhead transparencies, take the time to place them in transparency frames. Use masking tape to hold them in the frames. Masking tape will also prevent sticking to your other frames. I happen to be a fan of transparency frames for a couple of reasons. First, they make transportation of the transparencies a snap. Most frames are already three hole punched and can be loaded into a notebook with the rest of your presentation. They also make handling the transparencies a lot easier. Moving them on and off the projector is much simpler with the frames. Without frames, transparencies can often slide around the overhead. With frames, they will not. There is also another key reason I am such a fan of transparency frames, but you will have to read Chapter 11 to learn that one!

Now that you have your transparency created properly and in a frame, let's look at your physical position. It is time to introduce a little bit of controversy to the subject of positioning. There are those who say you should position yourself at the screen and others who say you should be at the overhead projector itself. Being a somewhat opinionated soul, I will be glad to cast my vote as to which is right. Without question, I would recommend that you position yourself at the projector. The problem with working at the screen is that presenters are constantly walking back and forth. Every time you walk back, unless you practically do the moon walk, you will be turning your back on your audience. As you gesture to the screen, once again you will no longer be facing your audience. Additionally, most presenters who gesture to the screen usually make a little bit of contact and the screen begins to wave. Not good. An important point to keep in mind is to always try and talk facing your audience. Position yourself slightly back and to the side of the projector. This will allow you to only have to subtly look for the words you need while maintaining a sense of eye contact.

Once you have positioned yourself correctly at the overhead, you have one other pitfall to avoid. Try to stay out of the projector's light. I have seen presenters doing their version of what looks like the limbo to avoid contact with the light. Relax. Occasionally, you will need to get something that requires you walk through the projector's light. By all means, do it! It is not a big deal, and I would recommend you not call any attention to it. When I say stay out of the projector's light, I am referring to your stationary position. It is easier than you might guess to clip off a corner of the screen with your shoulder. However, if you find yourself constantly hopping back and forth through the light, think about repositioning the furniture within your room or at least change the location of the objects you are retrieving.

Layering is another overhead technique that can add polish to your presentation. Layering is a term I use to describe the process behind covering the amount of white light you are exposing your trainees to. Every time you take an overhead off the projector your trainees are faced with a bright white light. By layering, you are attempting to reduce the amount of white light by always having an overhead on the projector. Assuming you are on the right side of the overhead, this is done in the following manner:

- With your right hand, grab the new transparency by the bottom right corner.
- With your left hand, grab the transparency being currently shown by the bottom left corner.
- Place the new transparency over the current transparency and as you lower it down, slide the current transparency away.

This technique may seem a bit trivial, but the results are well worth it. The trainees are not distracted by constant blasts of white light, and the presenter demonstrates a little finesse with the overhead.

When using the overhead projector, two last subtle techniques come to mind. They deal with covering portions of the transparency, or masking, as it is often called. The initial question you must ask yourself is, Do I really need to mask portions of my transparency? Would additional information that I do not want my audience to see be better off on another transparency? If, after answering these questions, you still have information on one transparency that you want to reveal portions at a time, there are two techniques you can use. One technique is to tape paper flaps over the appropriate areas. This is especially helpful if you are masking larger chunks of the transparency.

The second technique is used when you are masking a list of information. This type of masking often gets presenters into trouble. Most presenters lay a blank piece of paper over the top of the transparency and move it down to expose information as they go along. The problem with this method is that as the paper gets closer to the bottom of the transparency, it may slip. Many overhead projectors have a fan blowing out at the bottom where the sheet is hanging down, which adds to the problem. How many times have you seen presenters do a pathetic kind of dance diving for the falling paper and embarrassingly covering their material back up again? The good news is that the solution is a simple one. Try placing the masking sheet *under* the transparency. The weight of the transparency and frame (I hope by now you are convinced to use frames), will keep the sheet in place. You will still be able to read through the sheet and see what is next. To be on the safe side, try to leave the bottom quarter of the transparency blank.

I chose to discuss overhead projectors first because of their prevalence and their misuse in training. Work with the equipment and follow a couple of the suggestions I laid out for you, and you will get through using one of the most misunderstood visual aids without a hitch!

FLIPCHARTS

If the overhead is the most dominant visual aid used in corporate training, the flipchart comes in a close second. It is the visual aid of choice for many presenters, and when you see its strengths, you will know why. Let's first look at weaknesses of the flipchart.

The first, and most obvious weakness is the flipchart's message size. Depending on the shape and setup of your room, chances are once your group goes over 50 participants, the flipchart will no longer be effective. For large groups, the flipchart is of little use.

Another major weakness of the flipchart is its inability to travel comfortably. I am not referring to working with blank flipcharts. These can be rented on site. I am instead speaking of prepared flipchart materials. Typically, flipchart work is prepared on heavier paper, allowing for the wear and tear of everyday use. This paper usually cannot be rolled and must be transported flat. If you frequently conduct training on the road, this visual aid is probably not for you.

The flipchart's final weakness can actually be traced to the markers being used. The problem that many presenters run into when using flipcharts is messages bleeding through. Depending on the markers and paper that you use, you may see portions of your writing coming through to the next page, creating a ghostlike image. This can be somewhat distracting, not to mention wasteful.

With all the weaknesses of the flipchart out in the open, let me tell you why this visual aid is such a popular tool in corporate training. For starters, it can be used very spontaneously. When a presenter is struggling, the flipchart is often just the ticket to help answer a difficult question or clear up a confusing concept.

The affordability of a flipchart also helps make it an attractive choice when considering visual aids. Markers, pads, and stands are inexpensive to purchase. Even rental of such items when working on the road is negligible.

Perhaps the biggest strength in working with a flipchart is its positive perception by the trainees. For some unexplainable reason, flipcharts carry with them an adult connotation when it comes to training. Why knock it?

Now that you have been shown both the weaknesses and strengths, let's focus on how you are going to use the flipchart properly. First, let's clear up the weakness of messages bleeding through. This can be accomplished two ways. If you insist on using heavier markers, you can staple the bottom corner of two flipchart pages together. This will allow you to turn the page without fumbling for two pieces of paper. Another suggestion (if you want to avoid waste) is to change markers. There are some water-soluble markers that I particularly like called "Vis-à-Vis." These are markers whose advertised benefit is that they can be washed off a transparency. I like them because they do not bleed through a flipchart pad, and they are a little smoother to write with.

In terms of the words you are going to write, try to structure your writing using an outline format. In other words, you do not need to write down every single word. You may choose to use bullets and abbreviated English. A second suggestion is to watch the actual number of words you choose. I try not to use more than 12 words. The 12 words is a rule of thumb, not a law. When I am writing the expectations of a class, or something that is more for my use than that of the class, I will write more.

Finally, to use a flipchart properly, you need to consider your positioning. To begin with, you should have the flipchart in a position that allows all trainees to see it clearly. You should be positioned to the side of the flipchart making sure you do not obscure the trainees' view. As with an actor on a stage, you should not be too far back as to upstage your visual aid, nor do you want to be in front of it. Ideally, the trainees should be able to see both you and the flipchart together, and not be forced to choose. Position yourself on the side of the flipchart according to your dominant hand. In other words, if you are left-handed, try to stay on the left side of the flipchart. If you are right-handed, work on the right side of the flipchart. The idea is to try and keep your dominant arm from reaching across the flipchart and turning you away from the trainees.

As always, room assignment may put you in a position of working with what is there, but it is my hope that you will have enough control to set up your room in a way that best meets your needs. Considering the audience support by adult trainees, the flipchart may be the way to go for you.

SLIDES

Slides are still quite popular among many presenters, but you must first contend with some of the weaknesses of this media. Prepared trainee slides can be expensive. Now understand, I am not referring to your family vacation to the Grand Canyon-type slides, I am talking about slides that have been professionally prepared for training. It may seem rather simple to create a slide and have it professionally done, but depending on the artwork, the price per slide typically runs anywhere from $25 to $40. It can also take a lot of time to create slides. With their required lead time, slides cannot be used spontaneously like so many other visual aids. Turnaround time on the creation of slides can be as long as two weeks.

Setup requirements for slides is also a weakness of this visual aid. You may once again be faced with finding extension cords as well as cords that allow you to remotely change slides. In addition, when you use slides you typically need to darken the room. That can get real scary!

The strengths of using slides, however, would have to begin with the quality you can achieve with a professionally prepared slide. When using slides in your training, you will notice that they provide a high-quality image. You will also find that the color and clarity of that image can be fantastic!

A key strength for presenters who do a lot of roadwork is the convenience slides offer. Carrying a tray or two of slides is no problem. They are durable and hold up well to continued use. Although a slide may initially seem very expensive, it is actually quite cost effective if you are planning multiple seminars with multiple deliveries. After the first slide is created, the cost for each duplicate slide comes down to about $1. That certainly makes it more affordable.

Using the slide projector properly only requires a few basic hints. The most important is more of a reminder than a technique. Get in the habit of reviewing your slides. This will benefit you in two ways. First, it will assure you that the slides are loaded properly. Have you ever seen how slides go into a typical slide tray? Gee, upside down and backward would have been my first choice, too! In fact, that is how they must be loaded. Do not take chances; screen your slides first. When you are looking over the slides, make sure that you pay close attention to any writing that may be on the slide. A slide that is loaded backward, is not always easy to pick out unless writing appears on it. It is subtle, but because it is backward, the writing will look more like Russian than English.

A second reason for reviewing the slides is to benefit your overall delivery. With most visual aids, you can see what is coming and prepare for it. For example, when using an overhead projector, you can see the next transparency and offer a smooth transition to work your way into that visual. Unfortunately, unless you are attached to your script, the slide projector offers no clues as to what the next slide will be. Reviewing the slides should help freshen their sequence and thus the smoothness of your delivery.

Another suggestion that you should remember when using the slide projector is to watch how many slides you use. Too many slides can be difficult to sit through and equally difficult to manage. It becomes awkward and nearly impossible to go back to certain slides that have already been shown.

As with the overhead, slide projectors can have problems. Slide projector bulbs can blow. It is a good idea to keep a spare in your briefcase or near your equipment. The other problem is a little more tricky. It involves getting the slide tray onto the projector. Slide trays are almost all universal, but that does not mean they are all the same. The principle behind the slide projector is for the tray on top to turn, and the tray on the bottom to remain in one place allowing slides to drop through. You might have noticed that when you want to remove your slide tray, you have to spin the tray back to the beginning and then lift off. What is happening is that the bottom tray and top tray are lining up. If these two trays do not line up exactly, the tray will not go back on the projector.

Often, presenters will roughly pull the tray off a projector with the tray slightly out of line. The bad news is, this tray will not go back on. The good news is, it only takes a minor adjustment to fix. If your slide tray will not go on your equipment, complete the following steps:

- ■ Make sure the locking ring is secure by twisting it clockwise.
- ■ Turn the slide tray over and look for two matching symbols. Sometimes these symbols might be dots, other times arrows. The key here is whatever symbols you see, line up.

With some advance lead time and preparation, the slide projector can be an excellent visual aid. Considering its strengths, slide projectors often become the visual aid of choice.

THE CHALKBOARD

Now, much has been written about the old chalkboard, and some of it has even been positive. We need to review the chalkboard in the same manner as the previously mentioned visual aids. When you consider the weaknesses of using the chalkboard, a few thoughts come to mind. First, it is messy. Chalk dust has a way of seeking out even the most unsuspecting presenter and making that individual look silly. It is particularly cruel to those who feel a need to train with something in their hand.

Another knock against the chalkboard is that it is temporary. When you are using outside facilities (specifically hotels), your masterpiece of the day might become a beer coaster for the "Grand Poo-bah" of the night. Often, other groups use the same room. Even your training on site may not be spared a cleaning death. Once, while I was teaching a class, I created a multicolor masterpiece. I even went so far as to write across the top, "Please Don't Erase This." Imagine my surprise when I showed up the next morning greeted by a clean chalkboard. The only words left on the board were, "Please Don't Erase This."

Finally, the most crucial weakness of the chalkboard is sadly something that is completely out of your control. What do you think of when you see a chalkboard? Exactly. The poor chalkboard cannot escape its association with elementary school teaching. We just cannot get certain visualizations out of our mind: the school marm; the terrible screech that she sometimes created; writing at the chalkboard when you had done something wrong (so I have been told). These perceptions literally haunt the poor chalkboard.

The chalkboard is not without its strengths. It is easy to work with. In my mind, one of the key strengths of any visual aid is how easily and spontaneously it can be used. The chalkboard passes this test with flying colors! Availability is the chalkboard's other strength. It is available when the electricity is not functioning. It is available when certain other visual aid equipment failed to be delivered. It is available from just about any hotel or training facility and often available at no charge.

On some occasions, the chalkboard may very well be the only visual aid at your disposal. With that in mind, follow most of the same rules that were established with the flipchart. Try to stick to an outline format focusing in on key words. As far as your actual lettering is concerned, three inches high is generally considered a rule of thumb. Also, keep your lettering consistent. If you write in all capital letters, stick with it. If you capitalize the first letter or no letters, that is OK, too; just stay consistent. You might also want to draw some faint lines on the board before you begin so your lettering is even and straight.

As far as dealing with the messiness of the chalkboard, discipline yourself to use the chalkholder. Although it is a good idea to teach yourself not to hold any markers or pens, with the chalkboard, it is imperative! Discipline yourself to not lean against your visual aid either. If you lean against a chalkboard, you might as well be walking around with a "Kick me" sign on your back for the rest of the day.

VIDEO EQUIPMENT

With the advancement of VCRs in the home came the video explosion at work. More and more companies are using videotapes to show rather than tell their messages.

Video can be very complex. A number of cables and cords can easily be pulled out or fiddled with by a curious trainee. There is also the risk of being stuck with the wrong equipment at the wrong time. In the home, it appears that VHS technology has beaten BETA. On the job, there is still a battle brewing between broadcast quality ¾" tape size and ½" VHS. It is not unusual to have a tape from one and a player from another. The final weakness is the cost: Some hotels and rental companies will charge as much as $400 a day to use their equipment. Since it is far too fragile and heavy to carry, you are at the mercy of these rates. In some cases, the video equipment (which may be used for 10 minutes) is more costly than the room that is used for the entire day.

To counterbalance the weaknesses listed thus far are some impressive strengths. Video offers you the opportunity to introduce a lot of creativity to your training. Motivational videos or even videos that are not directly related to your topic allow for a great deal of flexibility within your training. I attended a management training course once that used video brilliantly. The class was not really coming together, and there was little interaction or discussion. Then the presenter showed a segment from a movie called *Twelve Angry Men*. This old classic movie deals with the deliberations of a jury and the emotions that are brought out. The presenter related it to certain responsibilities that all of us had as managers, and the discussion was on.

A second benefit to using video within your training once again involves perception. Video is naturally associated with a more high-tech level of training and for good reason. Video allows you not only to see dramatizations of situations relating to your subject but to create them as well. You can accomplish this using a video camera, one of the most beneficial tools available in training. Despite what people might think and despite the appearance of an extra five pounds, the camera does not lie!

Regarding the proper use of video, you must get in the habit of testing the equipment before you use it. You must also check it early. When video equipment does not work, it is not the kind of visual aid that you can repair quickly. Five minutes before your seminar begins is not the time to check your equipment. Leave yourself enough time to take a stab at fixing it and then get a specialist in to help you.

When selecting a video, look for tapes that are not too long: "Emphasize everything, emphasize nothing." Too many strong messages get diluted by tapes that are just too long. Remember, it is a visual *aid*. Actual length can depend on several factors such as the length of the seminar or topic relevance. Tapes in the 10- to 15-minute range are good for most purposes.

OBJECTS FOR DEMONSTRATIONS

Sometimes, you might find yourself bringing in different objects to show your trainees. This scene could resemble an adult show and tell. It seems harmless enough, but done improperly, there could be some problems. Objects tend to be a huge distraction if not handled correctly. Try to get out of the habit of allowing trainees to pass around your object during your seminar. Not only does it distract the individual who is looking at your object, it also distracts the next couple of trainees who are anxiously awaiting their turn.

Positioning is also an important consideration when working with objects. If you are going to show an object to your trainees, show it to all of them and not just a few fortunate souls. Avoid working one side of the room and showing any type of favoritism.

If you want to show an object to your trainees, start at one side and physically walk the object around to each person. If you are showing a particular piece or movable part, continue to repeat the action and verbiage for each couple of trainees. When you have made your rounds, inform the trainees that you will place the object in a certain area for them to come up and take a look during the next break (a necessity for larger groups). This will allow you to keep the trainees involved and let them get a better look at your object if they so desire.

POINTERS

I remember when I first decided that I was going to be a trainer. The dreams I had! The thrills, the challenge, the discipline, and, oh yes, the pointer. What trainer uniform could be complete without the pointer, loaded and ready for action? This, of course, was before I met with the reality of a pointer. Yes, if you are working a large room with an overhead or slide projector across the room, you will probably need one. Otherwise, if I may say so in my delicate, opinionated way, forget it! Pointers are more trouble than they are worth. If you want to play a practical joke on a friend who is a trainer, give him a pointer right before he is set to present. It is nearly impossible for a presenter not to fidget with the pointer as he is speaking. Additionally, the pointer often becomes an unintentional weapon as the presenter wields it about the room, distracting those trainees who prefer their ears, eyes, and noses to remain unharmed. In short, pointers and pointer pens are good for the kids and are loads of laughs at parties, but this trainer would not wish one on my worst enemy.

SOME FINAL THOUGHTS

In this chapter I have discussed the pros and cons of working with some of the more common visual aids. I have also provided some ideas on how to use them properly. There are two other reminders that I would like to leave you with. The first deals with the amount of time you expose your trainees to your visual aids. I have a little motto concerning this very point: "Use it, then lose it." This means that when you are done showing your visual aid, get rid of it. You have control over where you want your trainees to focus. Try not to clutter up your message with visual aids that relate to earlier material. This is not to say that I do not favor strategically posting certain aids around the room. This is one of the unique strengths of flipcharts. As you go over important points, key elements of your presentation can be taped up around the room. I am really referring to visual aids whose messages were delivered but not moved away or covered.

My final suggestion for working with any visual aid is to rehearse. Practice with the visual aid so its use offers you confidence and not concern. If you are going to mask or shield, rehearse. Visual aids will make a statement. Used improperly, the statement is negative toward the presenter. Used effectively, the statement is positive. Rehearse, follow the techniques outlined, and your experience with a critical tool used in training will be a rewarding one.

Chapter 10

Giving Feedback and Coaching

$\mathbb{P}$robably one of the most emotional issues that any presenter must deal with, on a regular basis, is giving feedback to students. On the surface, this may appear to be a rather insignificant issue, but be assured, it most certainly is not!

To begin with, it is extremely difficult to judge just how well a student will receive the feedback you intend to give. This can be one of the major pitfalls that awaits a new presenter. On the outside, most students appear to readily accept feedback. It is socially and professionally unacceptable to act any other way. The problem is, students do not internalize such rules.

PITFALLS TO AVOID

The first trap a new presenter can fall prey to involves working with a student whose learning pace falls behind the pace of the seminar. Often, in an attempt to catch this student up, the instructor creates an overload of negative feedback. Not only can this demoralize the student, it can confuse the major items that need repair from the minor items. The old saying, "If you emphasize everything, you emphasize nothing," comes true in this scenario. The student typically tries to fix everything, and therefore ends up fixing nothing. Now the presenter is faced with a demoralized student who most likely will continue to drop further and further behind, and will resent your feedback as well.

The second mistake a new presenter can make involves working with a student whose learning pace is ahead of the rest of the trainees. This trainee could also be referred to as "the superstar." Everything he typically touches turns to gold. He is good at whatever you are teaching. You know it; he knows it; and the rest of the trainees know it. From the outside, his ego appears hard as a rock. With the constant showering of praise and respect, his ego seems indestructible. This is where the problem lies. The typical approach to evaluating this student can be a quick and frivolous brush with the positives, and a more extensive look at the negatives. Even with this type of student, there are negatives. This approach can have disastrous effects on a seemingly strong and confident student. Once again, internally, that ego may very well not be as strong as this student leads everyone to believe. Even the most seasoned "superstar" can become depressed and unsure when showered with negatives. To make matters worse, this is often the student who will tell the presenter he really is looking forward to the constructive criticism he will be receiving, and to please lay it on him. Many presenters will fall prey to that trap. Probably, only once.

The final consideration in giving feedback relates to careful control of any public feedback. By public feedback, I am referring to an old trick of allowing the trainees to give their feedback to a student in front of the trainees. In theory it sounds like a good idea, to involve the rest of the trainees and gain increased participation, but the problems created by the process outweigh its strengths. Trainees are not schooled in giving feedback professionally. They do not possess the discipline that you do in trying to be objective and fair. How would you like it if everyone raved about the presentation *before* yours and looked rather empty when you finished your presentation? The nonverbal communication alone can be more than some trainees can take. It may be the one trainee you have been working with and trying to build up confidence in for the past week who gets shot down publicly. Your efforts were now in vain. It just is not worth the risk.

GIVING FEEDBACK WITHOUT INTIMIDATING TRAINEES

So how do you give feedback to a trainee without suffering through these frightening problems? The approach I recommend is a four-step process that should alleviate all these fears.

Step 1: Ask the student for two areas that *he* felt he did well. It is human nature for students to be overly critical of their own performance.

Additionally, because of inappropriate past feedback sessions or even to avoid appearing arrogant, 90 percent of the time a student will focus only on the points that he did not like. By asking for feedback on issues he felt good about, you move this performance to a conscious competent level and stand a greater chance of having the student repeat these strengths in the future.

Allowing the student to go first eliminates the risk of a student simply repeating the feedback received from the presenter. A presenter is in a better position to identify unconscious incompetence when his feedback follows the student's. If a student identifies an area that you do not agree with, simply probe the student for more information. Usually, it is simply a misunderstanding by the student and he will take it off his list of two. Make sure, however, that if you do question a strength and it is removed, you ask the student for another.

Step 2: Ask the student for two areas that *he* felt he could improve in. Nothing is gained by allowing a student to ramble on and on unfocused. Force the student to net out these two deficiencies and probe for suggestions on how he intends to fix them. Sometimes a good way to get this step started is to ask the student what two things would he do differently if he could do the observed task again.

Step 3: Give the student two areas that you observed as strengths within his performance. Model the same rules that you established for the student. Remember, these are areas of strength and not an opportunity to fix what has already been done better. So often, good feedback is wasted when a presenter says, "This was really good, if only you had . . ." There will be other opportunities to make something good even better. If this is one of the only two areas that you are identifying as good, leave it at that!

Step 4: Give the student two areas that you observed as weaknesses within his performance. Words that work better here are words like "alternatives," or "suggestions." Be direct and not apologetic. Try using words such as "I saw" or "I heard." Avoid feelings and stick to facts. Try not to use words such as "I feel" or "I think." If you feel it is vital to bring out a third point to be worked on, make sure you capture a third strength as well and vice versa.

What should you have accomplished when this process is over? First, by forcing the students and yourself to limit each area of the process to two points, there is just enough to feel good about, and just enough to work on. Taking a student through every point on your evaluation form complicates everything. The old saying fits here again, "If you emphasize everything, you emphasize nothing."

The second strength of this process is that in an area of extreme sensitivity, it assures fairness. Some students (and presenters for that matter) do not take criticism very well. When they know what to expect and know others around them are being evaluated in the same manner, criticism is much easier to accept.

Finally, in a relatively short period of time, the process becomes second nature to all involved. Feedback becomes so natural that the presenter need only monitor the process. Typically, after two or three times with the same student, the presenter needs only to sit back and listen as the student methodically lays out what he did well and what he needs to improve on, and how he intends to make that improvement. Feedback is no longer feared, and egos are set aside.

COACHING USING THE THREE Ss

Giving feedback to a trainee is similar to coaching the trainee. I am saddened that for most of the trainees I work with, their initial reaction to the word coach is, "Have I done something wrong?" I believe this is caused by most of our experiences from being coached. Most of us in business have learned to relate coaching to a problem behavior. Management often steps in to coach when an employee needs to be disciplined.

In corporate training, there is a different mind-set. In the training room, coaching should conjure up other words such as "opportunity" and "inspiration." The old school of thought was to show and tell someone how to accomplish a task, prompt him along, and then release him to accomplish that task on his own. Somewhat productive, but not what I would call inspirational.

The keys to good coaching are similar to those of giving effective feedback. I like to refer to my own model using "The Three Ss": situation, support, and solution.

Situation

To begin with, there must be two-way communication throughout. This point is especially critical when discussing the first "S": *situation,* or the issue in question. Coaching cannot be me dictating what the problem is and what it is you need to do. There must be a mutual acceptance of the situation, or we are wasting our time. Open probes relating to the subject and active listening are helpful here.

Support

The next "S" in effective coaching is *support*. Not all situations are negative. Coaching often can center around a task that is being successfully accomplished, but possibly can be done better. "If it ain't broke, don't fix it" is thankfully a dying sentiment. Too many companies subscribing to that theory have been caught flat-footed by other companies who believe, "If it ain't broke, try to fix it better." A critical factor to any coaching session revolves around the second "S," support. Regardless of the task, positive or negative, individuals deserve and need your support. Maybe it is a reference to a previous success or perhaps it is a mention of another area of strength. Sometimes, it may even be an expression of confidence by you and a willingness to help if help is needed. Coaching often treads on egos, and support is a way to soothe those egos.

Solution

The final "S" stands for *solution*. This is the "S" that so many presenters want to leap toward in a hurry. As with the description of the situation, this must once again involve two-way communication. If the trainee accepts the situation and feels the sincerity of your support, he may very well be able to offer realistic solutions. Once again, your ability to probe in the areas where you wish the trainee to look for solutions can assist you in getting the trainee to focus on necessary issues. Work with the trainees in making the solutions tangible and realistic. If possible, try to finish your coaching session with some kind of follow-up strategy to measure effectiveness.

SUMMARY

Coaching and giving feedback have the potential to be highly emotional tasks. They are, nonetheless, critical skills for all presenters. My hope is that my suggestions for handling these processes will give you the support you will need to carry out these vital skills. Many times, feedback and coaching may feel more like having to give your trainees a shot of medicine. Remember this: There are a lot of people who can stick a needle in another person's arm and give a shot. There are, however, a skilled few who can give that same shot creating the same physical pain but, through their people skills and their empathy, make its acceptance easier. That is often the real goal behind giving feedback and coaching. Perhaps the real pain is in our minds.

Chapter 11

Tricks of the Trade

Up to now, I have attempted to show you some solid, conventional approaches to corporate training. As with most professions, once you master the technical aspects of your position, you need to learn certain tricks of the trade. In this chapter, I would like to present you with a number of these "tricks." Depending on your style, topic, and trainees, some may be appropriate for you. Tricks that do not seem helpful now may be of use to you someday down the road when you are the presenter with your career on the line.

1. Use Transparency Frames

In Chapter 9, I recommended that presenters use transparency frames. Some of the reasons I mentioned were to better handle the transparencies, help keep them from sliding around on the overhead, and simplify their ability to be transported. I did not, however, tell you my favorite reason for using transparency frames. They are fantastic to sneak notes onto! Depending on the module, I will typically write a key question to ask, a transition, notes from the curriculum, or a logistical reminder. If your positioning is correct, and you are at the overhead and not the screen, all you need to do is peripherally peer down and you will have what you need. To the trainees, it will appear you are merely taking a peek at the overhead. To an observer, it will appear you must have done a lot of night study to be so close to what the curriculum says and yet not be a slave to the lectern and instructor guide.

A similar procedure can also be used with a flipchart. Often, when presenters use flipcharts, they are unsure of what is on the next page. As they or a trainee are speaking, they will slyly attempt to peek behind the uppermost flipchart sheet and look at what is next. Then they are in a better position to transition to the next page. Figure out what side you are going to be standing on and lightly pencil in some notes to assist you. These notes may be a reminder of what is on the next page, a key question to ask, or any other numerous reminders. Write lightly, use only key words and write large enough so you will not have to squint to read it.

2. Avoid Too Many Visuals

Have you ever attended a seminar only to have the wind knocked out of you noticing the towering stack of visual aids? Transparencies and slides are the most common culprit. Your job is to sell your topic and the course, not to whine about all the visuals you are forced to show. The trainees are not the least bit interested in who designed the course.

What is the solution? *Hide* your excess visuals. If you are showing transparencies, take enough to get you to the first break and stow the rest away. You might want to keep the rest of the morning's supply inside your lectern or close by just in case you begin running fast. Every time the trainees leave for a break, replenish. For slides, I would recommend you invest in extra trays and fill each one about one-third of the way. Each tray may represent a half day to a day of training.

This idea even works for curriculum. Some presenters will bring in enormous notebooks stuffed to the gills. If that is not enough to turn trainees' stomachs, presenters also typically travel through the curriculum slowly during housekeeping and introductions. Seeing a presenter take 20 minutes to turn the first page of a 400-page book may be too much for some people to bear. Strategically break the instructor guide into less intimidating, manageable books and keep those not in use out of sight!

3. Build a Sequence of Information

Here is an idea to help trainees who like to write down everything that appears on a visual aid. It seems that no matter how many times you tell certain trainees not to write everything down that appears on a visual, they do it anyway. You can plead with them that everything that appears visually is located in their participant guide, and they will still write it down. Having to wait for those trainees who are not listening but rather copying the visual aid down into their notes can often break the rhythm a presenter is trying to establish. (As an aside, this form of learning never appealed to me: However, I appreciate that this is a proven learning method for certain types of people.)

To work with these trainees and keep your pace up as well, try building sequence by ghosting information into your visual aid. This can be easily accomplished using just about any type of visual aid. Each visual should have what was on the previous visual plus a new item or line. The only difference between this and a typical list is that the previous information should be faded back and the new information should literally jump out at you. This will allow those who wish to copy everything down an opportunity to do so, while allowing you to move along as well.

4. Know the Value of a Nickel

When delivering training seminars, sometimes it is truly the little things that can pull a presenter through. Consider the nickel. It makes not one, but two contributions to your training. First, as mentioned earlier in Chapter 8, it provides you enough collateral to pay for answers to questions that get trainees involved in your presentation.

Second, it allows you to focus your overhead projector. When you are following a previous speaker or walking into a room where trainees are already waiting for you, you need to make a decision. Do you want to project a transparency on the screen to center and focus your overhead? Admittedly, this does not sound like a question that should keep you up at night, but we are talking about tricks of the trade and we are talking about looking polished. Often, I do not want my trainees to see certain visuals until a strategic time. In such cases, pull out a nickel, lay it on the overhead, center and focus your projector on the nickel. Once this is done, put your nickel away, turn off the projector, lay your transparency on the glass and you are ready to go!

5. Create Professional Flipcharts

They say a picture is worth a thousand words. Well, a professional-looking picture on a flipchart might be just the answer you are looking for in creating the right kind of mood in the training you conduct. I know, I know . . . you are not artistically inclined. I have heard all the excuses before because I used most of them until I learned this technique.

Start by looking for a picture that relates to your topic. You might find it in a magazine, newspaper, or book. Next, make a Xerox copy of it (sorry, it's the Xeroid in me) on a transparency. Focus your transparency onto a flipchart from close range and begin tracing. Instant artist! You can trace your lettering as well.

For a real professional look, do not stop here. Put some color into it. The problem with markers is they typically come in primary colors. Red, black, blue, and green. To get the pastels that are necessary for skin tones and other more realistic looks, try using colored chalk. The final piece to the puzzle that will keep the chalk in place is hair spray. Lightly apply about three to five applications to your artistry, and you will lock in your masterpiece.

6. Ask a Trainee to Act as Scribe

One of the most frustrating positions to be in as a presenter is to be at the flipchart scribing with one hand while twisting around trying to make eye contact. It is enough to give even the best of us a headache. Try selecting a trainee to scribe for you while you stay in the pit and work. I usually quietly scout out who has clear handwriting by looking at notes that have been taken. Sometimes you can strategically rotate trainees allowing you to work more effectively with some of the trainee roles. With a scribe at the flipchart, you can now stay in control of the room, involve trainees in the presentation, and perhaps even be let off the hook if your own handwriting or spelling is not what it should be.

7. Focus on That Screen

This next recommendation goes out to presenters who are projecting visual aids onto a screen. Specifically, those who are projecting from an area below the screen. What happens, in this case when a visual is nearly impossible to focus on? If you focus on the top, the bottom is blurry and if you focus on the bottom, the top is blurry. The solution is rather simple. Try matching the pitch of the projector by taping or pinning the bottom of the screen to the wall behind it. Most screens are hung a few feet away from the wall behind them. Bringing the bottom of the screen to the wall compensates for the pitch of the projector.

8. K.I.S.S.

It is an old saying, but a good saying just the same: "Keep It Simple, Stupid." This saying not only pertains to the written word, but the spoken word as well. You must be careful with the language you choose. Start by determining the knowledge level of your audience. Do they share the same company terms? Do they share the same business terms? In no way am I recommending you talk down to your audience. You must determine where their knowledge level is, use terms they are familiar with, and try to keep the words simple.

9. Avoid the Ache of Acronyms

When I taught flood insurance for the government, I used to start the course this way. "Hi, I'm Rob Jolles. I work for CSC who administers the NFIP for FEMA." I was not out of my introduction, and I had worked in three acronyms! No one likes them. People are intimated by them. Trainees get demotivated by them. I am referring to the dreaded acronym. Although we might wish we could avoid them, the solution, unfortunately, cannot make that an option. As presenters, your job is to teach the trainees everything, and if they will be exposed to acronyms once they leave the seminar, you must prepare the trainees by teaching them.

There are a number of approaches, and each has its strengths. The difficult assignment for a presenter is that they not only have to use them, they have to teach them. The most effective technique I ever used was to keep a separate Acronym Chart off to the side; each time I used an acronym, I would write it down in acronym form. Before and after each break, I would walk over to the Acronym Chart and have the trainees recite their meanings.

My recommendations to you are to avoid using acronyms whenever possible. Acronyms have the potential to get you into trouble. The flood program had many acronyms; one was BFD, standing for Base Flood Depth. This was a rating term used often in the program. Once, while routinely testing the National Flood Insurance Programs hotline, a government monitor had her son call up to test the system. The customer service rep routinely asked "What's the BFD?" The monitor's son was of an age that made another interpretation very clear. When the son told his monitor parent his interpretation of the BFD, memos went flying, meetings were held, and that acronym was stricken from document and dialogue at an expensive cost. Moral of the story? Watch out for those acronyms!

10. Try "Parking" Topics for Discussion Later

Here is the situation. You are teaching a group of trainees, and, you are on a roll! The trainees are just beginning to warm up so you want to be extra careful to respond to questions appropriately. A hand goes up. You call out the trainee's name and receive your question! The only problem is the question pertains to something that you do not cover for two more days. What's worse, once you enter that topic, it will probably be extremely difficult to get back to your original topic without eliciting more questions. The stage is set. Avoid the question, and you might send out signals that discourage your most precious ally: participation. Answer the question, and you run the risk of throwing the seminar into an illogical, confusing tailspin. This is the real world. This is another situation that places you underfire.

So, what's the solution? Park it. In a remote section of your room set up a flipchart pad or sheet with the words "Parking Lot" on it. Every time a trainee has a question that would be better answered later, use this approach:

TRAINEE: I was wondering if you could tell us how to handle a situation that required the computer and the administrator.

PRESENTER: That is an excellent question. We are learning about the computer's role in policy handling, but what about the administrator? Tomorrow afternoon we discuss the administrator's responsibilities. I think it might be a good idea to revisit and answer the question at that time. Let me write it down over here in the "Parking Lot" so we do not forget to answer it at that time.

I suppose you could just tell the trainees that you will answer the question at the appropriate time, but often when the appropriate time comes, all we remember is that someone had a question relating to this topic. When you write it down, you give credibility to the trainee who asked it, and assurances that you will not forget to answer it. The responsibility becomes yours to keep an eye on the "Parking Lot" and answer the questions at the appropriate time. You might even want to check the answers off as you address them to alert the trainees that you are actively answering their questions.

11. Use Post-its to Remind Yourself of Problem Areas

Every presenter typically has a few habits they are trying to break, no matter how proficient they may appear. Just as with a strong round of golf, you can always do better. The first task is to determine what you want to work on. A lesson can be learned from Wilfredo Pareto, father of Pareto analysis. Hundreds of years ago Pareto became interested in the distribution of wealth and determined that a significant few people, 20 percent, were controlling a vast majority of the wealth, 80 percent. It is certainly more profitable to fix a significant few problems than some of what Pareto called "the trivial many." This goes for training as well. Do you have a significant few problems that would be more profitable to fix than the trivial many? Dropping a marker on the floor once would be considered a "trivial many" problem. Rocking back and forth constantly would be considered a "vital few" problem.

Once you have determined which important areas you want to work on, try using "Post-its"™ to help you. If you want to smile more, post the word "smile" on the lectern. Even though you may be turning pages in the curriculum, the word smile remains in place. Often, correcting problems starts by becoming more conscious of them. The note will make you conscious throughout, allowing you to start correcting even the most difficult problems. One last point. Do not overdo it and clutter your lectern with these notes or you will be back at square one. Two or three at a time should be sufficient to correct even the most stubborn problems.

12. Use a Lectern

Time once again for a little bit of controversy. Arguments have been made for and against the use of lecterns for some time now. The key argument against the use of a lectern is that nervous presenters have a tendency to hold onto them. Without a question, that is a habit you need to avoid; however, when you look at the advantages of using a lectern, that problem becomes somewhat trivial.

The lectern's most important advantage is that it actually allows you more mobility. There are those who say using a lectern will cause a presenter to remain stationary behind the lectern, but in reality, the opposite is true. Let me explain to you why. Let's begin with the assumption that you need to look at your notes or some sort of guide. With a lectern, you can actually get comfortable strolling back and forth, in and out of the pit, working your way back to the lectern when you need to glance at your notes. The key here is glance. A lectern is typically higher than a desk or table, allowing you to subtly peek at your notes. That ability to sneak a little peek makes the lectern worth its weight in gold. It gives you the confidence to leave your notes knowing that help is a few steps and a glance away. If the material is located on a desk, unless you have super vision, you will have to bend over to take a look. Through my years as a trainer and many, many subtle glances as I have strolled by the lectern, I have developed super vision. The only side effect is that I truly can read my notes better from alongside me than straight ahead of me.

Another advantage the lectern provides you with is the ability to conceal strategic materials from the trainees. As mentioned in item 2, when you are saddled with too many overheads or slides, the lectern becomes an excellent place to hide them. If you are planning a competition with some prizes, once again the lectern is a place to store the prizes. You name it, and it often can fit inside a lectern. As a matter of fact, without seeing a presenter speak, I can learn an enormous amount of information about that presenter from what is inside the lectern.

One last little point that I would like to clear up. People often confuse the words "podium" and "lectern." Ninety-nine percent of the people you meet will call what a presenter stands behind, a podium. For the record, *Webster's New World Dictionary* defines podium this way:

A low platform, esp. for the conductor of an orchestra.

To my knowledge, although presenters can perform many exciting tasks in a seminar, none have conducted an orchestra. Lectern is defined this way:

A stand for holding the notes, written speech, etc., as of a lecturer.

Used properly, a lectern can be one of the most helpful training tools available to you in the seminar. You can even purchase portable lecterns that fold up and can be carried like a briefcase. So, when it comes to using a lectern, my recommendation is, don't leave home without it. As for the habit of holding onto the lectern, leave yourself a note on the lectern and stop doing it!

13. Stay in Character

As you can tell from reading this book, I am quite a fan of mobility and training from inside the pit. One major fear many presenters have is forgetting where they are in the curriculum and having to take that long, long silent walk back to the lectern to look at their notes. Take a tip from the acting profession and stay in character.

When I got involved in theater and landed my first sizable role, I learned an unforgettable lesson from a fantastic director. This lesson has helped me as a trainer and is one that I pass on to all my Train-The-Trainer classes. I was dutifully studying my lines night and day. At rehearsal, the director began asking me some nagging, rather silly questions about the character I was playing. "What is his favorite television show?" "What beer does he drink?" "What is his favorite breakfast food?" How ridiculous! I was learning my lines, why not just leave it at that! No wonder acting is perceived as such a strange profession; or is it? One of the theories behind what that director was doing was preparing me not only for success but for failure. I began to know my character better and became a better actor. I also later realized how this technique saved my life when there were problems on stage. No words can describe the terror an actor feels when he or someone else on stage forgets his lines. It is very similar to the terror a presenter feels when he forgets where he is in the curriculum. There is an audience, and there is fear. Learning all about my character in theater allowed me to stay in character. Now, for a few precious seconds, I may have been confused as to what line was next. If, however, I stayed in character, it was impossible to forget what my character was doing. In other words, I was still acting as the character I was playing, although I might not be delivering what was written in the script.

As a trainer, I can guarantee two things. One is that you will occasionally forget what comes next in your curriculum. The second guarantee is that you will not forget the basics. The basics are who you are and what topic you are talking about. That is really all you need. Stay in character (which means you do not have to announce to the trainees that you are hopelessly lost) and ask a question that pertains to your subject. "What do you think so far?" "Has this ever happened to you?" "Do you think this information will be of help to you?" These are not deep questions, but they can help stall. Your next move is to appear interested, backpedal your way to the lectern, nod, smile, and find out where you are. Following this technique allows you the confidence to prowl the pit where you belong. By the way, what does a presenter eat for breakfast?

14. Be on Time

This next suggestion may be more of a reminder than a training tip. When it comes to actually conducting your training, be on time. By the way, "on time" means get to your training early. Your best bet is to take no chances. I am not necessarily a superstitious person, but I would not tempt fate. As you are learning, you must deal with a number of variables before you actually begin teaching. Is the air conditioning or heating working? Are the projectors working? Did the materials that you were expecting get delivered? The list can go on and on. (Chapter 5 provides suggestions for what you should check out *before* your trainees arrive.) Arriving early allows you to accomplish all these tasks without that frazzled appearance. What if everything is as you left it and totally prepared? Get to your seminar early, relax, collect your thoughts, and enjoy the day. With that type of start for you, I know your trainees will enjoy the day as well.

15. Watch Out for Those Filler Words

Presenters do not like to talk about it. Trainees get distracted by it. Observers can get obsessed by it. What is it, you ask? Little words known as "filler words." These words can take on many forms such as "um," "ah," or one of the most common found in the training profession, "OK." They are used in place of pauses and can be a real headache for many presenters.

One way around this difficulty is to use the old Post-it trick. Unfortunately, some presenters will actually increase rather than decrease their use of filler words if they spot them in writing. An approach that worked for me was to join an organization called Toastmasters. Toastmasters is an organization that specializes in the development of those who wish to improve their communication skills. At a typical Toastmasters' meeting, roles are assigned to a number of participants. The role I so fondly remember is one called an "Um Counter." This person's job was to spend the entire meeting counting every single filler word that was spoken. At the end of the meeting, the "Um Counter" would call off the names of all the speakers, and the number of filler words each one had used. When it comes right down to it, the best way to correct the problem with filler words is to be conscious of it and discipline yourself to correct it. Toastmasters provided an excellent opportunity for me to correct this habit and simply pause instead of jamming my sentence with filler words. If you are interested, there are Toastmasters chapters in most metropolitan areas, nationally and internationally, with phone numbers as near as a phone book.

16. Don't Put Trainees on the Spot

One simple fact of life is that due to our slow rate of speech (about 175 words per minute) and our high rate of hearing (about 310 words per minute), students have a natural tendency to mentally check in and check out. This is often referred to as leapfrogging and can occasionally frustrate a presenter whose course material requires a lot of questioning and facilitation. Relax. It is natural and, to a limited extent, to be expected. The real danger is to the student who has been asked a question about material he has missed. All of us have been in that embarrassing rut before, blankly looking for an answer that will not come. Try a "Leap Chip."

At the beginning of each day, each student is given a round two-inch disk to keep on his desk. Its use is a simple one. Once a day, for any reason (be it leapfrogging, daydreaming, or simply not knowing), the student may hand the instructor the "Leap Chip" when called on for an answer. It is important the instructor not break stride and in no way call attention to this incident. The instructor simply moves to another student and carries on. The student is now left without a "Leap Chip" for the rest of the day which will force him to work a little harder at tuning in.

17. Reward Trainees

When teaching a class that requires participants to role play or do any task frequently, friendly competition can sure liven things up. At the beginning of the session, lay out ground rules. Each day, one participant will be selected as a winner based on any of the following criteria: most improved, best overall, best implementation of a new tactic taught, and so on. The award? Try a frisbee or card hung on velcro in front of the participant's seat, or even a mug that reads, "For today, I'm as good as Rob!" Needless to say, the award name can be whatever you choose, (although I am partial to Rob), but I recommend it not be too serious in nature. The idea is to create friendly competition. Cash prizes may be just the wrong idea here. Make it silly and fun!

For the rest of the day, that individual receives minor privileges such as determining when the class should take breaks, announcing how long to spend on reading assignments, and making other simple class decisions. At the beginning of the next day, the award is renewed to await another winner. The amazing thing about this simple idea is that rarely, if ever, will a student abuse these privileges. In addition, because the criteria for selection are left wide open, the award can coincidentally be spread around to all the individuals. As the class becomes closer, the students begin to root for and assist those who have not won. Now that's what training is all about!

18. Get a Look at Those Evaluations

This next idea is a simple but effective one. Most presenters I know (including myself early on) avoid looking at the evaluations that will be used following the training. Sometimes, the organization that conducts the evaluations is almost secretive about the content of these forms. I used to become frustrated after I finished a seminar and then found out what it was the trainees were evaluating me on. I would then vow to fix it for the next seminar. What about this seminar? If I look at what it is I am to be evaluated on before I speak, I benefit in two ways. First, it reminds me of what I need to be doing to be successful. Second, it gives me confidence when I know I am ready to comply with what is on the form. Take the mystery out of your training and address the evaluation criteria before you speak.

19. Watch Those Transitions

Once you have studied and learned your UPPOPPR and final review, there is one last piece of the puzzle that I recommend you work with. Most presentations cover three to five major points. What becomes key for you is your ability to smoothly move from point to point. These are referred to as transitions. When watching a presentation, you will notice that an unskilled presenter will literally bump his way from major point to major point. That transition might sound something like this:

PRESENTER: . . . and that is how the entire process began. Uh, if, um systems are important too. You see, when a system is hooked up correctly . . .

Once the presenter actually moves into the next major piece of curriculum, he is fine. It is getting there that gives the presenter some difficulties. Put in some extra time and write out your transitions. You can try to commit them to memory or simply write them out on a transparency frame or lightly in pencil on a flipchart (see item 1). Then your transitions might sound something like this:

PRESENTER: ". . . and that is how the entire process began. Now processes are all well and good in theory, but the system you create will be the true signal of your success. You see, when a system is hooked up correctly . . ."

20. Start and Finish Strongly

As I have already stated, you only get one chance to make a good impression. You only get one chance to leave a lasting impression as well. A lot can be forgiven when you start your presentation smoothly and end it just as smoothly. Chapter 6, on creating process-driven presentations, discusses the tools you need. Make it a priority, regardless of the condition of your curriculum, to start and finish strongly. That means right before you are scheduled to speak, do not study the entire presentation. If you do, you will be as confused as you were before you started. Look over the curriculum, but five minutes before you begin teaching, study the UPPOPPR. During your last break look over your closing review. After that, it's practice, practice, practice.

21. Learn Your Trainees' Names

Life just is not fair sometimes. Here you are, with another week of 10 new trainees. Their responsibility is to remember your name and maybe the name of a classmate or two. Your responsibility? Remember the entire class (within reason) and do it as quickly as possible. It comes with the territory. Nothing says more or less about you in trainees' minds than your ability to remember and use their names. We like to hear our name. Remembering it demonstrates you care and want to get to know us. Forgetting it can be taken as a slap in the face.

Name tags help a lot. Actually studying the names and committing them to memory helps even more. If this is difficult for you, try associating the trainees' names with something or someone that will help you remember. You might even want to take a memory course yourself, but make learning your trainees' names a priority and you will be perceived as a more caring presenter.

22. Watch Your Timing

In my humble opinion, I would not say that timing is everything . . . but it is pretty close! Ultimately, many groups will remember you more by your timing than anything else. Think about it.

In this book, I have attempted to illustrate key points by relating them to some of my successes as well as my failures. Let me now present a doozy of a failure. Many years ago, as a consultant, I was asked to conduct a one-hour motivational seminar to Farmer's Home Administration employees in upstate New York. What did I know about motivational seminars? I was a trainer, not a dinner speaker, so I turned them down. I do not like to bring money into this, but when they offered me $1,350 for the hour and expenses, I changed my mind. One hour, $1,350. I became obsessed by that figure. I had never spoken in front of more than 50 trainees, but what was another 450? I began making little jokes about the money. I would make obnoxious statements to my wife like, "I'd like to talk to you about that honey, but I'm not sure you could afford it."

The presentation? A piece of cake. I usually can speak for hours off a dinner napkin, but for this presentation, I would take no chances. I prepared about eight pages of material from poems to stories to help motivate them. I even, rather smugly, prepared two more emergency pages just in case. I had the world by the tail. Big shot motivational trainer at a resort speaking for one hour to motivate. I took my golf clubs, arrived a day early, and got set for the easiest money of my life.

As I approached the lectern, after being introduced, I was greeted with my first surprise. 500 people are not 50 people! I was experiencing unaccustomed "butterflies." Then came the big surprise. I began to ask my usual barrage of questions only to be greeted by a room full of blank stares. No one ever told me that 500 people do not talk back to the speaker. It was quiet, too quiet. I panicked. I began to churn through my material at an absurd pace. I now knew this was not training. There was no real topic. At 16 minutes, I finished my material. At 29 minutes, after slowing to a crawl, I finished my emergency pages. In my mind I kept thinking, $1,350 for one hour.

I began pacing back and forth, sweating profusely, offering a word or two about a message I had already delivered and demanding the audience "think about it." Over and over again I told them "it could happen to you . . . think about it." Followed by a profound, "because it has already happened to others . . . think about it." From there, I went into a number of "it might just happen to me . . . think about it!" At 44 minutes, and for the first time in my life, I had nothing left for an audience to think about. I walked off, in a daze, 10 pounds lighter, to polite applause. I was thanked and paid. I was also never invited back.

What did I learn from that experience? Like a good fighter, I needed to be beaten to really grow within my profession. It was a tremendous experience (easier to say years later) and one that I have benefited from immeasurably. When it is all said and done, timing is one of the most critical criteria on which you will be judged. The presentation is the routine. The timing is like sticking a good landing. It is a true measure of your professional ability. If you are running short, ask more thought-provoking questions and facilitate some discussions. If you are running long, trim away those discussions and net out what you need to say. Keep a watch inside your lectern and work your glances in subtly. Do not wait until the last five minutes to begin making decisions regarding timing. Remember, whether it is one hour, one day, or one week, that is what the customer requires and that is what you are underfire to deliver. Think about it . . .

23. Start with an Activity

For many presenters, one of the hardest aspects of training is simply getting started. Time and time again, you will hear someone say, "If I can just get past the first five minutes, I will be fine." Here is an idea that might help. Plan an activity such as a small group exercise relating to your subject. It could be as simple as splitting the room in half and allowing the trainees to come up with five benefits that they could receive from attending your seminar. With an exercise like that, you will not only have a head start on building your utility for your module, you will get a good indication for trainees' attitudes as well.

The key to this idea, is the time that a well-placed exercise will allow you to get your emotions under control. Once the exercise is over, chances are, you will have worked through a lot of your nervousness and will be in better position to nail down a solid UPPOPPR!

24. Cover Up and Shut Up

Why is it that when presenters make mistakes, there is such a great need to inform all those around? Perhaps it is nervousness, or maybe the perfectionist in all of us. In any case, it is unnecessary. Nobody is keeping score so just keep moving forward. How many times have you taken a course where the instructor seems to keep up a steady chatter every time he makes the slightest mistake, mumbling to the trainees and himself. Most of the time, the trainees are neither aware or interested. Keep moving on and roll with the punches. It is nice to have a presenter who is not perfect.

25. Try Using a Bell

The last suggestion I would like to make treads dangerously close to a style issue, but you might want to give it a try. For many years, I have kept a small call bell on the desk that my lectern sits on and have found it to be helpful. When do I use it? Obviously, it can be used to regain control when necessary, but there are other uses as well. I find myself using it to start and stop seminar breaks. I find myself ringing it when something funny is said, or a good idea is mentioned. I also find myself using it when something exciting happens in the seminar, or I have the trainees competing and want to signal a good response. In other words, there are endless opportunities for its use. Coincidentally, there are also about 35 Xerox trainers who have call bells perched next to their lecterns. Put one in front of your lectern, and I guarantee you will be amazed at how often you find yourself ringing your bell.

SUMMARY

In presenting these ideas to you, it was my intent to spare you from some of the harder lessons that can be learned underfire. Also, I hope that maybe I have inspired some of you to try a couple of ideas of your own. There is no risk in trying, only in complacency.

III

IMPROVING THE TRAINING PROCESS

Chapter 12

Inside the Mind of a Trainer: How to Present Your Best Self

Few jobs can match the role of trainer in the number of skills that must be displayed publicly by one individual. Training is one of those rare professions that is nearly impossible to understand unless you have actually done it yourself. As mentioned before, there are no real simulations for firsthand action underfire in the pit. The ultimate irony in most training departments, unfortunately, is that these departments are typically managed by individuals who have never conducted a day of training themselves. Empathizing with the feelings a trainer is experiencing is difficult, to say the least. It is therefore my intent to take a stab at giving you a tour inside the mind of a trainer to help you better understand some of the unique aspects of corporate training.

ALWAYS PRESENT A POSITIVE AND ENTHUSIASTIC ATTITUDE

Let's start with a trainer's attitude for the courses he teaches. To illustrate a point, I will be more than happy to tell you my attitude toward teaching a Train-The-Trainer. Usually the anticipation starts on about the Wednesday before the week I am to teach the course. It is only a little stir, but it counts. Thursday morning that little stir becomes more of an anxious hum anticipating next week's fantastic class. For some reason on Friday, I walk around with a kind of silly grin. It looks as if I just pulled off a practical joke on my co-workers when, in fact, I am already looking forward to Monday's start. Saturday, I try to avoid thinking about what is to come, but it is usually no use. I find myself happily day-dreaming about the first five minutes of the course. By Sunday, my day-dreaming takes me well beyond the first five minutes, with sleep not coming easily on Sunday night. I am always up well before my alarm clock goes off on the Monday morning of a Train-The-Trainer, anxiously looking forward to the start of what I am expecting to be a cohesive group of trainees coming to town for what I consider the best course ever written!

Do you think that is a true story? If you asked me to answer that question, I would tell you quite simply: What does it matter as long as *you* believe it is true? That is the bottom line when it comes to a trainer's attitude toward his curriculum. He has no choice, he must fall in love with what it is he is teaching. He must acquire this love affair for two reasons. First, when a trainer does not like the curriculum he is teaching, it flat out shortens the life span of that trainer. Once again, think of a salesperson. Most good salespeople will tell you that they can overcome just about any obstacle you put in front of them to make the sale if, and only if, they truly believe in their product. If a salesperson does not believe in the product he is selling, no matter how he tries to deny it, those feelings eventually act as a cancer ending that individual's career. It soon becomes nearly impossible for him to get up day after day and sell ideas that are poorly put together or that he does not agree with. It becomes imperative that a trainer sit down with the supervisor, manager, or whoever is responsible for the curriculum and work out a solution he is comfortable with. This is by no means a time for manage-ment to adopt a "my way or the highway" approach. For the sake of the trainer, both parties must use patience until they can reach a compro-mise. Remember, you are looking inside the mind of a trainer, and noth-ing shortens the career of a trainer faster than bad curriculum with no compromise.

The second reason a trainer must sell to the seminar his love for the curriculum is a little more selfish. The trainer's attitude plays a major role in the trainees' attitude toward the curriculum. That goes for every module as well! When a trainer stands in front of the trainees and says, "This next module is a little on the slow side, but we are supposed to teach it, so hang in there," the trainer does a terrible disservice to the trainees. This does happen often. Next time it does, look around. I will tell you what you see. You will see an entire audience tune out every-thing that is taught for the duration of this "slow" module. If that does not scare you, let me try this one on you. As you now know, I believe it is quite rare for a trainee to come to training prepared to snipe the trainer. It is not rare, however, for trainees to come to a seminar discouraged, depressed, frustrated, or unhappy about training. Most trainers learn the hard way that a bad attitude on the trainer's part acts as a catalyst to trainees who are one step away from acting as snipers. For the trainer's own well-being, it is imperative that he adopt a healthy attitude toward what he is teaching.

DON'T ADVERTISE ANY LACK OF EXPERIENCE

In most professions, it is absolutely normal for a person to tell fellow workers information that affects him on a day-to-day basis. In training, for a trainer, nothing could be farther from the truth. A trainer's personal life, his health, his job satisfaction is irrelevant. Training is a position that does not afford you with that type of closeness to your trainees.

For instance, if you were to teach a course you had never taught before, would you tell your trainees it was your first time? Better think this one over for a second. Let's get the reasons "in favor" out of the way first. Most trainers who inform their trainees that they have never taught the course before are looking for a crutch. They may not word it quite that way, but that is what they are counting on: "Well, it is his first time"; "He was pretty good for his first time." The thinking here is if you want some empathy and understanding, you will probably get it if you inform your trainees you are teaching their course for the first time. Sounds pretty good to me, if it were not for the word "probably."

You see, you probably will get a lot of empathy if you announce you are teaching a seminar for the first time. The downside to this sudden dose of honesty is you may get just the opposite. If you have trainees within your seminar who are disgruntled or potential snipers, you have just given them a loaded pistol and asked them to aim it at your head. To that handicap, add the difficulties that some trainees who are natural skeptics may bring to the training seminar. Also add the probability of being constantly challenged on virtually every point you attempt to make. Your disclosure to these individuals may represent a serious challenge to your credibility as a trainer.

The risks involved with disclosing this type of information just are not worth it. So what is the answer, lie? Absolutely not! I would never suggest such a thing. How does selective disclosure grab you? In the example we just looked at, I would assume most trainers would at least have had an opportunity either to see the course taught or to work with the developers if the course has never been taught. How does this sound to you:

> TRAINER: As for my experience with this course, I have been work-ing in various capacities with the course for some time now and have a good knowledge of the program from both a trainer and trainee perspective.

In other words, "Don't mess with me; I know my stuff!" So many trainers get themselves in hot water disclosing information that not only is no business of the trainees but is of no value as well.

I worked to cross-train an individual once on a program I currently teach for Xerox, which is an insurance type sales course for property and casualty agents. Although the individual I was cross-training had a tremendous amount of knowledge about the curriculum and the topic, she had no experience selling the actual product the trainees sold. Cer-tainly, it would have been preferable to have some specific product ex-perience, but contrary to popular belief, it is not that critical. Selling is selling; and although product experience may represent added credibil-ity in the trainees' eyes, it can and must often be worked around when forced to train underfire. In this situation, I begged the individual I was cross-training simply to tell the trainees that she had a lot of experience within their field, from home office duties to work in the field (the indi-vidual had gone on numerous sales calls with salespeople). What the trainees did not know would not hurt them. I do want to emphasize here, if the trainees asked directly about sales training experience, this individual was prepared to respond, "None." As the three-day training was to begin, I sat back like a proud father waiting to see the fruits of my labor. Instead, the individual I was cross-training decided to toss out what we had discussed and informed the group the only experience she had within the area they sold in was as an underwriter. The trainees became so agitated with this person and her lack of "real" experience, that the individual called it quits by lunchtime. The proud father was then forced to conduct the training for the duration of the course, and the individual never attempted to teach the course again.

You see, when all is said and done, the precious credibility that every trainer strives for is not given, it is earned. Selective disclosure only allows you the opportunity to gain enough listening time with your students to earn that respect. The rest is up to you. As a footnote, I have been teaching this course to property and casualty insurance agents for over three years, and the course is receiving the highest marks it has ever received in the nine years that Xerox has conducted it. I mention that simply to prove my point. I have no experience in nor have I ever sold property and casualty insurance in my life!

HOW TO HANDLE ILLNESS ON THE JOB

Illness is another example of an issue a trainer can be torn over regarding how much they want to share with the trainees. As with the first-timer example, one side of telling an audience about your condition is the feeling that trainees will be sensitive and supportive. True enough. These same trainees will also scrutinize your performance and every action you take: "Not bad, considering the trainer was sick," they will say. "Too bad, our trainer was sick. I wonder what this course is like with a healthy trainer." For someone who does not have a positive attitude coming into the seminar, the comments could be much harsher.

Let me give you a rather macho example of a trainer dealing with an illness. Once I flew to Madison, Wisconsin, to conduct a three-day sales training course for Xerox. Twelve trainees were flown in from all over Wisconsin and some of the bordering states. The night before the training was to begin, I began to feel strange. I say strange instead of sick because (please knock on wood as you read this), I seldom get sick and am never really sure when I am. As a child, I came down with no childhood illnesses despite my parents making me play with every child who was exposed with or was coming down with any of the classic childhood diseases. Well, at 5:00 P.M. I was feeling strange, and by 7:00 P.M., I was sick. As I lay alone in my hotel room sweating one minute, freezing the next, I began to wonder what I was going to do in the morning. After a couple of trips to the bathroom, I decided to try and sleep on it. After enduring a rather long night of discomfort, I made my decision. With so many trainees coming from so far and clearing their schedules for these three days, I decided to go for it. In training, as in the theater, the show must go on! I would tell no one of my illness, try to not get too close to anyone, and give it my best.

My best was spending about 90 percent of the time I was teaching sitting in my chair in the middle of the pit, drinking fluids constantly, and wheeling myself around to different trainees from inside the pit to answer their questions. Occasionally, I would summon up every ounce of strength and make a token move out of the chair to cross the room, shaking my fist in a pathetic attempt of enthusiasm, and then return to my chair. Remember, no one in the room had ever seen me train before and they had no idea this was not exactly my style of teaching. The only other times I would get out of my chair would be to call a break, wait until the trainees left the room, and go throw up. I did a pretty good job coming up with excuses as to why I could not go out with the trainees at night, but I could not get out of the final dinner celebrating the conclusion of the training program. Those who know me know that for a 160-pound man, I can put away a lot of food when I want to. That night I reverted back to my childhood days, ordered a shrimp and rice dish, and proceeded to push my rice around the perimeter of my plate successfully hiding my shrimp. If my childhood dog Brandy had been there, I would have been funneling my scraps to him as well.

When the training was all over, I had gone almost three days without eating anything and had lost eight pounds. This I am not proud of. I had no real idea how sick I was, and if I had known I was not going to be getting any better during the training, I probably would have called it off. What I am proud of, however, is that I received 12 evaluations from the trainees who raved about the training they had just received. A couple of the evaluations specifically made reference to the enthusiasm I displayed throughout the training. When all the trainees left, and only the person who coordinated the event remained, I told this individual of my condition. He remarked, "I thought you were nervous. I saw your hand shaking some of the times you went to take a drink."

The point I am trying to make through this story is that inside the mind of a trainer lies an individual who must keep his feelings and emotions to himself to be successful. Trainers move. Trainers have fights with their spouses. Trainers have bad days. None of this information is relevant in a seminar environment. In reality, the decision at hand is not whether to tell the trainees or not to tell the trainees. The decision really becomes whether to teach the seminar, or not teach the seminar. In my mind, barring a dire emergency, the show must go on.

SURVIVING WITH A SPLIT PERSONALITY

In looking inside the mind of a trainer, I have attempted primarily to show you the public side of the trainer. I think that it is important to explain to you right here and now that anyone who conducts training on more than a casual basis is forced to acquire a split personality. There is a public side the trainees see, and a private side friends and family see. The longer an individual remains a trainer, the more pronounced the split becomes. The more professional trainers I meet, the more I find this to be true.

The reasons for this splitting of personalities is really quite simple. When a trainer is doing the job he is paid to do, he is putting everything he has into his work. His attitude must be perfect, his control flawless, his focus acute. To carry this type of concentration out of the presentation environment would cause a trainer to burn out very quickly. It can also drive those working around the trainer a little wacky. Every now and then I will come home, forget where I am, and say things like, "I would like the salad, then the dressing. After the salad is served, everyone at the table may then eat the main course. Let's begin." Fortunately, I have an understanding wife who will basically tell me to join her in reality and the episode ends rather abruptly!

STAY IN "TRAINING SHAPE"

Due to the energy required to properly conduct a seminar, it is rare to find a trainer with a substantial delivery schedule who has a weight problem. A trainer literally gets into "training shape" when he begins to teach courses. Maintaining the proper type of focus for eight hours a day, five days a week is no easy matter. For a trainer to handle a typical schedule, (four weeks on, one week developmental), it typically takes about three weeks to get in shape. The work can be so exhausting that often when trainers take off for as long as a month at a time, they will need to get back in "training shape" again.

BE CONFIDENT—NOT ARROGANT

Perhaps the most misunderstood aspect of a professional trainer involves the confidence this individual exudes. For many, this confidence appears more like arrogance. When looking inside the mind of a trainer, you begin to have a better understanding as to why.

Trainers who have been underfire in the pit know that the most dangerous mistake they can make is to appear unsure of themselves in front of the trainees. This lack of confidence can be detected in their voice, their facial expression and even in their physical movements. It is imperative, for the trainers' own survival, to learn to remove doubts, or at the very least, to mask them.

As with most sports, training is a profession that is actually very mental. Successful field goal kickers in the NFL all have their own strange little quirks and superstitions; however, they all share one common action. Listen to any kicker talk about his thoughts prior to kicking the ball and he will tell you that he has a vision of actually seeing the ball going through the uprights. He must not let doubt sneak through.

One of my favorite sports heroes is Mike Tyson. In my mind, Mike is the greatest prizefighter who has ever lived. It saddens me to hear about some of the troubles he has gotten himself into, but enough has been written about his "out of the ring" troubles. I would like to focus for a moment on his attitude toward what he does inside the ring. In my mind, he is one of the most misunderstood athletes of all times. His comments before and after a boxing match are often misinterpreted and taken out of context by those who do not understand. A professional trainer does understand. Before a fight, you will never hear Mike Tyson say he thinks he might win with a little luck. He will look whoever is asking him about the fight right in the eye and tell them without question he will destroy his opponent. Many are frightened by some of the comments Mike Tyson makes before a fight, but no one will question that without a shadow of a doubt, Mike Tyson thinks he will win. Almost all the boxers that Mike Tyson fights are taller, heavier, and have a longer reach. If Mike ever stopped to wonder about the physical attributes of the men he fights and then questioned his own abilities he could be in trouble. Fortunately, he does not. There is no question that Mike Tyson's boxing skills are amazing. However, I believe one of the biggest assets he brings into the ring is his confidence. Mike Tyson tells you he cannot lose; he believes he cannot lose; and therefore he almost never does lose.

When a trainer goes into a seminar believing he will absolutely positively be successful, he too will almost always succeed. Once, while working with Xerox, I was observed and then interviewed by a group that wanted a representative from the private sector to address about 700 participants. The purpose of the presentation was not only to speak for two hours on how we (as a company) negotiate with our customers but to be motivational as well. This was an annual event with a list of previous presenters that read like a who's who of famous speakers. After watching me deliver a presentation, we sat down and they began to ask me some questions. I did not realize it, but every answer I gave them included statements such as "Without question I will do this" and "I can definitely make that happen."

Finally, one of the people conducting the interview stopped and said, "We have asked you 10 questions, and 10 times you have given us a definitive answer. How can you be so sure of yourself?" This was one of the first times I had ever stopped and consciously analyzed the behavior I was exhibiting. Still, the answer came out rather easily: "How can I get up, and in two hours convince 700 people who have never heard of me that I am for real, my material is worthwhile, and they should be motivated and excited if I do not believe in myself?" Their search ended with that comment as the individual who asked the question smiled at me and told the others, "We've got our man."

I recently watched an interview with Joe Thiesmann who summed it up well. Thiesmann said, "I have been accused of being both egotistical and arrogant. To this I say, pshaw. I'm simply the best at what I do." As a lifetime Redskin fan and an admire of Mr. Thiesmann, I must say, I could not say it better!

Arrogance? No. Confidence? You bet. A trainer would look awfully silly if he got up in front of a group of people and told them that he thought the ideas he was presenting might help them, but then again they might not! I want trainers who work for me to be team players. I also understand that a large ego comes with the territory. With that large ego comes the confidence to face even the most difficult situations courageously and without hesitation.

COPING WITH DOUBT

I suppose the last aspect of the mind of a trainer involves the five-letter word that frightens trainers the most. The word is "doubt." This word can haunt some trainers into early retirement from corporate training. There is no other profession that subjects an individual to as much scrutiny and judgment. The successful trainers do not remove doubt; they coexist with it. They know that doubt can actually inspire them to work harder and give more to a seminar. When these trainers are actually in front of trainees, thoughts of doubts are pushed away and confidence takes its place. Sometimes, doubt can remain dormant for a long time, but no matter how well it is hidden, it is often only a bad seminar away from surfacing. This only serves as a reminder to anyone who goes underfire that a trainer is only as good as his last seminar. Strangely, in retrospect, doubt actually becomes the catalyst that makes training so exciting to so many trainers.

WORKING WITH ANXIETY

Anxiety regarding speaking in front of a group of people should not be taken lightly. It happens to be a very common fear among most people as illustrated in the following study:

The Ten Worst Human Fears (in the U.S.)*

1. Speaking before a group.

2. Heights.

3. Insects and bugs.

4. Financial problems.

5. Deep water.

6. Sickness.

7. Death.

8. Flying.

9. Loneliness.

10. Dogs.

One of the biggest concerns most trainers, or public speakers, have to deal with when working is anxiety. You will notice that I do not like to use the word "nervousness." I avoid using that word because it conjures up a lot of negative thoughts and fears. Anxiety, on the other hand, is a better word and one that we all can live with. You see, anxiety is a natural occurrence that you can actually use to your advantage. Before a big presentation, I am often pacing about in another room attempting to channel my anxiety into energy. To this day, I still visualize a racehorse, loaded in and ready for the gate to open so it can be free to run. That is what anxiety can be directed to: energy and drive. The

* David Wallechinsky et al.: *The Book of Lists* (New York: William Morrow & Co., Inc., 1977)

only time I actually do get nervous is when I am not feeling any anxiety. That is when you run the risk of being flat! Here are some other points you may wish to consider when coping with anxiety.

Welcome to the Club

The first tip to remember is that everyone experiences the same phenomenon that you do. True, sometimes it is to a greater or lesser degree, but everyone experiences it. Some of the most famous television and movie stars have documented their dealings with anxiety. We all experience it. It is natural and to be expected. Do not deny your feelings. Simply accept them and realize that we are all in the same boat.

They're Rooting for You

Another point to remember when coping with anxiety is to realize that your trainees want you to do well. You don't believe me? Then I will prove it to you. Think back to the last time you were a trainee and attended a training seminar. I refuse to believe you rocked back in your chair and whispered to the person sitting next to you, "I hope this seminar is terrible. I hope the trainer is boring and we get nothing out of our week here." You might not have been conscious of it, but I think you might have been saying just the opposite. If it were verbalized, I think it would have sounded a lot more like "I hope this seminar is good. I hope we got a good trainer. I want to maximize my time out of the field and learn as much as possible." You see, I believe in a basic principle (please do not take this as being too cynical): People are greedy. We appeal to that greed by stating utilities. We are soothed by that greed, knowing most trainees would prefer not to waste their time in training and want to maximize their experiences. Before you even speak, those trainees are rooting for you!

Get Moving

One of the best techniques I know of to better control anxiety is movement. You already know that movement is a natural for helping maintain interest within your training. Now, movement is back again as an aid to dealing with anxiety. Different circumstances will dictate just how much movement you can use. If you are teaching a new curriculum that you do not know well, obviously your mobility will be somewhat reduced. Question, discussion, anecdotes, and presentation aids can still allow you to move in even the most difficult times. The bottom line is, if you want to cope with anxiety, get in that pit and move.

Study the Start

I mentioned it earlier and I will mention it again: Study the start of your presentation. If you put in the time to get comfortable with the first three or four minutes, your anxiety will come down. Think back on the presentations you have given in your life from grade school on, and one memory will most likely be constant. Those first couple of minutes were difficult and then things got easier. Study those first couple of minutes, and I assure you things will get easier and you will become more confident as well.

Prepare, Prepare, Prepare

In real estate, they say the three most important factors in buying a house are location, location, and location. In coping with anxiety, some of the most important factors a trainer needs to deal with are preparation, preparation, and preparation. More than anything else, anxiety is a fear of the unknown. The more unknowns you can eliminate, the more confident you will become. Want to make sure you use your overhead projector properly? Prepare. Want to ask the right types of questions at the right time? Prepare. Want to deliver a meaningful UPPOPPR? Prepare. The list can go on and on. Want to thrive under-fire? Prepare!

Take a Breath . . . or Two

Everyone experiences anxiety, and on particular occasions, you may be fortunate enough to experience "butterflies." That feeling in your stomach called "butterflies" is really nothing more than a lack of oxygen in the middle region of your body. This is caused by a stress response sending more oxygen to the larger muscles in your body. This feeling can be reduced by taking one or two deep breaths, holding them, and letting them out slowly. Remember, that is one or two deep breaths. I do not advocate hyperventilation as a technique to conquer anxiety. There is an old saying regarding the management of butterflies. "If you get butterflies, the trick is not necessarily to get rid of them, but rather to just get them to fly in formation."

Put on Your Game Face

If all else fails, allow me to give one suggestion of what not to do. Try not to give in to the anxious feelings. Do not feel obligated to tell your audience how nervous you are. If I could report to you that I have seen this technique work, I would. You can let everyone in the training seminar know how nervous and afraid you are and the reality is, the training will not be one bit easier for you. There are just too many trainees who will take advantage of that type of situation. So, you do not feel 100 percent confident. Welcome to the club. Put on your game face, which, by the way, is a confident, enthusiastic face, and have a ball!

Chapter 13

The Value of Good Training: Hiring Effective Trainers

When was the last time you left a retail store thinking to yourself, "That is the last time I come back to this place?" Was it because the item you were considering buying was not up to par, or was it something else? Perhaps it was a futile search for an item that was no longer in stock. Maybe it was that it took so long to be waited on. Maybe it was a feeling of indifference by the individual waiting on you. All these possibilities add up to one thing: lost revenue.

Now, let me ask you another question similar to the first. When was the last time you left a retail store thinking to yourself, "That was a pleasant experience; I really enjoyed that?" In this second scenario, perhaps it was the courtesy extended by the salesperson. Maybe it was the organization's ability to convince you that you were important. One thing is for sure. You will return.

I am not saying that every time you have a favorable experience, it is a direct result of good training . . . exactly. I am saying that statistics speak for themselves. A general rule of thumb used in business today is that when it is all said and done, about 15 percent of a company's problems relate to people, and about 85 percent relate to process. I am a firm believer that one of the goals of good training is to teach repeatable, predictable processes to assist on the job. The sad truth that reinforces this point is that most people will actually tolerate a level of service that is sub par, as long as it is consistent. A lot of people really want no surprises. It is often inconsistency that causes rejection from our customers.

Statistics also show a rather frustrating correlation to the impact of a less than favorable experience. Depending on your source, you will find the experts saying that a disappointed customer will tell anywhere between 9 and 15 people about his dissatisfaction. The frustrating portion of these studies is that a satisfied customer will tell anywhere between 2 and 5 people about the experience. It would seem only fair for customers to tell an equal number of people about their experiences good or bad, but it just does not work out that way. One way or another, after that first experience, the honeymoon is over.

With those numbers in mind, it is now time to turn your attention to the training that is or is not up to par. Gone is the notion that an individual who does not have frontline contact with the customer is somehow insulated from responsibility to that customer. No matter how far down the line of internal customers, or removed from direct customer contact these individuals are, the results of their actions eventually affect the customer. Therefore, not only can the training that employees receive have a major effect on how these employees do their jobs, it can have a major effect on the customer as well.

MEET THE NEW BREED OF PRESENTERS

With more and more companies beginning to realize the impact of good training, a revolution is occurring in corporate training departments. The old idea of the corporate trainer being a stuffed shirt who "could not do so he teaches" is evaporating.

Corporate trainers touch the company and customer more than any president or CEO. Who is the first employee that most new hires are exposed to in a mentor position? It is seldom the manager, because new employees are usually too overwhelmed and intimidated with management. Co-workers send too many conflicting signals. Even early on in a new hire's career, there can be a sense of competition among employees or even just a lack of time to really show a new person the ropes. The only group aggressively approaching the new hire is one I like to refer to as the "We Hate It Here and Think Anyone Who Likes It Here Is a Fool" club. It consists of employees who for some reason or another are fed up with the company and want out. Like junkies, one way they make themselves feel better is to prey on the vulnerable and try to turn them to their way of thinking. As soon as a new employee joins the company, these club members go on a membership drive. Starting a new job is traumatic enough without aggravating the stress by doubting the decision to take the job in the first place. Often the person who can most quickly come to the rescue is this new breed of presenter.

How about the more tenured employee who has been with the company for a suitable period of time performing at an acceptable level? Nothing flashy, you understand, just quietly doing his job. Do you realize how many people go about their lives quietly doing their jobs? In my management training experiences talking with many frontline managers, all seem to agree that in any given work situation the numbers break down about like this:

- Ten percent of the employees are superstars. They do a wonderful job, receive constant recognition, and will continue to perform at that level.

- Ten percent of the employees are regarded as (for the lack of a better term) mistakes. They most likely should never have been hired, are probably hanging on, and will eventually quit or be terminated.

- Eighty percent of the employees are competent. There is nothing flashy about these individuals, they are the ones who just seem to quietly do their jobs. The discouraging point is that so many managers simply forget about these employees. As a matter of fact, the vast majority of these employees end up quitting for that exact reason; a lack of recognition.

So here we have this silent mass within the workplace that for all intents and purposes remains untapped. What would happen if we made a point of recognizing their work? Nothing to recognize you say? Oh come now, look harder. Maybe they are not flashy and do not excel in some of the more obvious areas, but there must be something they are good at. For instance, maybe they simply come in on time every day. It does not seem like much, but they do come in on time every day. Do you think if they were recognized for it they would be late the next day? No way! Essentially, what you would be accomplishing is solidifying good habits. As a matter of fact, you may actually help to open the floodgates that will inspire the employee to do other jobs better as well. I want to be sure that I am sending out the correct message here regarding the intent of recognition. It is a way to inspire employee performance. It is not a way to have a discussion to improve performance in other areas. That is the quickest way to negate any positives that may come out of this experience.

You may be asking yourself what does giving recognition have to do with training? Before I answer that, let me first tell you why most managers I have come in contact with do not give recognition. It is not because there is a feeling that there is not enough recognition to go around. It is because there is a feeling that all employees want is more money and that there is not enough money to go around. This is where the possibility of training can come in. When training is truly effective and has the kind of reputation that it should have, it can be used as a reward. I count on the new breed of presenters not to let you down.

$15,000 is a standard that most companies will use when quoting the effects of hiring and then firing a new employee. The stakes are high when it comes to making the correct decision regarding the hiring of a new employee. It would be a crime not to do all you can to save the employees on the edge of failure. The new breed of presenter can come through here, too.

Let me now introduce you to the new breed of presenters. The new breed exhibits a number of unique qualities. To begin with, you are dealing with quick studies who can become subject matter experts, regardless of the curriculum, in a matter of one or two seminars. Add to that, enormous energy and enthusiasm for their curriculum and students, regardless of the topic. The new breed consists of risk takers who will stop at nothing to make their messages understood and retained. A tremendous amount of empathy for their students sends trainees out motivated and ready to apply the principles learned.

Successful companies are now, finally, putting the same level of attention into who is teaching the material as they are into what material is being taught. The fact of the matter is, the curriculum is only as good as the presenter delivering it. The stakes are high, and the consequences are real. No one in the company directly affects as many individuals as most trainers. Hiring the right individual has become essential.

WHO TO HIRE

A question that is often asked of me by other training managers is, "What do I look for when hiring a trainer?" As with most mysteries of hiring, there is not a patent answer. If there were, I would dedicate this entire book to it, and I would be retired and wealthy as well. Different trainers have different styles that they make work for themselves, which complicates the answer even more. Let me instead answer the question by telling you some traits I would be most interested in spotting during an interview.

The first quality I would be looking for during my questioning would be the individual's ability to think quickly on his feet. The majority of my questions would be case study scenarios with many possible answers. As an experienced interviewer will tell you, the intent of these questions is not necessarily to spot the best response. There really should not be a best response, but rather other less obvious areas to look at. First, watch the logic pattern the individual is following. Are you detecting good problem-solving skills? Good trainers are good problem solvers. Also, see just how well this individual can make you believe in his answer. It will be one of your best opportunities to judge how articulate and persuasive the individual is. It will also be an opportunity to get a sense of whether the individual can make you believe in his point of view. Sit back, and allow yourself to be swayed if the selling of the answer is a good one. This will demonstrate one of those rare skills that cannot easily be taught to a new trainer. Some skills you either have or you don't. It is not imperative, but I sure would like to feel persuaded.

Another quality I look for is one I personally emphasize a great deal. A crucial quality that is a common link among the finest trainers in the world is compassion. It shows up in the seminar room again and again as a sense of empathy for the trainees. This trait is not an easy one to spot in an interview. However, you may want to try this idea. To begin with, due to the unique nature of the position of trainer, a portion of the interview must consist of a presentation. Fifteen minutes should do the trick, with the subject a topic of the interviewee's choice. Now, I would like to see strong stand-up training skills incorporating good questioning, but it certainly is not imperative. Most of those skills can be taught to the trainer. They do not have to be instinctual. Compassion is a difficult lesson to teach. To get a sense of how much your interviewee possesses, ask a question that intentionally would make you look a little foolish. Humor me for just a minute. This question may be about a point that was just covered, or perhaps something that really does not relate to the subject. What I would look for is to see just what type of instincts this interviewee has for showing empathy to his future students. Does he maintain his composure and attempt to find value in your question? Does he acknowledge the question as a good one to have been asked? How would you feel as a trainee in a room with 20 other strangers after this individual's response?

A third critical quality I would look for and consider essential would be a feeling of enthusiasm from the interviewee. I would like to feel this during the presentation, during the question-and-answer period, before we start the interview, after we finish the interview, and in the hallway. As with compassion, it is difficult to teach enthusiasm.

There are some final qualities that I would look for when hiring a trainer or seminar leader. Individually, however, these traits might fall in the category of "nice to have," as opposed to "need to have." I would start by looking at an individual's ability to be flexible. This is not a position for a perfectionist simply because, in the pit, as well as behind the scenes, seldom do things go perfectly. Those who venture into that pit must bring with them many skills that are often taken for granted and, if possessed, are barely noticed. Presenters can be taught a great deal, but verbal skills, problem solving, and leadership are some intangibles that quite simply, some possess and some do not. Structure your interviews to include a glimpse of these final traits and you will find the individual you are looking for.

SUMMARY

To wrap this up, with regard to backgrounds conducive to training, I have seen enough stand-up trainers with diverse backgrounds to avoid making any definitive statements as to where the best trainers come from. Yet, with all due respect, I am convinced that the highest percentage of successful trainers typically have sales backgrounds. My own theory for this phenomenon is that these individuals have had to make a living by getting people to listen to and agree with their messages. When turned loose in the seminar room, their typical response is to do the same thing. What a marvelous quality these people bring into the room with them. They not only naturally teach their material, they unconsciously sell it to the trainees!

Chapter 14

Avoiding the Training Trap: Problems with Relevance and Respect

Company training departments can take on many appearances. Some look strangely like personnel departments, while others look more like marketing departments. Still other training departments appear so far removed from the rest of their organization, they attempt to reside as a separate entity. This would all be well and good, if it were not that the more removed a training department appears from the rest of the company, the less credible it appears in the eyes of those who depend on it.

HOW TO BUILD CREDIBILITY AND GAIN RESPECT FOR TRAINING

One of the biggest problems any training department must take on is the notion from "the field" that the training department is "out of touch" with what is really happening within the company. Therefore, we must confront problem number one: *relevance* within a training department.

This is one of the first, and often cheapest shots that a training department must contend with. At first glance, it appears to be a pretty good argument. How can this individual teach me something he is not currently doing? A particularly poignant example would be that of sales training. Products change, as do customers and their demands. How does an individual who has not been actively selling in the field effectively teach someone who is? There is an answer, albeit a somewhat disappointing one.

Build a Qualified Training Staff

The training department must develop a staff where the majority of individuals have experience within the subject to be taught. This is a rather basic principle, but often not adhered to. This will begin to establish the elusive credibility that is a "must have" in a good training department. You will notice I said a majority. I disagree that the department must consist entirely of successful field personnel. I firmly believe that a realistic combination of talents can often keep a department from tunnel-visioning ideas and techniques. With all due respect to the Smith family, who wants to live in a world where everybody's name is John Smith? Diversity breeds change and creativity, which are imperative within any department, especially a training department.

A formula that I have grown comfortable with is more like 75 percent out of the field teaching exactly what they have done previously, and 25 percent who have had related experiences. Perhaps they have sold, but not that particular product, or they worked with systems, but not that particular system. The percentage would obviously change depending on the subject to be taught. The numbers I am speaking to reflect a "field, nonfield" environment.

Make Sure Trainers Are Knowledgeable and Up to Date in Their Field

Next, to build this precious credibility, training departments should undertake a plan to keep the department relevant. This is often mistakenly adhered to by providing the presenters with copies of all the literature, magazines, memos, and various other correspondence involving their particular topics of expertise. Nice idea, and I would recommend it highly, except unfortunately, that alone is not nearly enough. Presenters are faced with more pressures in a day than most people will face in a month. Coping with the pressures of good delivery and literally eating and sleeping the subject matter on a daily basis make a lot of the correspondence placed in the presenter's mailbox meaningless. Even considering the most disciplined presenter, the chances of truly being able to absorb the information that is building on that poor, piled up paper stack once referred to as a desk, is remote. I am not for an instant saying this information is not important and need not be read. I just think if it is that critical, go over it in a team meeting or rotate individuals to synopsize and redistribute the information. What I am also saying is stick with the most successful approach to retaining relevance. Get that presenter out of the office on a regular basis and into the field where he belongs. One day of field observation or coaching will go a lot further than the out-of-control documentation disaster waiting for that presenter in his mailbox. What a strong statement to those who question the credibility and "out-of-touch" nature of your department. It also does wonderful things for a presenter's confidence as well. All are served with a steady diet of fieldwork.

TRAINING CAN'T SOLVE ALL BUSINESS PROBLEMS

Probably one of the most frustrating misconceptions that most training departments must contend with is the notion that practically anything that cannot be explained away must be a training issue. This brings us to problem number two, hereby referred to as the "training dumpster."

The ironies of training are astounding. First, this poor department, searching desperately for an identity, must work day and night to establish its own credibility. Then, almost as quickly as the department accomplishes this, it must begin to contend with the idea that everything can now be fixed with good training. Performance problem? Send them for training. Losing good personnel? Must be a training issue. Customers unhappy? Training. Apathy within another department? You guessed it, training. I could go on and on. The important point here is that, contrary to popular belief, not everything is a training issue. Unfortunately, if the training department is not careful, it will find itself taking on issues it cannot and should not solve.

A series of four steps should accompany any request for training:

1. Consult.

2. Analyze.

3. Investigate.

4. Pilot.

Consult to Find Out Whether Training Is Really Needed

The idea of consulting takes on a slightly different connotation when reviewing a request for training. By consulting, I simply mean before wasting a tremendous amount of time and energy, you should ask some questions regarding the request. Interview skills would be particularly helpful during the consulting stage. It is time to start questioning all those who are even remotely involved with the situation.

Let's look at a typical example. Let's say you are managing a telephone hotline and the director notifies you that there has been an increase in customer complaints about rudeness from the operators. This director immediately has the situation pegged as another "training problem." Before wasting a lot of money on a problem that may not be, it's time to ask some questions of a lot of people. I would be most interested to hear from the customers—the dissatisfied and the satisfied. I would like to hear from the operators—those with a record of some complaints and those without, also tenured operators, and new hires. I want to hear from supervisors as well as management. Basically, I want to hear from just about anyone who has a relationship with this department and its duties, and there is a game plan to this questioning. There are several questions I want answered:

- How long has this been going on?
- How often has this occurred?
- How severe is this problem?
- What are the repercussions of this problem?
- What other actions, if any, have been taken in the past?

What I want to make sure of with this sampling of questions is first whether the problem really exists, and second that I am not reinventing the wheel. Often, a generation ago (that's about two years in a typical training department), similar problems may have existed that were dealt with in any number of successful or unsuccessful ways. I want to know about them.

Analyze the Potential Audience for the Training Program

It's not that I'm a skeptic . . . exactly. It's just that to be totally sure a problem exists and to add some real-world experiences to the potential training, it would be a good idea to observe and analyze the expected audience. This should settle any last-minute doubts and begin to direct you to selecting the appropriate training package.

Research the Training Curriculum

Now that all involved have been consulted and the situation in question has been analyzed, it is time to research and select the curriculum. If time is an issue, benchmarking may help. Selecting the format of the training is almost as important as the curriculum itself. How long will your program be? How interactive and participative would you like to make it? Often, you can answer questions like these by looking at the background of the audience and the size of your intended seminar.

Pilot a Test Training Program

Once the curriculum has been chosen, it is finally time to conduct the seminar. If the course is going to be taught more than one or two times, it is vital to take a look at its effectiveness. It is rare for restaurant chains to introduce new selections nationwide without setting up a few test sites first. Better to make a little mistake than a large one. Studying and reading a curriculum is one thing; teaching it is another. A pilot will allow you to test the curriculum and its effectiveness. Be warned. Pilots are not a whole lot of fun. There are a few rules that must be followed.

First, to make a fair observation, the curriculum must be delivered as written with little to no deviation by the instructor. No war stories, no analogies, and no embellishments. The idea is to see if the curriculum is strong enough as written. This is especially critical if more than one instructor is going to be teaching the seminar. The curriculum must be able to be hypothetically handed off and taught effectively. An addition that will complicate the evaluation is a presenter's style that may not be duplicated by other presenters. This sets up a scenario that has students evaluating style and not curriculum. The fact of the matter is a good presenter can make the art of paint drying an interesting topic, if allowed to embellish. The problem is, such presenters do not grow on trees, and it does not help with the evaluation of new training curriculum. Piloting means that curriculum is delivered word for word as written. That allows for a true test of the curriculum's potential success or failure. There are not a whole lot of presenters who will volunteer for this hazardous duty (this author included), but it is what is necessary to truly test the material.

Finally, when preparing to launch this new training campaign, it is important to set up some sort of measurement system to evaluate its effectiveness. Thinking positively, what are you going to use as evidence that the course is a success and the original problem has been fixed? Taking these measurements before the actual training takes place allows for a fair and unbiased appraisal once the program kicks off. For obvious reasons, whatever measurements are established before training must be taken after training. Nothing can be objectively proven without an apples-to-apples comparison.

Trying to solve all of life's problems through a dumpster called training is a hazard that awaits most training departments. Be careful. It will weaken the credibility of a training department as well as damage the morale of the presenters who represent it.

VALIDATING YOUR TRAINING PROGRAMS

One of many obstacles that a training department has to face is proving its own validity. It seems that American corporations either believe in the idea of training or they do not. There are not a large number of individuals who do not have a strong opinion supporting one side or the other. The unfortunate truth is those who oppose training can make a fairly strong argument as long as they are not pressed too hard. The argument often made involves a somewhat harmless, even insignificant little word. It is really all training foes have to do battle with, but for those who oppose training as a solution, this word is a battle cry. That word is "results." It's not that I am opposed to results. I often think individuals are looking in the wrong area for results; however, let me provide you with a story that may help clear this up.

In high school and college, I had a passion for basketball. I loved to play the sport, and the sport liked me. I say liked and not loved because although I had the desire to play with some of the best, my 5'10" 150-pound body took an enormous beating. After years of breaks, sprains, twists, and pains, I decided to hang up my high-tops and participate in a far less violent sport—running. After being dared into my first race, a half marathon no less, I realized I needed someone to help teach me the ropes. A friend of mine put me on a rather strict running program of about 5 miles a day. Same course, 5 miles a day. He preached to me that if I stuck with this course and this mileage, I would notice appreciable results after one week. That sure sounded good to me, so off we went on my first training run. When we finished, I was tired and panting as I checked my watch. About 35 minutes, and was I ever out of breath. We drove home, and as I stood under the shower, still panting, I realized I had a long way to go. Night after night, I ran alone. The same course, the same 5 miles. What really frustrated me was that my time was not improving that dramatically, and I knew in my heart I was giving it my all. My spastic panting at the finish line told me that! Finally, frustrated as I neared the end of my second week, I called my friend to voice my displeasure with his techniques (and my physical prowess). He seemed confused and promised a run together the next night. Together, again we ran the same course, the same 5 miles. Almost gloating with an "I told you so" sarcastic attitude, I pointed to my watch and showed him the time. It had not improved much at all. He was somewhat bewildered as he looked at me and said he never told me my time would improve dramatically in one or two weeks. He told me I would see results. He then suggested I look at my rate of breathing. We had finished the run one minute before, and I was breathing as if we had not even started. It was a classic case of looking in the wrong place for the wrong results.

The problem that most training departments must cope with is similar to the preceding story. Those who fund and support training must show results. Those who are seeking this information often look in the wrong place.

Sometimes, we look to see just how much more an employee is selling after training, and we do not see an appreciable difference. Certainly not enough to warrant the enormous expense of training! What we may fail to look at, however, is the immediate and major improvement in customer service with a salesperson who is perceived as polished and confident. Those are results that pay dividends for many years. Long term, that represents big bucks.

We may be automating an office environment and conducting technical training. Short term, it costs money to send a presenter out, and it costs even more in lost production. The argument is made that these employees could learn from each other, or on their own time. After training, the speed of those who participated has not gone up. Maybe the error rate has dropped, however. Certainly, if nothing else, morale has improved with good, effective training. The last time I asked my management training colleagues, the figure of $15,000 was still being quoted in the workplace as the cost to hire and then lose an employee. If you were looking for short term, there it is. Long term, it is no contest.

Remember, long term means you are going to have to wait for those results. This could potentially take years. Unfortunately, for those who do not enjoy a good mystery, tracking and measuring these results can cost more than the training itself. Regardless, let's at least make sure we are looking in the right place and taking the correct measurements.

Convincing those within your organization the importance of training can be a challenging sale, to say the least. For the most part, we must be reminded over and over again that as with a good stock, results are more accurately and more fairly measured long term as opposed to short term.

Chapter 15

Developing a Training Staff

Traditionally for most companies, a training department is born more out of necessity than careful planning. You can call it budget problems, or you can call it credibility problems. You can even call it identity problems. Typically, when a training department really takes off, it is more for reactive reasons than proactive reasons. Assuming your decisions are based on the latter, here are a couple of thoughts you may want to consider.

EMPHASIZE THE QUALITY OF YOUR TRAINING PROGRAMS

As with any department (or corporation for that matter), the first emphasis should be on *quality*. I know that seems to be a buzzword for businesses at this time, but it is a reality. As with any other customer-related business, word of lack of quality spreads at a much faster rate than word of quality. There is no reason to whine or complain about what is or is not fair about that statement, it is simply reality.

To establish a reputation for quality, the first thing a training department must do is make a statement to the other departments or outside organizations of its competence. There is really only one way to do this and that is to start training. Most likely, this will come from a request or need from another department. Once it is determined that, in fact, there is a need, be sure the department is not on the line to do too much. Training is not the end-all, cure-all. It exists simply to improve performance, not to solve world hunger. The sooner a training department and those around it realize this, the better.

MAKE SURE TRAINERS WORK WITH THE
CURRICULUM DEVELOPERS

Another important factor involving the creation of a training department is the function of its employees. One of the first things that managers seem eager to do, when running a training department, is to separate the presenters from the curriculum developers. If I may borrow an old phrase let me make one thing perfectly clear: This is a terrible mistake. It follows the same old logic that states we keep sales and service people apart. It seems many forget about the potential for one to teach the other, increasing both employees' value. Sadly, it remains an unwritten law in most companies. Suppose we keep those who work on your car's engine away from those who work on its chassis. I once owned a car where this was so much a reality that I actually had to stock two separate sets of tools. Metric for the engine and linear for the chassis. Where the two connected, it was anybody's guess! This also explains why, for some cars, changing the oil filter is like heart bypass surgery. I guarantee, before that engine was placed inside that chassis, it was a piece of cake. So why is it so many training departments keep presenters away from developers? Certainly, the argument can be made that if presenters needed only to concentrate on the delivery, their focus and presentation would be better. The problem is, I made that argument, and I do not even believe it.

The benefits of allowing the two departments to work hand in hand are many. If the presenter assists the curriculum developer, there is the potential for a faster start-up for the presenter to master the curriculum and delivery. Next, not only does the pride factor give an instructor more confidence, it translates to the credibility that presenters and training departments are often seeking. Also, you eliminate the potential for an "out-of-touch" curriculum developer missing out on real-world information. Typically, presenters have experience in the field they are teaching, and involved presenters can help monitor the relevance of a curriculum they work with on a daily basis. The chance of an attitude problem among your presenters is also held in check when they have a say in the final project. Finally, once a program is up and running, the department essentially has a sea of subject matter experts to draw upon when needed. Keeping these channels of communication open can help ensure the curriculum is not becoming outdated. It can also help to make sure your department is not wasting a valuable resource.

PROMOTE CONSISTENCY IN COURSE CONTENT AND TRAINING STYLE

The last obstacle training departments must clear, once a program is up and running, is consistency. By consistency, I am referring to multiple presenters teaching the same curriculum. This scenario is a pretty typical one. An instructor sits through a pilot with other instructors to learn how the curriculum is to be delivered. The students come to town and are bowled over by the training (perhaps I'm a little biased here). The instructors celebrate those first couple of tough weeks and each begins to settle into the curriculum . . . his own way. Now I am an advocate of each presenter developing his own style. What worries me is when a presenter crosses the style line and begins to change the curriculum. This often occurs due to boredom. It is a lot like an actor who delivers his lines dutifully night after night. When the part is new, so too are the lines.

After weeks of the same lines, night after night, the words begin to sound stale. The actor changes the lines to freshen up the part a bit and is lulled into believing the lines are now better. Some actors truly believe that they have somehow improved their Shakespeare. Fortunately, there are directors in theater whose main job is to act as the actor's eyes from the back of the theater, and remind the actor that although the words do not change, the audiences do. For them, the actor is saying these words for the first time. Each audience deserves the best. In business, the actor's script is replaced by the presenter's curriculum. The director is replaced by either a manager or observer. In either case, take comfort in knowing the student's reactions and questions will no doubt take the curriculum to new and exciting places.

If it were not for the fact that students talk to each other constantly, inconsistency among presenters would not be such a major problem. Students have egos also, and each wants to assure the other that they have the best seminar and the best presenter. I have actually observed students involved in heated arguments over which presenter's interpretation of the curriculum was most accurate. Often, the students are forced to pick sides because both interpretations cannot be right. The loser's morale can be adversely affected along with the corresponding presenter's reputation and that of the department.

To make matters worse, the most challenging task involving consistency is not curriculum. It is subjective evaluation by presenters. Subjective evaluation involves interpretation by the presenter. In school, most of us were subjected to this type of interpretation when we wrote papers or completed essay exams. There is not a large call for this type of testing in corporate training. However, a number of courses involve role play, demo, or case study evaluation. In this type of testing, the presenter interprets an action or series of skills and judges the student's effectiveness. Perhaps now you can see the potential difficulty when more than one instructor is evaluating this type of behavior.

The good news is there are solutions to both of these scenarios. Solving the problem with curriculum is best handled with the proactive approach of establishing a benchmark right off the bat. This will often be served best by using your most tenured or senior presenter. The simple truth is that it really does not involve rocket science to carry out this task: It will, however, act as the final word involving gray areas of the curriculum and their interpretation. The only reason I suggest it be a tenured individual is that few fields hold higher egos, and this designation, handled fairly, may help to prevent a mutiny. Once this person has been put in place, it should be his further responsibility to assist in cross-training any new presenters, act as a contact for the curriculum developers, and if possible, rotate to the various seminars to observe on a random, routine basis.

The more difficult of the two scenarios involves achieving consistency among the subjective portions of the instructors' evaluations. The most effective approach I have ever used involves a few steps and a few late nights. To begin with, video- or audiotape a few samples of whatever you are evaluating. By a few samples, I am referring to samples of what is considered excellent, good, and not so good. The next step is assemble your team of presenters, order in some pizzas, and prepare for a late evening. What you need to accomplish is a consensus among those in the room as to what to interpret as what. Just a reminder: Consensus does not mean everyone in the room must agree 100 percent with the group's interpretation, merely that he can "support" the actions of the group. Gone are the days (and thankfully so) when consensus meant those in the group could "live" with the decision. That one word led to a lot of "I told you so's" by disgruntled individuals who did not get their way.

The mark of any good training department is its ability to achieve and deliver consistency. With the early establishment of a benchmarked individual, and group consensus on the interpretation of subjective portions of the curriculum, a training department can sell credibility and effectiveness to whomever it interacts with.

Chapter 16

Evaluation and Support

Let's assume that you have diligently studied a proposed problem and have decided that training is in fact necessary. It is now time to look at how you are going to evaluate your training. This is by no means an optional step. Without feedback, you are wasting a valuable resource to help assess your training. First, we will examine the evaluation options that are available for your trainees.

EVALUATING TRAINEES

When most of us think about student evaluation, often the first word that comes to mind is "test." Years of schooling condition most of us to fear the dreaded evaluation. In corporate training, thankfully, a few more options are often available. Certainly, written tests or verbal tests are viable alternatives to evaluate the trainees' retention of information. I only have one question: Do you feel written or verbal tests enable you to evaluate trainees' performance? My answer to that question is no; these forms of evaluation usually do not give the presenter a true insight into performance. Corporate training is typically put in place to teach information that trainees need to apply on the job, so there is a bit of a disconnect between those forms of evaluation and corporate training objectives.

Another form of evaluation used in corporate training is called ability testing. This form of testing is commonly used in more technical situations and requires that the trainee merely parrot the skills being taught. Demonstrating a technique on a computer or other piece of equipment would be examples of this form of evaluation.

When it comes to evaluation, the trend in corporate training seems to be toward implementation testing. Can the trainee actually utilize the information being taught? This form of testing attempts to pit the trainee in a real-world situation requiring him to apply what has been taught. Often, this form of testing will even prod trainees to make decisions in areas that have not necessarily been taught but are real world and relate to their task. Some common examples of implementation testing would be role plays and my personal favorite, simulations. Now the trainee must think on his feet using the skills that have been taught as well as his instincts for the topic.

EVALUATING THE TRAINER

Let's turn our attention to another important evaluation topic: You. Most training evaluations attempt to separate course content from the evaluation of the presenter. Your interest in the content portion of the evaluation will most likely be dependent on your relationship with the curriculum development side of your training. Content is usually evaluated on a 5- to 10-point scale that attempts not only to measure the trainees' proficiency after the training but also to measure their level of proficiency before the training. A sample question may look something like this:

Hardware Configuration Knowledge:

Before Training	1	2	3	4	5	6	7	8	9	10
	(Poor)			(Average)				(Excellent)		
After Training	1	2	3	4	5	6	7	8	9	10
	(Poor)			(Average)				(Excellent)		

Using this technique to evaluate content allows you to measure the end result of your training, and in addition, it gives you a more accurate accounting for the level of improvement your training is providing.

The evaluation of the presenter is often a more controversial subject. This controversy lies in two areas. The first centers around who should actually see the evaluation. Some say only the presenter. It is his seminar, and he is most affected by the results. Others say just about everyone should see the evaluation *except* the presenter. Once the evaluations have been tabulated and logged, the presenter is then typically given what amounts to a quarterly rundown of the numbers.

I see value in both methods, but neither exclusively. When evaluations are compiled, the presenter gets a better sense of possible trends. The fact of the matter is that some seminars are difficult. It could be a bad mix of trainees or a bad week for the presenter. These things happen. That is why it is so important to look for trends and not isolated occurrences. On the other hand, it is a big mistake to not allow a presenter immediate feedback as to how he is doing. Why wait two months to start fixing or adjusting? The solution must be a combination of the two. It should not even be an option to look over the week's evaluations. Study them, learn from them. Then turn them over to be tabulated to get some perspective regarding trends.

ADVANCE PREPARATION USING PRESCHOOLS

Another form of evaluation of the trainees can be made using preschools and pretests. Every presenter has his own fears. Mine happens to be preschools. I have grown to cower when I hear that term for a couple of reasons. Before I frighten anyone who happens to be reading these words, let me tell you some of the positive aspects of a preschool.

To begin with, preschools are designed with one very basic goal in mind—to allow trainees to do certain work ahead of time that they can easily do alone. The concept is a simple one. If trainees look over the materials, are responsible, and study hard, they can begin together at a more advanced level. "Hit the ground running" is a popular phrase for what you are attempting to accomplish with the preschool. No need to waste valuable time with certain basics that do not require a presenter's help. More can be accomplished in a shorter period, thus saving money and time. Sounds too good to be true? It just may be.

I have several concerns with preschool. First, they are a little tricky to administrate. Remember, a preschool has to be timed out so that those who are taking it have enough time to adequately complete it. It is easy to have one of the preschool packages fall between the cracks and not go out properly or at all, and with that one miss can come a boatload of trouble for the presenter. The seminar training pace can be knocked off stride, and it is certainly no fun "hitting the ground running" when one or two trainees are lagging behind.

Another concern with a preschool is the trainees' realistic ability to finish it. To this day, a reality of training is that although many companies are finally seeing the light about more quality training, the majority of seminars still consist of new hires. Ask yourself this question: "What were you doing for those first precious, memorable, couple of months on the job?" I'll tell you what I was doing, along with most of you—sorting through file cabinets, closets, and any other neglected areas they could get "the new guy" to clean up. There often is not a whole lot of time for "the new guy" to study preschools. And now it really gets scary.

Problem: How do you get trainees to responsibly study preschools? You could use an honor system, but if you believe that, you probably believe you really can shave a whisker one more time before it snaps back! Sorry to break the bad news to you, but my experience with honor system preschools says if you get 75 percent of the trainees to complete the preschool, you are way ahead of the game. That still leaves 25 percent of the trainees not able to move ahead. Although the temptation is there to move ahead and leave those who did not complete the work behind, the potential difficulties that would cause makes it an impossibility. What most training courses are left with is a preschool with no credibility, which translates to fewer and fewer students completing it.

The most common solution to the preceding problem is a pretest. A positive side to pretests is that you can count on the rate of completed preschools rising dramatically: The negative side is there must be a consequence to not passing.

Here is where I start getting squeamish. You see, it is not the preschool that I really object to. It is the *pretest* that so often accompanies it. The most common device used by corporate training departments is the practice of "send homes." Fail the preschool test, you go home. Sounds simple enough. The ramifications are staggering. As a child, I always marveled at how wonderful it must have been to be a teacher and have the power to pass some youngsters and fail others. To literally give life, or take it away (I had some rather rocky years)! Teachers must love that control over their students' destiny. Little did I know what a real nightmare that kind of power can bring. I have seen students on a send-home pretest involving a typewriter demo forget how to shift to capitalize the first letter in their own name! A sleepless night of fear can bring out some very strange results in trainees. If they pass, you can often rule out any real learning due to emotional fatigue. If they do not pass, it gets even worse. Let me draw a rather emotional scenario. A student flies to your training facility and faces a send-home pretest to see how well he has studied the preschool. With so much riding on the exam, he tenses up, and although he really does know the information, he does not achieve the passing test score of 80 percent.

Instead he receives a grade of 75 percent. With tears in his eyes, he approaches the presenter and begs to be allowed to stay. Rules are rules however, and he is sent home . . . humiliated, discouraged, and suffering from an emotional blow he may never recover from. The presenter is often not doing that much better. In some ways, it actually takes on the feeling of a death in the seminar to those who remain.

If I did not frighten you emotionally, let me take a shot at it financially. Let's take the same scenario as before, but reexamine it from a legal angle. Let's suppose that same student fails the same test. He received a 75 percent and needed an 80 percent to stay in the course. On that long ride home, this student begins to ask some questions: "Who says an 80 percent indicates you know enough of the information to stay in town?" "Who says every question asked was a fair one?" "Who says every question asked related to the preschool that we were given to read?" By the way, that student goes home, is fired from his company, goes on unemployment, and loses his home and eventually his wife. Sorry to paint such a bleak picture, but it is of such stuff that massive lawsuits are made of.

The only way to counteract such a suit is to have the preschool test legally validated before anyone is sent home. To do this is no easy chore. It typically requires the assistance of a couple of clinical psychologists employed by companies who study each question against the material given in the preschool. They then go through a procedure that can take months of testing the exam. A norm is established and the test is then literally blessed as legally validated. To administer a test that is not legally validated is the equivalent of playing Russian roulette with a major lawsuit.

Even after the test is legally validated, you still are not out of the woods. You are going to have to have a talk with all the presenters who are involved in this testing. You must explain that the conditions of the testing (i.e., time limits, use of additional materials) must be consistent. One other message must be delivered as well. There can be no exceptions to who stays and who goes. By this, I mean if 80 percent is established as the passing point, 79 percent is a send home. *No* case-by-case interpretation is allowed. I would also recommend that a senior presenter or manager oversee the entire operation. That also includes the individual who has become distraught and is pleading with the instructor to let him stay. As I said before, reinforcing this rule is one of the most difficult aspects of a presenter's job. It is often better for all involved if a third party can intervene and make the necessary arrangements. Any deviation due to these factors once again opens the door to potential lawsuits from those who did not receive these same considerations.

It may seem as if you are damned if you do and damned if you don't, but there is one compromise I have become comfortable with. Rather than send home the student who does not pass the preschool test, intensify his workload. By this, I mean allow the person to take another test the following day that requires additional work outside the regular seminar load. If he does not pass the test, perhaps an essay or paper might be in order. The idea is to bring the person up to speed as humanely as possible. By humanely, I simply mean showing compassion while allowing a trainee to continue to work and try with dignity.

Another idea that is particularly effective for a one-day course is simply to put in the preschool a letter that states test results will be sent back to the individual's mentor. Sometimes lessons from academia do work in the training world!

REALISTIC EXPECTATIONS

As training approaches, it is always a good idea to solicit expectations of those involved in the training. Often, training cannot live up to some of the advanced billings it sometimes receives. Unrealistic expectations can be set both for and against training.

What comes to mind when I think of expectations that are unrealistically conservative is the old saying that I still hear in a lot of the courses I teach: "If I can learn one or two new ideas in this training, then it will have been worthwhile." Yuk! If, during the course of your seminar, the average individual learns only one or two new ideas, I would consider your training a failure. Recently I attended a one-day seminar dealing with managing different personality types. At the end of a disappointing day, I looked over my notes and handouts and determined I had only learned one new idea that I could use. I do not recall jumping up and down for joy thinking what a productive day I had. I do recall being disappointed and feeling I had been taken advantage of. I assure you, we can dream for more!

Now the flip side to this expectation argument is to assume too much will come out of training. Good training will not move mountains; it will not cure the incurable. The human brain can withstand only so much; even with the best written curriculum delivered expertly, there will be nice-to-knows and need-to-knows. Realistic expectations for training should call for stimulating training, delivered professionally (implementing a host of ideas from this book) that leaves the participant motivated and satisfied.

The realities of management support are a little like a fair-weather friend. When the money is there, often management will stand on soapboxes and preach the value of training. "Do what it takes, I want these people trained right!" they'll say, or "Money is no object, my people have to learn the right way!" Sadly, when budgets are cut and times are lean, what is the first to go? You guessed it, training. This book's intention, however, is not to paint a doom-and-gloom picture of corporate training. As a matter of fact, it is quite the opposite. I want to point out the realities of expectations when you are preparing to train. My real intention is to explain how to make your training so unforgettable and effective, through good times or bad, that your training and trainees will thrive.

Chapter 17

Adventures in Cross-Training

Once a presenter has mastered the necessary teaching tools, that presenter then has to begin to learn the curriculum he will deliver. How long is enough? There are many theories and opinions as to what is the best method for teaching a presenter a new course. Frankly, I have to say that in all the courses I have learned and then taught, I cannot remember any two cross-training approaches being the same. I will be more than glad to offer some recommendations, but first let me tell you some of the factors involved.

FACTORS TO CONSIDER BEFORE CROSS-TRAINING TRAINERS

To begin with, a key determining factor is the material type. I have witnessed cross-training of new presenters on courses that require extensive technical knowledge and training that can take over a year before the presenter is ready to teach without assistance. Some less technical courses can have a presenter ready to go in a week.

Another factor to consider is how frequently the course will be taught. If you only plan to teach the course a couple of times, it will not be very cost effective to spend months just learning the curriculum.

It is my intent to look at situations that represent more of the norm. Every course is different in its own way, but hopefully you will be able to adjust your timetables and techniques using some of the recommended ideas.

HOW TO CROSS-TRAIN A NEW PRESENTER

Let's look at a classic course that requires little technical information. It is one week in duration and is taught on a consistent basis by four presenters. On most teams, there is a lead or senior presenter, who should be running the show. As mentioned in Chapter 15, it is important that someone take responsibility for consistency, which is critical when cross-training new presenters.

The mistake many training departments make is to throw the new presenter into the back of a new course, have him watch the presenter conducting the seminar without telling him what to look for, and ask both presenters to debrief after each day. On paper, that seems to be a sound approach. The problem is that it just does not work effectively. To begin with, try sitting in the back of a seminar without saying a word for a week and see how much you get out of it. Add to that, the fact that at the end of a day, the presenter teaching the seminar is not exactly fresh as a daisy and raring to go. The net effect is a new presenter absorbing little during the day and picking up even less during the debriefs.

The best approach I have ever used is a combination of ideas. To do the job in a quality fashion, you are going to have to free up more than one presenter to help. Having the new presenter sit in the back of the room watching is not a bad idea, but get the senior presenter to conduct the debriefs. This will benefit your cross-training in two ways. First, you will provide your new presenter with someone who is not totally exhausted, and second, you will achieve the consistency you must strive for when multiple presenters are teaching the same course. Look over the curriculum carefully. See if there are any areas that would allow you to have the debrief sessions while the seminar is going on. Some classic spots that can often be used are seminar reviews, small group exercises, lab work, and individual study. If at all possible, try to conduct your debriefs during one of those times. New presenters get exhausted also. Sometimes, I can honestly say that I am more tired at the end of the day after watching a seminar than I am delivering a seminar. I cannot actually provide any logic as to why that is true, but it is. I have not met too many presenters who do not agree.

Another classic mistake of many training departments involves the preparation, or lack of, that new presenters receive before watching the seminar they have been assigned to teach. Giving a new presenter a copy of the instructor guide, a highlighter, and well wishes is not my idea of preparation. The new presenter must be prepped on just what to look for while watching the seminar being taught.

Start out by telling your new presenter to watch for areas of the curriculum that might be confusing or difficult to teach. If, while observing a portion of the curriculum, the presenter is confused, that material will most likely be confusing to the trainees he teaches. The frustrating part of cross-training is that if you do not make a note of these areas, you will probably forget where some of them are. Remember, by the time you study your way through these areas and work with the individual who is conducting the cross-training, you will know far more than the trainees know about your subject. You have put in more time and effort than the trainees will ever put forth. Once you become familiar with those areas, you will have a natural tendency to fly through them. If you make a note of these areas, not only will you become more confident knowing you can answer the most likely questions, you will have a permanent reminder to slow down and make sure everyone understands.

Other things to watch for when cross-training are areas in the curriculum that you find yourself daydreaming through. As with the areas that gave you difficulty, if you are losing interest, so are a number of other trainees. Look around sometime, and you will see what I mean. Almost all curricula have dead spots. These are areas that, for whatever reason, tend to lose their audiences.

A classic example of this phenomenon can be found in movies as well. When I was 16, the first job I ever had was as an usher at a movie theater. This is where I first noticed dead spots. During the movie, I would stand in the back of the theater and watch the backs of 200 heads remain totally riveted on the screen. At certain points in the movie, often when the action changed, literally 90 percent of the people would move. It would often be just a stretch or a crossing of the legs, but almost everyone would move. Then they would settle back again and get drawn into the action. Curriculum is the same way. Not every part can be totally spellbinding, but you do not want to lose your trainees either. As you have already learned in Chapter 7 of this book, you can always come up with some interest-sustaining ideas that might provide some punch without changing the curriculum at all.

The final, and most important area to focus in on when cross-training has to do with logistics. In most situations, new presenters bring with them a certain amount of experience within the topic they are to train in. Certainly, some degree of brushup is required, but for the most part, the product knowledge is there. The real challenge becomes learning the logistics of the course in question. Here are some examples of logistical concerns:

- ■ Timing (probably the most difficult of all), included in all the examples.
- ■ Small group exercises.
- ■ Trainee materials.
- ■ Handout materials.
- ■ Visual aids needed.

When a new presenter is cross-training, it is critical for him to focus on these issues. Nothing can take the place of experience, but achieving logistical competence sure can do wonders. To begin with, a new presenter who knows what is coming next and is prepared with all necessary materials avoids a lot of anxiety. This preparation and newfound confidence translate into a more polished impression left with the trainees.

With the importance of logistics in mind, here is a suggestion that might make your cross-training more effective. Try using two or three different color highlighters when following a curriculum in a cross-training environment. Set up a key and stick with it. Perhaps red will indicate movement, either group activity or breaks. Green may represent handouts or direct references from the trainee's participant guide. Yellow can signify the use of visual aids. This is by no means a new trick. The problem is that most presenters who start out with an idea of this concept in mind, end up with so many colors and symbols, their highlighted notes wind up being no help at all. As the old saying goes, "If you emphasize everything, you emphasize nothing." Be selective in what you highlight and in the colors you use, and you should not have any difficulties.

DON'T BE A PERFECTIONIST

So we are now back to the first question asked: "How long is enough?" Hopefully, by using some of the ideas that were discussed, you now have a better idea of how to gauge your response. Let me just leave you with this one friendly warning. Be on the lookout for the perfectionist part of your personality taking control over your actions early in your training. When I use the term perfectionist, I am referring to the individual who insists that he must do everything perfectly and that he must know everything there is to know before training begins. It is hard to criticize an individual for this type of work ethic. The problem is that perfectionists age very quickly in the training profession. I have often referred to years in training as dog years. The 7 to 1 ratio in years is about right when you look at a presenter going underfire with an active stand-up delivery schedule. Presenters who attempt to prepare for every potential situation in their training usually find the results sadly disappointing. Let me provide you with an analogy to illustrate to you why I say this.

As I mentioned earlier, for some time now I have been a runner. For various reasons my running has slipped a bit now, but from time to time I take my running quite seriously. I am not alone. One of the reasons I run is that, although I enjoy running for its own sake, I love racing. Each year I enter a certain number of races, and although I have not run a marathon in a few years, it still remains my favorite race. A lot can be learned about runners by the way they train for this distance. I do not exactly consider myself a maverick, but my training has always been considered a little bit unique. To this day, when I am getting ready for a race or working with someone else to help him get ready, I preach a straightforward philosophy. Work hard, take good care of yourself, show up strong, and trust in your abilities. That may appear to be a whole lot of rhetoric, but the thinking is rather simple. If you work hard and do what you need to do to take care of yourself—call it adrenaline or whatever else you like—you will find the strength to persevere.

What helped mold this theory was watching the complete opposite in those I would compete with. Many would put in more miles training, would make sacrifices that caused them to feel miserable, and basically would show up at race time looking like death. Certainly, you have seen these people running along the side of the road looking as if they are ready to find a bridge, jump off, and end it all! Too bad. There are plenty of runners like myself who actually look as if we are somewhat enjoying ourselves. The most interesting news of all is despite all the training and neurotic behavior, these athletes often lose to knuckleheads like myself. Why? Because they are too tired, run down, and often injured to do their best. Their best efforts were spent weeks ago around some dark, lonely track.

The perfectionist personality runs the same risk. The ultimate irony is that as with the neurotic runner, often you reach a point where the more you prepare, the less prepared you become. Repeat after me: *You cannot prepare for everything.* Relax. Put in a reasonable amount of time in your preparation and show up for training sharp and ready to think on your feet. Ask a soldier from combat and they will tell you there is no way to truly simulate live underfire conditions. There is no way for a presenter to simulate conditions underfire as well. Study your notes, feel confident about your logistical preparation, and trust your instincts.

POWER AND ITS MANY MISUSES

The final lesson that needs to be discussed before you deposit this book on some dusty shelf (hopefully in a prominent location) deals with one of the by-products of being a presenter and finally becoming comfortable with the curriculum and delivery: *power.* Sadly, one of the first, and often most tragic, pitfalls a newer presenter experiences is the lure of power.

As a new presenter prepares, his eagerness is unmatched. Working with as many new presenters as I do (or even some grizzled vets who come in for a checkup), I see the same pattern often repeating itself. Presenters leave with a win-at-all-costs attitude. A desire to tailor the message to the trainees, to be enthusiastic, and without question or hesitation, to do what it takes and go the extra mile to make the trainees' experience a rewarding one!

When does that desire stop? When do we begin to doubt our own message?

After successfully coping with the pressure of those initial experiences, a kind of metamorphosis takes place. After reaping the rewards—the praise of our participants and peers—we begin to believe in our own immortality. We truly are talented! We truly are powerful! Coincidentally, about this same time, the trainees we are sent begin to lack the motivation and drive we were accustomed to. Or do they?

This addiction to power now takes on a more cruel appearance. If trainees cannot keep up, they are to be admonished for it. If classwork does not meet our expectations, there will be a serious price to pay. And there we stand, pathetically believing our own misguided feelings. "Boy, trainees just aren't what they used to be. It's a good thing they have me to kick them in the pants!" *Don't do it.*

Epilogue

What's Next?

Well, that is about it. It is my hope that after reading this book, you are better equipped to not only understand the realities of corporate training but perhaps be in a better position to instruct if called underfire.

The appeal of corporate training is that few other careers offer as much excitement or allow for as much creativity. No two days are the same. Countless variables affect what goes on "in the pit." As a professional presenter, you can die from the pressure or thrive under it. I have attempted to give you as many different forms of ammunition as possible.

Experiment! If one idea does not work, try another. To this day, I keep a pad of paper inside the lectern dedicated to nothing else but possible changes to the Train-The-Trainer I teach. As a result of changes in curriculum and delivery techniques, this course currently has seen a roughly 900 percent increase in participants from before I rewrote it. As they say, "If it ain't broke . . . fix it better!"

The possible frustration that often goes along with "fixing it better" is the reality that while you are trying to implement new ideas and processes, for some period of time, you will probably get worse. For example, take the UPPOPPR overview process. It is not easy to master immediately, yet anyone who watches it in action will swear by it. The real problem is not actually being convinced to use it, but rather being convinced to stick with it through the conscious competent blues. The first time you attempt to use a number of the ideas I have layed out for you, you will probably be worse not better!

Before you lose your temper, and swear off the name of Rob Jolles, let me leave you with one last story that may help clear all this up. When I was about 13 years old, I was watching some new tennis prodigy named Jimmy Connors on television. Because I was left-handed, extremely competitive, and somewhat obnoxious, I decided that Jimmy Connors was my new sports hero and was inspired to play the game myself. I went on a begging spree that ended with the purchase of a "Wilson T-2000" just like my hero's. I would not say that many sports came naturally to me, but for some reason, tennis did. Without ever taking any lessons, I was immediately able to beat all of my friends who also got into tennis at about the same time. Years later, when I went out for my high school tennis team, the coach asked me if I had ever taken any lessons. I proudly told him, "No." He asked me to work with another teacher on my serve. What puzzled me was that my serve was fast and consistent. When I went to the other teacher, the first thing the teacher did was twist the racket in my hand to what amounted to a backhand grip. He went on to explain that although my serve was fast, it was too predictable. He wanted to teach me how to spin the ball and create what in tennis is known as a "kick" serve. It was extremely frustrating trying to hit the ball with one-tenth of the racket but I remember him patiently telling me not to worry where the ball was going, just to use the correct technique and it would eventually go in. Perhaps the toughest part of learning this serve was playing against my friends with it. I double-faulted constantly and lost to people I had never lost to in my life. I would constantly look down at my grip and dream about switching back. I could get the ball in that way, and it was fast. I also realized I could play tennis every day of my life and my serve would never improve. It took discipline, but I refused to change back to my old grip. Now, serving is effortless. My serve is more accurate, better than it ever was in the past, and the more I practice, the better it gets.

What's the moral to that story? Using a number of the techniques that I have attempted to teach you will require you to leave your comfort zone, and most likely you will get a little worse before you get better. You will probably find yourself muttering under your breath reasons for going back to your old ways. I hope you don't change your grip back but instead pay the price for improvement!

Watch out for the unconscious incompetent spirits that prey on more tenured instructors. Keep pushing yourself to "fix it better" and read those evaluations. Those are your customers speaking, and as with any other business, they will ultimately determine your success or failure. I would love to hear from you so fill out the reply card and drop me a line. Good luck and may these ideas as well as your energy and enthusiasm serve you when you go . . . underfire!

INDEX

◾ Index ◾

■ Index ■

■ Index ■

Please rate this book using the scale below.
Enter the appropriate number under the Rating column.

Unsatisfactory	Fair	Satisfactory	Favorable	Very Favorable
1	2	3	4	5

Rating

1. How effective was this book in teaching you the fundamentals of corporate training? _____

2. If you have used the UPPOPPR process, how would you rate its effectiveness? _____

3. In what ways was the book most valuable to you?

   Comment: _____

   _____

4. What would you like to see improved about this book?

   Comment: _____

   _____

5. Please describe your relationship to training (type of training, frequency, etc.)?

   Comment: _____

   _____

6. Can you share a success story based on any ideas implemented from the book?

   Comment: _____

   _____

   _____

Your name & address (optional): _____

_____

_____

Send your comments to: Robert L. Jolles
P.O. Box 22
Great Falls, VA 22066

Fold _

Robert L. Jolles
P.O. Box 22
Great Falls, VA 22066